RESPONDING TO THE SACRED

Responding to the Sacred

An Inquiry into the Limits of Rhetoric

EDITED BY MICHAEL BERNARD-DONALS AND KYLE JENSEN

The Pennsylvania State University Press
University Park, Pennsylvania

Library of Congress Cataloging-in-Publication Data

Names: Bernard-Donals, Michael F., editor. | Jensen, Kyle, 1981– editor.
Title: Responding to the sacred : an inquiry into the limits of rhetoric /
    edited by Michael Bernard-Donals and Kyle Jensen.
Description: University Park, Pennsylvania : The Pennsylvania State
    University Press, [2021] | Includes bibliographical references and index.
Summary: "A collection of essays examining the extent to which rhetoric's
    relation to the sacred is one of ineffability and how our response
    to the sacred integrates the divine (or the altogether other) into the
    human order"—Provided by publisher.
Identifiers: LCCN 2020050643 | ISBN 9780271089577 (hardback)
Subjects: LCSH: Holy, The—Philosophy. | Rhetoric.
Classification: LCC BL51 .R466 2021 | DDC 210—dc23
LC record available at https://lccn.loc.gov/2020050643

The Pennsylvania State University Press is a member of the Association of
University Presses.

It is the policy of The Pennsylvania State University Press to use acid-free
paper. Publications on uncoated stock satisfy the minimum requirements of
American National Standard for Information Sciences—Permanence of
Paper for Printed Library Material, ANSI Z39.48–1992.

CONTENTS

The idea for this collection emerged from a professional friendship, and a common set of interests, held by its co-editors. That connect began by chance, when the editor of *JAC*, Lynn Worsham, brought our work to one another's attention. We are both grateful for that professional connection, which has resulted in a rich collaboration, one of the results of which is this volume.

We would like to thank our contributors, all of whom enthusiastically responded to our call and worked diligently and often with good humor to our requests for proposals, contributions, revisions, more revisions—and in some cases more revisions still. It has been a pleasure working with such a talented group of scholars, whose originality of thought, inspired writing, and commitment to difficult ideas exemplifies the very best of what inter-disciplinary scholarship in the rhetoric, and the humanities more broadly, can look like.

Our institutions have generously supported our work. In the case of Michael Bernard-Donals, this project was initiated and completed while he served as the vice provost for faculty and staff at the University of Wisconsin–Madison. The provost who appointed him gave him license to maintain his scholarly work, and the provosts who followed him reiterated that promise, one that Bernard-Donals cashed in on to complete this collection. He was also supported, on this project and others, by the English Department and the Wisconsin Alumni Research Foundation through the Nancy Hoefs Professorship and the Chaim Perelman Professorship of Rhetoric and Culture, respectively. Bernard-Donals also wishes to thank his colleagues—in the Department of English, in the Mosse-Weinstein Center for Jewish Studies, and in the Office of the Provost—for their generous engagement with the ideas that serve as the foundation of the project, and for their ethical and moral support when it seemed impossible for him to do his day job in the Provost's Office while also moonlighting as an academic. With Bernard-Donals's return to the faculty this year, he is grateful to his colleagues for their warm welcome back.

In the case of Kyle Jensen, this project was initiated at the University of North Texas and completed at Arizona State University. The University of North Texas provided a rich intellectual environment, especially where its unusually bright students were concerned. Special thanks are due to Sarah Adams, Tori Thompson-Peters, Michael Young, Jen Buchan, Charlotte Lucke, Ryan Kendall, Andy Heermans, Cody Hunter, Nicole Campbell, and Kimberlyn Harrison. In very short order, ASU has proven to be a place where creativity is valued and where every student has an opportunity to learn. The college and department's leadership team made the transition seamless, and considerable gratitude is owed to Jeffrey Cohen, Kris Ratcliffe, Doris Warriner, Ellie Long, Brad Ryner, Adelheid Thieme, and Demetria Baker. Finally, Kyle is grateful for colleagues who have made academic research so rewarding over the years. In addition to his co-editor Michael Bernard-Donals, he thanks Ron Fortune, Kris Ratcliffe, Jack Selzer, Roxanne Mountford, Dave Tell, Jess Enoch, and the group of scholars that regularly meet at the Theory Conference at the University of South Carolina.

Working with Penn State University Press has been a pleasure. At the outset, Kendra Boileau encouraged our submission of the project and was enthusiastic about its promise, giving us much-needed support when it was only a glimmer of an idea. Ryan Peterson handled the project as it made its way from an idea to reality, and helped us negotiate reader reports and the project's submission to the Penn State University Press board with a firm but light touch, and with equal doses of honesty and supportiveness. Alex Vose is a rock star of organizational acumen and responsiveness, and her shepherding of the project through the editorial process was stress-free. Thanks, too, to Jessica Freeman, indexer extraordinaire.

Finally, we are grateful to our families, whose love and support is the very best kind of gift, that of generosity itself.

Introduction

Taking Rhetoric to Its Limits; or, How to Respond to a Sacred Call

MICHAEL BERNARD-DONALS AND KYLE JENSEN

Rhetoric has always had a vexed relationship with the sacred. If the sacred is defined as that which exceeds human capacity—aspects of experienced reality that are beyond human understanding and that defy one's ability to communicate them—then the sacred poses a limit to rhetoric. Experiences of the divine, recognition of aspects of the material world exterior to discourse, the sense that agencies are networked and beyond the control of any single actor, all suggest both what is problematic about the sacred (its exteriority to rhetoric) and what is compelling about it (its exposure of rhetoric's limits). The rhetorical and the sacred are both powers and capacities, distinct but also inextricably linked. The sacred can be seen as a call that compels a response, and so one important aspect in tracking rhetoric's relation to the sacred is locating the tension between the sacred as a manifestation of the divine (with a focus on a call or compulsion that makes itself apparent as a break with the material and human order) and the sacred as a *manifestation* of the divine (emphasizing the human and material dimension of the response to the call). René Girard captures this tension in *Violence and the Sacred* when he notes that ritual or liturgic expressions as responses to the sacred do not involve the identification of an already sacred object, but rather the production of a sacred object through ritual acts. The sacred object is not sacred independent of the response. What this means is that rhetoric is crucial and necessary not just for the *call* of the sacred itself but also for the crafting of the *response* to the sacred mandate. It is not just that the response is rhetorical; it is that the call (however impossible that call may be) can only be understood in rhetorical terms. The sacred is rhetorical, and the rhetorical is (made) sacred.

This paradoxical relationship can be put another way. If the sacred is something set apart, a caesura that makes itself visible by means of the rhetorical, one must be able to ask *how* the sacred becomes manifest in discursive material. This notion of the sacred is visible in the Hebrew term *kadosh*, which translates both to "holy" and to "set apart." But if the sacred is an expression of ritual, then it is also worth considering the means by which the caesura is made manifest in discursive (in Girard's schema, ritual; in a rhetorical register, figural) terms. The Greeks' understanding of potentiality (*dynamis*) and *kairos* provide us with a set of concepts with which to note something that inheres in and exceeds the capacity to make it manifest. It is in this sense that the sacred not only poses a limit to rhetoric, but also potentially does violence to it. The sacred makes the limit visible and confounds those schemes by which we would make sense of it. It makes those who contend with the limit vulnerable, because the rhetorical limit, the sense that we are only ever partly able to capture what is beyond human language in discursive terms, also marks a limit to the capacities of the human subject. In the face of the sacred object or the sacred word, the subject is laid bare and open to aspects of material reality that are only dimly glimpsed.

In the following pages, we will describe rhetoric's relation to the sacred—as a capacity or openness to what is beyond us, and as a means by which to respond to that call—and define a set of key terms that will be used throughout the collection, though in slightly different ways by each of the authors. In the first section, we examine the extent to which rhetoric's relation to the sacred is one of ineffability—in which the divine, as manifest in the sacred, causes a kind of material break in the human relation to the world—while in the second section, we take up the ways in which our responses to the sacred, in rhetorical terms, could be likened to Girard's sense of ritual, an attempt to integrate the divine or the altogether other into the human order by means of repetition, albeit a repetition, in a Lacanian turn of phrase, that returns with a difference. In the third section, we describe how the essays in the collection serve as responses to the sacred.

RHETORIC, THE SACRED, AND THE DIVINE

Rhetoric's relation to the sacred has two dimensions. The first is a capacity or openness to that which appears to us as altogether other. In rhetorical terms, that "appearance" might be called "exigence," or quite literally a call—as quasi-discursive—that, while it seems to be beyond our capacity for response, nonetheless demands one. In her work on the relation of rhetoric and ethics, Diane Davis has called this relation "rhetoricity," "a constitutive persuadability or responsivity that testifies, first of all, to a fundamental structure of exposure" (*Inessential Solidarity*, 3). Davis's book argues that rhetoric is an attitude as much as it is an instrument, one that takes as its first principle that the human is defined by its relation to something beyond it—a person, a circumstance, a power—and that rhetoric is the means by which humans engage in that relation. Michael Hyde, in much of his work, describes the relation between rhetoric and the sacred as one that creates a void or a space that quite literally *opens us up*. The divine, in its call to the subject *as* the call of the other, casts out that subject as one is compelled to respond, and casts out—makes strange—their language as well. Subjects become exiled from themselves, exiled from the community, and in rhetorical terms move outside the confines of the polis. To be called by the divine is to be called away. The divine call creates subjects sanctified by a violent ejection from what was believed to be true both about themselves and about their ability to speak. In *The Inoperative Community*, Jean-Luc Nancy describes this sacred break as a "laceration," a laceration not of being or of reason, but rather "the communal fabric," "immanence" (30). The cruelty of separation—the radical setting apart—makes plain that our *sense* of community, and our sense of ourselves as recognizable by name, has been dis-placed. For Michael Hyde, the confrontation with the altogether other creates a space, a "dwelling place, the Hebrew term for God, *makom*" (*Call of Conscience*, 114). The term is not a synonym but a synecdoche: God is *not* the place; the place is a displacement—God is here no longer—and so *makom* marks a displacement; the divine encounter *displaces* the one who responds. The divine is made manifest *in the midst of* what we take to be reasonable and deliberative.

The second dimension of rhetoric's relation to the divine is as the means by which we respond to the call in the midst of that displacement. One of the canonical descriptions of this second dimension of rhetoric's relation to the divine—as a response to a call—can be found in Plato's *Phaedrus*. Plato's Socrates is called to respond to a task that he's not quite sure he's up to, and in order to do it, he manages to break a number of the rules he sets down for his task (albeit retroactively). Socrates is asked by the younger Phaedrus to show him how to persuade a person about the benefits of physical love, and so he does. But within Plato's treatise, Socrates also hears a different, more compelling call, and goes on to speak—and to succumb to the power—of what he calls "divine madness," the madness of lovers and poets. Socrates's response to the call indicates places and times—which are not spatial or temporal locations at all—unknown to the speaker and listener but recognized (recalled) nonetheless. In fact, that call unmoored Socrates, quite literally displaced him, as he finds himself disturbed by Phaedrus's call, and forgets where he is as he speaks. A second canonical instance of a rhetorical response to a call can be found in the Torah, in the Akedah (Abraham's ritual near-sacrifice of Isaac). In that account, God directs Abraham to travel with his son Isaac to Mount Moriah, and once there, commands him to sacrifice his son. In her book *Stupidity*, Avital Ronell sees this call as doubly problematic. Not only is the circumstance of the call disconcerting; it puts the one who is called into question altogether: is this even meant for me? It is this calling into question that distinguishes the call of the sacred. Linking the sacred and the divine, Ronell asks, "Is this not an essential trait of God, to dispossess, to be the cause of one fall after another and, in so doing, to render ridiculous the very possibility of self-possession?" (307). If the call of the sacred is a *bêtise*, an interruption of the real, then the *content* of the response does not matter nearly as much as the openness with which it is offered: "Abraham's intention . . . does not need to be sealed in an act. . . . Intention is enough. Proneness to intention would suffice, a certain numbness that answers to a name prior to the constitution of any subject or any faculty of understanding" (309). His response amounts to a deterritorialization, an exile of sorts. Abraham's "Here I am" is not an agreement to go through with the sacrifice; it is the ultimate act of exposure in the face of a force that is as demanding as it is incomprehensible. As narratives marked by a singular call, and as requiring a singular response, *Phaedrus* and the Akedah show that it is not only the call of the sacred but also the response that causes a kind of discursive disruption, and a spatial and temporal dislocation that begs to be made less frightening and disorienting. It is in this way that the sacred serves as a limit to rhetoric: as that which compels a response, albeit an unsettled one, and as the response itself, which does not do justice to or contain adequately the compulsion to respond. The limit is made manifest in the response that could be characterized as a way to wed the human, rational, and material aspect of our surroundings and its inhuman, irrational, and immaterial dimension.

Three Definitions

Before we go much further, it is necessary to define some terms and, in particular, to describe precisely what we mean when we call something sacred. There are three terms that are often used together, if not synonymously—"divine," "sacred," and "ritual"—whose definitions, while they differ somewhat in the essays that are included in this collection, remain fairly consistent throughout. While these terms have been imported from disciplines outside rhetorical studies (such as anthropology, religious studies, philosophy, and theology), they have been taken up in our field in nuanced and sophisticated ways.

Of these terms, the "divine" may be the most difficult to pin down, if only because, as a concept, it is elusive. In a brief chapter near the end of *Negative Dialectics*, Theodor Adorno writes of philosophy that "if thought is not measured by the extremity that eludes the concept, it is from the outset in the nature of the musical accompaniment with which the SS liked to drown out the screams of its victims" (365). The extremity—what eludes our ability to conceptualize it, as phenomenon that exceeds our ability to think it, to give it attributes, to place it into language—was for Adorno that which causes a philosophical or conceptual anxiety (see "Commitment," 93). Jeffrey Kripal puts it similarly. In *Authors of the Impossible* he writes, "By the sacred, I mean what the German theologian and historian of religions Rudolf Otto meant, that is, a particular structure of human consciousness that corresponds to a palpable presence, energy, or power encountered in the environment. Otto captured this sacred sixth sense, at once subject and object, in a famous Latin sound bite: the sacred is the *mysterium tremendum et fascinans*, that is the mystical (*mysterium*) as both fucking scary (*tremendum*) and utterly fascinating (*fascinans*)" (9).

For Kripal, it is hard to pry apart the structure of consciousness from the palpable energy or power to which it corresponds; it is also notable that in Kripal's definition, as in Adorno's "extremity that eludes the concept," the divine cannot exist apart from the consciousness or intellectual apparatus through which it is made apparent or registered. Peter Berger writes that the sacred is a quality of power that is visible on objects and experiences that "stick out" from the normal routines of everyday life but that depend on that ordinariness—something "other than man [*sic*] and yet related to him" (*Sacred Canopy*, 25)—in order to be apprehended. It is also notable that for Kripal, as for Berger and Adorno, there is an attraction and a repulsion associated with the sacred: it is an awesome power, something "extraordinary and potentially dangerous" (Berger, *Sacred Canopy*, 26) that causes Adorno's anxiety, and what Mircea Eliade calls fear (*Patterns*, 14). As Michael Bernard-Donals has put it, the divine, "carrying with it a certain urgency and also a disruption rendered by that urgency," "compels the subject to engage with" it, a "manifestation of a radical otherness that interrupts discourse, that does not let you go, or that you cannot let go of, and that challenges what you thought you knew" ("Divine Cruelty," 405–6).

For the divine to be apprehended there must be a structure of human consciousness to which it corresponds. Eliade, a philosopher of religion, spent a lifetime attempting to understand this paradox, and in his book *The Sacred and the Profane* describes the relation of otherness and ordinariness as a *hierophany*, from the Greek meaning the bringing to light that which is holy or divine. The divine shows itself by punctuating the ordinary, whereby what had been previously considered profane—mundane, purely natural, ready-to-hand and readily assimilable to our previous experience—is endowed with another quality, something beyond, mysterious, and unfathomable ("the extremity that eludes the concept") that is nonetheless here, unmistakably present in one's midst and calling for a response. Antonio Cerella, writing about Émile Durkheim, describes the ambiguity of the sacred as that which results from its "all-pervasive tendency to penetrate into the profane world," forcing whatever is imbued with sacred character— its hierophanic quality—to "embod[y] (that is reveal[ ]) something other than itself" ("Myth of Origin," 214–15). To return to Kripal's description of the divine, what is so "fucking scary and utterly fascinating" is the fact that the divine has transformed that which was just a moment ago a normal part of our everyday worlds and has now become something else. The sacred is a manifestation of the divine in our everyday worlds, and because of its violent eruption into that world—because it has displaced us, forcing us to recognize an otherness that cannot easily be squared with our current understanding—it becomes something other, and potentially makes us something other as well.

Putting things slightly differently, for Giorgio Agamben—writing about Roman law and the "state of exception"—the sacred object moves from the realm of the human to the realm of the divine, where something previously recognized as profane has now become sacred. The sacred—in the form of the *homo sacer*, the person cast outside the law—takes the form of a double exception, in which the sacred is neither divine nor human, recognizable as neither a material object nor a person, nor entirely an other. This strangeness, the sacred's scariness and its fascination, calls for a kind of institutionalization or regularization, since confronting that which is altogether other is not only "fucking scary" but also potentially destabilizing and violent (a point to which we will return). The political theorist Kent Enns, writing about political violence from the perspective of Girard's theory of the scapegoat, describes the process where secular societies attempt to make sense of instances where the profane has been punctuated by the divine via ritual, as a "deliberate repetition of elements of the crisis and collective dedifferentiation to stave off repetitions of full-scale dedifferential crises" ("René Girard," 84). Ritual is one possible response to instances of the eruption of the divine into everyday life as manifestations of the sacred, a response that does not so much repeat the violence of the eruption itself so much as keep it at bay in a way that recognizes the instance's otherness while also reintegrating it into the fabric of everyday life.

This brings us to the third term in need of definition, "ritual," and while the next section of the introduction will take up the idea in more detail, here we describe how it serves to make sense of the divine as it manifests in the sacred object or event, and its relation to rhetorical practice. By ritual we mean expressions of the sacred, either those that attempt to confer order on that which is beyond it, or those that express qualities of the divine through the creation of objects or practices. Returning to Eliade's term *hierophany*, the eruption of the divine into the everyday calls for practices in which those eruptions are given meaning, and over time humans have developed practices that repeat those eruptions—either as representations, narratives, or ritual practices—so that the "conscious repetition of given paradigmatic gestures reveals an original ontology," whereby the "gesture[s] acquire meaning, reality, solely to the extent to which [they] repeat[ ] a primordial act" (Eliade, *Cosmos and History*, 5). Ritual is the "paradoxical coming-together of sacred and profane, being and non-being, absolute and relative, the eternal and the becoming" (Eliade, *Patterns*, 29), making what is beyond our understanding meaningful and affective through bestowing on natural objects or commonplaces a quality of the divine. What is important to note here is that rhetoric—finding the available means, the discursive and gestural and visual power to *move*, to respond to that which is other to us, including the altogether other—provides us with a way of shaping and regularizing those divine manifestations, while also through those expressions leave room for the divine's capacity to interrupt and potentially hold open the rational and the material. Peter Berger correctly recognizes that "other worlds" are "not empirically available for the purposes of scientific analysis. They are only available as meaning-enclaves within *this* world, the world of human experience. . . . Put differently, whatever else the constellations of the sacred may be 'ultimately,' empirically they are products of human activity and human signification" (*Sacred Canopy*, 88–89). It is by means of rhetoric—human signification—that we respond to the divine call through the sacred, which may take the form of ritual, or may be shaped altogether differently.

Creating the Sacred in Ritual

The most common way we respond to the sacred is through the observation of sacred rituals. Qualitatively speaking, the nature of our response hinges on the level of faith we assign to the sacred being who compels it. To the faithless, a sacred ritual may be one type of action among many; they may respond with agnostic attention, a mocking gesture, or a simple shrug. But to the faithful, sacred rituals transform objects, human actions, human bodies, and physical spaces into "the receptacles of an exterior force that differentiates it from its milieu and gives it meaning and value" (Eliade, *Cosmos and History*, 4). According to Eliade, such meaning is tethered to a point in time when a sacred being revealed itself as "incompressible, invulnerable" (4). By staging the "rebirth" of this sacred revelation, sacred rituals "provide the moral renewal of individuals and groups" (Durkheim, *Elementary Forms*, 276). The faithful accept moral renewal as necessary to the health of their community and thus treat sacred rituals as the appropriate response to a dangerous threat.

Because sacred rituals are commemorative imitations of a sacred being's actions, those who perform them are aware that the originating actor— hero, god, or otherwise—is off the spatiotemporal grid. This performative fact explains, at least in part, why sacred rituals require repetition. Because they are not performed by the sacred being proper, because those charged with repeating rituals exist in profane time and space and are thus exposed to the vicissitudes of history, the social order that sacred rituals establish will inevitably degenerate.

Achieving self-awareness in profane time and space is not the point of a sacred ritual, of course. But even if it were, self-awareness would not be possible. According to Catherine Bell, ritualization "does not see how it actively creates place, force, event, and tradition, how it redefines or generates the circumstances to which it is responding" (*Ritual*, 109). It only sees the desired outcome, "the rectification of a problematic" (109). In the attempt to rectify a problematic, sacred rituals "expose the limit that defines the very possibility of representation, the blank or blinded time/space that enables all representation to *take* time and space" (Stewart, *Poetry*, vii–viii). They do so by establishing a differential relationship between the sacred and the profane.

Insofar as sacred rituals are, "above all, an assertion of difference" they "effectively *create* the sacred by explicitly differentiating such a realm from a profane one" (Bell, *Ritual*, 157). Such differentiation is, in our view, qualitatively rhetorical in nature. Sacred rituals produce a "fragmentation of practices" that defer meaning as they travel into new times and spaces (Stewart, *Poetry*, viii). For this reason, Gregory Bateson asks critics to observe the dynamics of sacred rituals as they unfold over time: "When our discipline is defined in terms of the reactions of an individual to the reactions of other individuals, it is at once apparent that we must regard the relationship between two individuals as liable to alter from time to time, even without disturbance from outside. We have to consider, not only A's reaction to B's behavior, but we must go on to consider how these affect B's later behaviour and the effect of this on A" (*Naven*, 176).

Even though the administrators of sacred rituals can only see "the rectification of a problematic," their responses are not reducible to a desired outcome. According to Emile Durkheim, sacred rituals are "celebrated because the ancestors celebrated it, because people are attached to it as a venerable tradition, and because they leave it with an impression of moral well-being" (*Elementary Forms*, 281–82). Sacred rituals thus carry at least a dual meaning where ethos is concerned. On the one hand, they "involve [the] symbolic fusion of ethos and worldview" that conceives a ritual response "as the natural or appropriate thing to do in the circumstances" (Bell, *Ritual*, 109; see also Geertz, *Interpretation of Cultures*, 113). On the other hand, because "people are attached" to sacred rituals "as a venerable tradition," the ritual's ethos is tied to the dynamic maintenance of in-group relationships that extend in and throughout history. In the first sense, sacred rituals imagine the sacred being as the audience; the ritual action thus needs to be felicitous with the sacred call. In the second sense, sacred rituals imagine the community as the audience; the tradition of ritual action must therefore maintain or augment social relationships in a manner that is felicitous with the group's collaborative expectancies.

The dual meaning of ethos in sacred rituals indicates how they can be both a structured and structuring response to environmental demands. They are structured in the sense that there is a specific and predictable protocol for responding to an environmental demand; they are structuring in the sense that they alter the environment that has placed an unwelcome demand on them. Victor Turner has argued that prevailing social structures both facilitate and fail to fully explain the structured and structuring relationships created by sacred rituals. To underscore the processual dynamics of sacred rituals as they respond to the limits of prevailing social orders, Turner uses the term *communitas*, which he argues "liberates [individuals] from conformity to general norms" by enacting "undifferentiated, equalitarian, direct, extant, nonrational, existential, I-Thou . . . relationships" (*Ritual Process*, 274). Such anti-structural relationships challenge the tendency of prevailing social structures to "hold people apart, define their differences, and constrain their actions" (275). We pay attention to the interplay between structure and anti-structure, then, in order to identify the transition points that connect the profane with the sacred. Such identification relies, at least theoretically, on the existence of a liminal space.

The liminal space between the sacred and profane is crucial to understanding how sacred rituals respond to environmental threats and sacred calls. Turner argues that liminality is easiest to theorize in sacred rituals where community members transition from one life stage to another. For example, there are sacred rituals designed to elevate the status of a community member or to signify times in the year when those of low status can enjoy authority over their superiors (Turner, *Ritual Process*, 167). In either case, it makes sense to think about liminality in terms of Kenneth Burke's study of transformation in *A Rhetoric of Motives*. Within this framework, the liminal constitutes the "dead center of motives" insofar as it defines the space of undecidability and, thus, the capacity for dialectical reversal. As such, it reveals "the moment of motionlessness, when the axe has been raised to its full height and is just about to fall" or, if you prefer, "the pause at the window before descending into the street" (294). Of course, liminality can only be posited theoretically since, as we have argued, the differential relationship between sacred and profane creates the conditions whereby one may document the transformation from one representative state to another. Nevertheless, liminality must be posited in order to account for transformation of symbolic and material in profane time. Independent of such transformation, there is no way to evaluate the efficacy of sacred rituals.

The social structure that precedes and is maintained by sacred rituals is *hierophanic* in quality. A hierophany, according to Eliade, "expresses in some way some modality of the sacred and some moment in its history; that is to say, some one of the many kinds of the experiences of the sacred man has had" (*Patterns*, 2). The revelation of the sacred is important, obviously, because it inaugurates the relationship between the sacred being and its community, as well as the relationships among community members in light of a sacred revelation. Eliade stresses the historical dimension of sacred hierophanies because this focus allows critics to track the "attitude man has had toward the sacred" over time (2). "A given hierophany," Eliade explains, "may be lived and interpreted quite differently by the religious elite and by the rest of the community" (7). As a result, those who are in greater or lesser proximity to the sacred being (e.g., those who administer sacred rituals vs. those who observe them) will convey different attitudes in response to a sacred call. Within a given community, there may therefore be a number of different types responses to a sacred call. Even where homogenous responses are prevalent, there may be heterogeneity in the attitudes of the various actors both in the immediate application and over time; one's attitude may change, for example, over the course of one's life or in response to non-sacred historical circumstances. Thus, a rhetorical orientation toward the sacred must be nimble in how it conceives the structural cohesion established by sacred rituals with as much flexibility as possible.

Rhetorical critics can remain flexible by remembering that the performance of sacred rituals is an embodied phenomenon. Obviously, sacred rituals involve physical gestures that carry symbolic meaning. Our reference to embodiment signifies, as well, how an environmental threat exposes the nexus of social structures that shape and connect the bodies of believers and nonbelievers alike. This fact becomes readily apparent in anthropological accounts of conflict that results from the application of sacred rituals. For example, in *The Interpretation of Cultures* Geertz describes how a sacred burial ritual in Java produced conflict among the different members of the community. Geertz is clear that "there was no argument over whether the slametan pattern was the correct ritual, whether the neighbors were obligated to attend, or whether the supernatural concepts upon which the ritual is based were valid ones" (164). The conflict emerged as a result of "discontinuity between the form of integration existing in the social structural ('causal-functional') dimension and the form of integration existing in the cultural ('logico meaningful') dimension" (164). In other words, the embodied experiences of the kampong people as an evolving urban culture was increasingly placed in conflict with their folk history (164). We could interpret this conflict in symbolic terms, of course. But Geertz emphasizes that the embodied experiences of the kampong people—their evolving economic, occupation, and bureaucratic structures—caused the sacred rituals to appear retrofit even as the belief systems and their application structures remained relatively consistent. Evolving economic, occupational, and bureaucratic structures had disciplined the bodies of the kampong people in ways that made the sacred ritual seem more or less successful as a sacred response to an environmental demand. The upshot is that the rhetorical study of sacred rituals must account for the entanglement of bodies within political, economic, occupational, and bureaucratic systems that may be attached to the hierophanic structure that calls a community to respond. As we have noted, such entanglement must account not only for the structures that shape the bodies in question but also the dynamic unfolding of attitudes that grant insight into their motivations.

It is tempting, given the prevalence of dramatistic criticism in rhetorical studies, to latch onto Victor Turner's claim that sacred rituals enact social dramas. Although we would not want to discount the value of the dramatistic method, it does not encourage a theoretical engagement with the limits that sacred rituals place on rhetoric as much as we would like. So, we offer the rules of thumb presented in this section to emphasize sacred rituals as both an object and method that bring rhetorical theory to its limits. We know from scholars both within and outside rhetorical studies that sacred time and space is uninhabitable; we have learned, as well, that the performance of sacred rituals bends time and space to achieve ameliorative outcomes. So, perhaps we should ask what makes rhetoric such a habitable capacity of human existence. Or, if that question is not interesting enough, we might consider how rhetorical acts such as sacred rituals can reconstitute time and space in a manner where each becomes something other than itself. This collection is not designed to settle such questions once and for all, but rather to show how such questions may reframe what is possible in rhetorical theories and methodologies.

Rhetoric and the Limit

In the remainder of this section, we will describe the ways in which the sacred changes how we understand rhetorical notions of space and place, our sense of time (both chronological and *kairotic*), and the extent to which humans are defined—as subjects—by relations of vulnerability and violence. In all three contexts—space, time, and relation—the sacred serves as a *limit* to rhetoric, a point beyond which rhetoric cannot proceed, as the axis toward which an asymptotic curve reaches but with which it can never merge. Mircea Eliade introduces the idea of the sacred as a limit condition for space and place when he describes *hierophany* as a kind of chimera, a both-one-and-the-other, producing a heterogenous space: "Every sacred space implies a hierophany, an irruption of the sacred that results in detaching a territory from the surrounding cosmic milieu and making it qualitatively different" (*The Sacred and the Profane*, 26). In fact, sacred space, heterogenous ground, is called forth in precisely the same way that the divine call is made manifest as Hyde's "call of conscience" or Davis's rhetoricity. Eliade writes that "some *sign*" makes itself visible, that the sign serves as a compulsion to respond, and that the result is the creation of a space—"countries, cities, temples, and palaces"—that serves as a center, evincing the divine "center of the world" (27) but in fact carving out a kind of void, the same kind of void that was cleared by the divine in the mystical version of the creation story in Kabbalistic Judaism. It is this space that serves as both sacred and deterritorialized void, working as both a centripetal unifying force as well as a threshold for the chaotic, disordered cosmos. It is a disorder that serves as the impetus for a mobility, a destituent force that is troubling and potentially violent. Like the concept of "nomadism" in Gilles Deleuze and Félix Guattari's section on the topic in *A Thousand Plateaus*, the hierophanic place has the capacity for upheaval, for radical change, that is not ultimately tied or susceptible to the power of ritual or the laws of the community in which it is located. Deleuze and Guattari write that such spaces "give time a new rhythm: an endless succession of catatonic episodes . . . and flashes or rushes" ("1227," 356). They redistribute our bodies' relations to habit, its relation to other bodies, and its relation to the material circumstances in which it is embedded, forcing a radical reconsideration of that material topography, and *moving* those bodies in a reconfiguration of space. Even the frame of a door, for example, makes manifest not just a way to get from one room to another, but "an unstable position, acting as an intermediary" (Teyssot, *Topology*, 270) between one space and another, two potential locations and moments, a border or a passage, a kind of "membrane" that defines and serves as a passage among "many opposite sets of spaces: the exterior and the interior; the illuminated and the adumbrated; the visible and the invisible; the manifest and the hidden" (255). These moments of dwelling—what might be called the fact or event of moving through the materiality of the material world—create *passages*, moving the subject in such a way that she is disoriented, in which she forgets the map of the location, where the fixed makes way for the transient, and where she is at home but never at home.

In the same way that the sacred dis- and reorients space, it does the same with temporality. Again it is Eliade who provides the best summary for how this happens. Time, he explains, has two dimensions, the profane and the sacred: "The one is an evanescent duration, the other a 'succession of eternities,' periodically recoverable during the festivals that made up the sacred calendar" (*The Sacred and the Profane*, 104). As with any hierophany, the two are not discrete; the latter interrupts and disturbs the former, creating a "transhuman" quality to liturgical time, in which the discontinuities of the "succession of eternities"—reminiscent of Walter Benjamin's description of *jetztzeit,* or "now time" in which the chronology of historical time is blasted open in a flash (see *Illuminations*, 255–66)—become entangled in and find a place in the more normal temporal rhythms of chronological time. The interruption of chronological time by time's void—what might, in rhetorical terms, be called *kairotic*—is described by Giorgio Agamben as "destituent," a kind of in-between circumstance that "constitutes a threshold, passing through which domestic belonging is politicized in citizenship and, inversely, citizenship is depoliticized in familial solidarity" ("Elements," 4). Stasis marks a temporal point of decision that "works like a reagent that discloses the political element in the final instance, as a threshold of politicization that itself determines the political or nonpolitical character of a particular being" (5). Stasis is not the same as a temporal suspension; rather, to be at the point of stasis—at the threshold of choosing, at the verge of both *oikos* and *polis*—is to be both the object and the agent of the process. Stasis is in a temporal zone of indetermination in which the subject is one that "constitutes itself only through the using, the being in relation with another" (7), in which the terms use refers to the "affection that [the body of the subject] receives inasmuch as it is in relation with another body (or with one's own body as other)" (7).

In stasis, the human person, in serving as both agent and patient, becomes a kind of potentiality, "devoid of any specific vocation: a pure potentiality (*Potenza*), that no identity and no work could exhaust" (8). Think, says Agamben, of the Christian feast day or of Jewish Shabbat: during these days, human activity is "liberated and suspended from its 'economy,' from the reasons and aims that define it during the weekdays" (9). Stasis, as inoperative, functions as a middle state between doing and being done to, in which the subject is potential and *destituent,* in which mobility is not readily captured by the law and has the potential to call the law—and state power and its attendant ideologies—into question.

To put into question is to be put into a position of vulnerability. One element that definitions of the sacred have in common is the sense that it induces fear, or awe, or—in Agamben's formulation—inoperativity and a kind of stochastic (rather than directional) movement. In his essay on Giorgio Agamben and René Girard, Antonio Cerella writes that for both thinkers, theorizations of the sacred were attempts to understand an ontological origin, in which—for Agamben—one speaks oneself into personhood: subjects *"invent themselves ethically"* (Cerella, "Myth of Origin,"

222). Referring to Agamben's short book titled *The Sacrament of Language*, about the oath's place in the moment of ontological origin, he writes, "The structure of the oath . . . reveals its original gesture that does not consist in merely binding together individual and society, private and public, but rather in the establishment of a '*subjectum*' on which to place the order of things and discourse. Language would be the mark of an ethical foundation: To become speaking beings, humans must make room for the *logos*, must open themselves *on* themselves and to the challenge of the world, continually binding things and words together not to lose them" (222).

This opening renders the speaking subject vulnerable. The capacity to be other—what Danielle Petherbridge calls "a general openness to the other" ("What's Critical," 591)—is a condition that is as enabling as it is limiting. Petherbridge sees the possibility of willing together underwritten by a basic mutual affirmation between subjects, which is in turn understood to be necessary because of our "biological under-specialization," the "fact of our biological or physical vulnerability at birth" (595). While there are situational vulnerabilities—those brought about by uneven distribution of material wealth, or by injustice, or by violence and oppression—they are premised on a common vulnerability that we all share by virtue of being human. But vulnerability *itself* has a kind of force, if not power, because its definition of the human agent is founded on the notion that we will *with* others, whether we want to or not; that those interactions are not overdetermined but are radically open; and that any instance of deliberation that comes as a result of the invitation to engage with others is also radically open, insofar as it involves an aporia between the compulsion to speak (in Avital Ronell's terms, the call) and the utterance itself. The constitutive openness—a kind of pure potentiality—initiated by a sacred call suggests that there is no necessary direction that rhetoric has to take. That openness has the capacity to undo rhetorical patterns of thought, can lead us to and fro with a lack of direction that is potentially liberating and also—because it suspends direction in favor of intensity and undoes fixity, because it is exogamous, brute, and forces us to be on the move. It is (in Kripal's terms) "fucking scary."

OVERVIEW OF THE BOOK

In order to determine how rhetoric is responsive to the sacred, this collection of essays examines rhetoric's limited capacity to render phenomena that simultaneously demand and resist conceptual understanding. The purpose of this collection is to engage a deeper theoretical and methodological study of the limits of rhetoric by focusing on how rhetoricians have responded to the sacred throughout history. Insofar as our collection is focused on the limits of rhetoric, it is not meant to be representative of religious faith traditions. Even if it were, it simply is not possible to treat forms of the sacred from all religious traditions; the present volume strives to include diverse views and acknowledges other views not treated directly.

The collection is divided into two parts. In the first, "Sacred Encounters," contributors contend with ontological matters: how rhetoric and the sacred are defined, where and how they overlap, how they interact, and what kinds of claims can be made about the force of the sacred and of rhetoric and how those claims themselves have rhetorical or sacred force. The second section, "Sacred Practices," takes a pragmatic turn. There the authors examine how rhetorical and sacred practices—through writing, divination, governance, forms of reasoning—make clear the ways that rhetoric and the sacred, as capacities, challenge one another *as methods*. Each of the contributors take up the relation between the rational capacity of rhetoric to understand the past and its irrational capacity, the *immanent* power of rhetoric as rhetoric's surplus, in both theoretical and historical terms. Their contributions will address topics such as the status of signs as a rhetorical category, the notion divination in the work of Plato and Pascal, the rhetorical status and power of sacred texts, and the question of rhetorical knowledges that exceed the rhetorical apparatus (such as, for example, big data and historical materialist science). A fuller description of each of the contributors' chapters follows below. Taken as a whole, this study of rhetoric and the sacred is fundamental to how we define rhetoric's relationship to the unknown, the impossible, and the incomprehensible.

In the book's opening chapter, Cynthia Haynes looks at the work of the philosopher Hélène Cixous. By definition, Haynes writes, the *sacred* belongs to no category or system of representation. It is beyond what can be communicated, perhaps beyond all knowing. Rhetoric, on the other hand, takes that barrier as its foremost challenge: seeking to permeate the impermeable, to relate to the unrelatable, to unveil so as to enlighten. It is a kind of sacred act. Rhetoric acts *within* the sacred, in words other than it otherwise would. This chapter aims to examine this unruly character of rhetoric by situating the two in a different kind of relationship, one that forms an organic bond—a passageway through which things come and go, ebb and flow, to and fro. To enter this forgotten passage, one needs *passwords*. Hélène Cixous likens them to "wizard words, that deliver love's password in parentheses, in clandestinity." We must not only remember this passage (it having been forgotten), we must learn (again) how to pass through it. This chapter intends to weave rhetoric and the sacred into a *passing through* various forgotten passages and the passwords with which we gain entrance to "the answer itself. The one that was waiting for us" (Cixous), even the one that is *unholy*.

In subsequent chapters, the contributors examine how the sacred, as a concept of the ineffable, shows itself in the work of several thinkers, from theology to politics, as a way to theorize a role for a power that eludes our ability to make it plain, to describe it, or to respond readily to its call. David Frank makes the case that the God of the Hebrew scriptures and the humans this God created are rhetorical creatures affected by the vagaries of time, culture, and exigencies that invite argumentative exchanges using rhetorical reason. Hebrew scriptures and the Torah depict God and humans as inflected with sacred touchstones that reveal themselves in divine mystery, the ineffable, the permanent, and things spiritual that place limits on the reach of rhetorical reason. Rhetoric's relationship with the sacred in the Hebrew scriptures form a philosophical pair that undergoes continuous dissociation. As Chaïm Perelman and Lucie Olbrechts-Tyteca contend, the act of dissociation maintains the existence and importance of conflicting values and places them in nested opposition. In the case of the rhetoric-sacred philosophical pair, dissociation retains and honors both when they are in conflict, but seeks innovative compromises, negotiations, and hierarchies that account for the peculiar factors comprising rhetorical situations.

Turning from Judaism to Christianity, Steven Mailloux examines the attempt to develop, in the 1960s, a dialogue between Christian and Marxist thinkers in the West, an attempt that included the work of Gaston Fessard, a Jesuit to wrote a commentary on the Jesuit tract *The Spiritual Exercises*, which was an attempt to establish a Jesuit pedagogical rhetoric. In this essay, Mailloux argues that Fessard's focus on the language in contemporary partisan debates about religion and politics led to the development of a framework for discussing the possible conditions of dialogue in general that depended on the role of "sacred mystery" and "supernatural symbolic structures" in Communist as well as Christian discourses. The essay examines Fessard's framework for activism and explores how the rhetoric of dialogue is both limited and enabled by his appropriation of the sacred, particularly as the dialogue relates to the Jesuit adage of "seeing God in all things."

In the chapter that follows, James Martel takes note of a point in common in the work of Thomas Hobbes and Walter Benjamin: for both writers all texts are potentially sacred, and often those texts that we consider to be sacred are not necessarily so. Sacredness lies in our *reading* of texts; it is an attribute—a state of radical possibility, which has the capacity to undo our sense of what language does—that individuals bring to the discursive act. Martel argues, apropos Benjamin and Hobbes, that the sacred is not so much a theological force as such but a site in which force is marked as unknowable, serving to give the power of interpretation over to communities that Hobbes is often seen as robbing of that power. The sacred, in this articulation, evinces an anarchist tendency wherein the power to declare something sacred is a political one resisting demands by sovereign authorities to determine the dimensions of political and social life in a community. Finally, Richard Doyle and Trey Conner's essay notes that most of those who study the divine and the sacred begin with Mircea Eliade's genealogies of religion, which create a clear divide in human experience between the sacred and the profane. Typically, such analyses of the sacred proceed by means of the practice of division: the sacred is that which is ineffably but unmistakably different—and divided—from the profane. Other religious traditions—particularly those from the East—posit the sacred as immanent, as the "treasure beneath our feet," as described in the Chandogya Upanishad. In this iteration, the sacred beckons not from some elsewhere, as a rupture of the ordinary, but must instead be explored through a "turnabout in the field of consciousness," in the words of American philosopher Franklin Merrill Wolff. Doyle and Conner explore the patterns and practices of such turnabouts, wherein the sacred is understood to be hidden in plain sight, and the rhetorical practices such turnabouts require.

The essays in the book's second part articulate the ritual or practical dimension of the sacred and the ineffability of the sacred in the realm of science and other disciplines. To begin the section, Jodie Nicotra claims that like big data, the relatively new science of the microbiome depends on vast sets of information that run through algorithms, relying on "wide, dirty" datasets that stymie classical statistical techniques. But because of the complexity of the datasets, the outcomes of machine learning algorithms have an inevitable opacity, resist human attempts to know and understand, and make the algorithms of contemporary machine learning "uncanny." Big data makes visible a struggle between the unknowable and the known. Nicotra takes a close look at the use of big data in microbiome science as a rhetorical practice, one that uses inferences based on attunement to the nature and interactions of the natural world that could be described as both mystical and to a certain extent sacred, a response, in the words of Teston, to imperatives that resist conceptual understanding.

In the following chapter, Michelle Ballif notes that rhetoric contains within it—in its tripartite distinction between the epideictic, the forensic, and the deliberative—a process of divination that portends the future, which has traditionally been devalued as a form of "divine madness." Ballif addresses the suppression of divination in rhetoric and takes up how it is currently used in contemporary rhetoric as a way to challenge the binary of the rational and the divine. If deliberation is irrational, it is so only because it cannot count on logistical equations to make decisions; it is not so irrational, however, that it cannot make judgments. It can. The essay examines rhetorical strategies of divination—necromancy, telepathy—as methods from which the field of rhetoric can learn and that can inform the theorization of rhetorical practice today.

In the essay that follows, Ned O'Gorman and Kevin Hamilton note that the Nazi political theorist and jurist Carl Schmitt argues that the modern state, far from articulating a move toward secularization and away from the sacred, re-creates the sacred in the form of political sovereignty, a re-creation that is, as an act of naming, rhetorical through and through. Their essay argues that the re-creation of the sacred in the form of the sovereign is inscribed into late-modern American governance in the form of a "nuclear sovereign," a figure that holds unilateral and exclusive right to bring about global destruction, and examines the modern presidency in terms of sacred rhetoric. More than "civil religion" or a "rhetorical presidency," modern American presidential rhetoric is rooted in a commitment to the sacred status of the sovereign.

Turning once again to philosophy, Brooke Rollins examines "Pascal's Wager," the gambit in the *Pensées* in which the Christian philosopher Blaise Pascal justifies belief in the divine through the logic of risk and reward, noting that logic fails in the face of the divine. Rollins's essay makes the case that Pascal's wager should be understood in performative terms, one that exceeds and disturbs the content of its claims. As a rhetorical response to the sacred—an attempt to turn an audience of nonbelievers toward an unknowable God—Pascal puts his logical claims under erasure: it is an impossible response to the sacred and thus signals the limits of rhetoric. And it suggests that when confronted by the limits of knowledge, chance (in the form of a gamble) is a powerful, even emblematic mode of response. The essay traces the consequences of taking the gamble as a rhetorical turn in which the subject, unmoored from traditional experiences of space and time, turns to an engagement with the radically unknown.

The book's final two essays take up rhetoric as communication, and the extent to which the sacred may be made visible if not in ritual then perhaps in the discursive response to the divine call. Jean Bessette focuses on the notion of *kairos* as exemplifying the sacred's conundrum; it is a force on the edge of rhetoric that exceeds yet makes possible human agency and communication. Indeed, if *kairos* denotes the "right" or "opportune" time for intervention, it is not a time a rhetor can choose freely, predict in advance, or explain fully. There may even be two *kairoi* in any given rhetorical situation: the sacred call we both choose and are compelled to answer, and the retroactive—and rhetorical—identification of temporal "rightness" after the moment has passed and success has been gauged. To advance this reconsideration of the complexity of *kairos*, this chapter turns to the Stonewall Riots of 1969. On the face of it, Stonewall seems to exemplify the *kairotic* moment: after years of raids (usually thwarted or diminished by paying off the cops), this time was different. And yet the case of Stonewall's *kairos* reveals that what is right for the rhetoric is not always right for the rhetor. If the uprising succeeded in mobilizing the gay liberation movement (and so the time was right to riot), the rhetors who heeded the sacred call were not always so sure of its rightness. It is through the archive and its traces that we can see how *kairos* abuts the limits of rhetoric.

Finally, Daniel Gross turns to the idea of "interpersonal communication," an idea that emerged in the early part of the twentieth century as an impoverished humanism where the basic problem was bridging the gap between individual agents who appear to take turns as speaker and listener. "Extrapersonal communication" is a late modern countermodel—resonant with traditional versions of rhetoric (the sacred most prominently)—that can include next to individual human agents, collectivities, machines, institutions, objects, nonhumans, unconscious language, and spiritual entities. With reference to Aristotle's unartful means of persuasion, Gross outlines a genealogy of extrapersonal communication focusing on the pivotal work of Sigmund Freud and his persuasive contrivances, or *Veranstaltungen*, which he grounded in sacred practices, in order to offer a new, and practically suggestive, continuity in the rhetorical tradition.

In the end, all the contributors to this volume argue that the sacred not only poses a limit to rhetoric, but also potentially does violence to it. The sacred does violence insofar as it makes that limit visible and confounds those schemes by which we would make sense of it, and those who contend with it are rendered vulnerable. Each of the contributors to this collection takes up the relation between the rational capacity of rhetoric to understand the past and its irrational capacity, the *immanent* power of rhetoric as rhetoric's surplus, in both theoretical and historical terms and the vulnerabilities that the limit lays bare. Taken as a whole, this study of rhetoric and the sacred is fundamental to how we define rhetoric's relationship to the unknown, the impossible, and the incomprehensible.

Bibliography

Adorno, Theodor. "Commitment." In *Notes for Literature*, 3:348–63. Translated by Shierry Nicholsen. New York: Columbia University Press, 1992.

———. *Negative Dialectics*. Translated by Shierry Nicholsen. New York: Seabury Press, 1973.

Agamben, Giorgio. "Elements for a Theory of Destituent Power." Translated by Stephanie Wakefield. Living Together in the Heart of the Desert, 2013. http://livingtogetherintheheartofthe desert.files.wordpress.com.

———. *Homo Sacer: Sovereign Power and Bare Life*. Translated by Daniel Heller-Roazen. Stanford, CA: Stanford University Press, 1998.

———. *The Sacrament of Language: An Archaeology of the Oath*. Translated by Adam Kotsko. Stanford, CA: Stanford University Press, 2011.

———. *State of Exception*. Translated by Kevin Attell. Chicago: University of Chicago Press, 2003.

Bateson, Gregory. *Naven: A Survey of the Problems Suggested by a Composite Picture of the Culture of a New Guinea Tribe Drawn from Three Points of View*. Stanford, CA: Stanford University Press, 1958.

Bell, Catherine. *Ritual: Perspectives and Dimensions*. Oxford, UK: Oxford University Press, 1997.

Benjamin, Walter. *Illuminations*. Translated by Harry Zohn. New York: Schocken, 1968.

Berger, Peter L. *The Sacred Canopy: The Social Construction of Reality*. New York: Anchor, 1967.

Bernard-Donals, Michael. "Divine Cruelty and Rhetorical Violence." *Philosophy and Rhetoric* 47, no. 4 (2014): 400–418.

Burke, Kenneth. *A Rhetoric of Motives.*
Berkeley: University of California
Press, 1969.

Cerella, Antonio. "The Myth of Origin:
Archaeology and History in the Work
of Agamben and Girard." In *The
Sacred and the Political: Explorations
on Mimesis, Violence and Religion,*
edited by Elisabetta Brighi and
Antonio Cerella, 213–36. New York:
Bloomsbury, 2016.

Davis, Diane. *Inessential Solidarity: Rhetoric
and Foreigner Relations.* Pittsburgh:
University of Pittsburgh Press, 2010.

Deleuze, Gilles, and Felix Guattari. "1227:
Treatise on Nomadology—the War
Machine." In *A Thousand Plateaus,*
351–423. Translated by Brian Massumi.
Minneapolis: University of Minnesota
Press, 1987.

Durkheim, Emile. *The Elementary Forms of
Religious Life.* Translated by Carol
Cosman. Oxford, UK: Oxford
University Press, 2001.

Eliade, Mircea. *Cosmos and History: The Myth
of the Eternal Return.* Translated by
Willard Trask. New York: Pantheon,
1954.

———. *Patterns in Comparative Religion.*
Translated by Rosemary Sheed.
Cleveland: Meridian, 1958.

———. *The Sacred and the Profane: The
Nature of Religion.* New York:
Harcourt Brace, 1987.

Enns, Kent. "René Girard, Human Nature, and
Political Conflict." In *The Sacred and
the Political: Explorations on Mimesis,
Violence and Religion,* edited by
Elisabetta Brighi and Antonio Cerella,
69–106. New York: Bloomsbury, 2016.

Geertz, Clifford. *The Interpretation of Cultures.*
New York: Basic Books, 2017.

Girard, René. *Violence and the Sacred.*
Translated by Patrick Gregory.
Baltimore: Johns Hopkins University
Press, 1972.

Hyde, Michael. *The Call of Conscience:
Heidegger and Levinas, Rhetoric and
the Euthanasia Debate.* Columbia:
University of South Carolina Press,
2001.

Kripal, Jeffrey J. *Authors of the Impossible:
The Paranormal and the Sacred.*
Chicago: University of Chicago
Press, 2011.

Nancy, Jean-Luc. "The Image—the Distinct."
In *The Ground of the Image,* 1–15.
Translated by Jeff Fort. New York:
Fordham University Press, 2005.

———. *The Inoperative Community.*
Translated by Peter Connor,
Lisa Garbus, Michael Holland,
and Simona Sawhney. Minneapolis:
University of Minnesota Press,
1991.

Petherbridge, Danielle. "What's Critical
About Vulnerability? Rethinking
Independence, Recognition, and
Power." *Hypatia* 31, no. 3 (Summer
2016): 589–604.

Plato. *Phaedrus.* Translated by James H.
Nichols. Ithaca, NY: Cornell
University Press, 1998.

Ronell, Avital. *Stupidity.* Urbana: University
of Illinois Press, 2002.

Stewart, Susan. *Poetry and the Fate of the
Senses.* Chicago: University of
Chicago Press, 2002.

Teyssot, Georges. *A Topology of Everyday
Constellations.* Cambridge, MA: MIT
Press, 2013.

Turner, Victor. *The Ritual Process: Structure
and Anti-Structure.* New York:
Routledge, 1969.

PART 1

Sacred Encounters

CHAPTER 1

Sacred Passages,
Rhetorical Passwords

CYNTHIA HAYNES

I was sent forth from [the] power....
Do not be ignorant of me.
For I am the first and the last.
I am the honored one and the scorned one.
I am the whore and the holy one.
I am the wife and the virgin.
I am <the mother> and the daughter....
I am the bride and the bridegroom....
I am the silence that is incomprehensible....
I am the knowledge of my inquiry,
and the finding of those who seek after me,
and the command of those who ask of me,
and the power of the powers in my knowledge
of the angels, who have been sent at my word,
and of the gods in their seasons by my counsel,
and of spirits of every man who exists with me,
and of women who dwell within me.
—"THE THUNDER, PERFECT MIND" (EMPHASIS MINE)

I begin with an anonymous "female revealer" (deity) who, according to
translator George MacRae, proclaims and reveals herself using "antithesis

and paradox" ("Thunder," 271). We can only speculate about this Gnostic tractate's authorship, but of its style we can see rhetorical attempts to exhort readers to "hear and reflect" (271). MacRae suggests that such rhetorical devices as antithesis and paradox "may be used to proclaim the absolute transcendence of the revealer, whose greatness is incomprehensible and whose being is unfathomable" (271). Gnosticism arose in the first few centuries CE and concerned itself with *gnosis* (Greek, "having knowledge"), a particular knowledge achieved through self-revelation, or secret knowledge. Another characteristic of Gnosticism's various teachings, found in the spaces between the antitheses and paradoxes in "The Thunder, Perfect Mind," is the idea that both male and female deities shared in the creation of the world, as shown in the following passage:

> I am the mother of my father
>   and the sister of my husband
>   and he is my offspring.
> I am the slave of him who prepared me.
> I am the ruler of my offspring.
>   But he is the one who begot me before the time on a birthday.
>   And he is my offspring in (due) time,
>   and my power is from him.
> I am the staff of his power in his youth,
>   and he is the rod of my old age.
>   And whatever he wills happens to me. (McRae, "Thunder," 272)

For the early Christian "fathers" the idea of female deities cocreating the world was heretical, and Gnostics (and their texts and teachings) eventually declined, though variations of Gnosticism persisted underground, so to speak. In 1945, an Egyptian farmer discovered a large jar containing thirteen bound codices that collected fifty-two Gnostic tractates. These hidden texts have revived interest in Gnosticism ever since. In my view, Gnosticism serves as a conceptual passageway between the more ancient pre-Christian Eleusinian "mystery" religions that were cotemporaneous with the early sophistic and rhetorical tradition. All three of these traditions—Eleusinian mystery rites, sophistic rhetoric, and Gnosticism—share some key traits: the concealed (sacred) nature of knowledge, its relationship to the "feminine," and the role of language in both.

By definition, the sacred belongs to no category or system of representation. It is beyond what can be communicated, perhaps beyond all knowing. Rhetoric, on the other hand, takes that barrier as its foremost challenge. Seeking to permeate the impermeable, to relate to the unrelatable, to unveil so as to reveal (unconceal). Rhetoric reveals a kind of sacred (revelatory) act. Rhetoric acts *within* the sacred, in other words, in words other than it otherwise would. Wherever language *is*, rhetoric is there to trace its energy (or *energeia*, as Aristotle terms rhetoric in the Greek). Energy works to conduct thought, it moves thought through the passages between the historically masculine (violent) and secret feminine (revelatory) characteristics of rhetoric *within* the sacred. In the interstices afforded by paradox and antithesis, for example, an abundance of the sacred is revealed.

In this chapter, I examine the feminine character of rhetoric and/in the sacred by situating the two in a different kind of relationship, one that forms an organic bond—a passageway that reconciles. I have in mind a passageway through which things come and go, ebb and flow, to and fro. To enter this forgotten passage, we will need *passwords*. Hélène Cixous likens them to "wizard words, that deliver love's password in parentheses, in clandestinity" ("What Is It O'Clock?" 76). For Luce Irigaray, this passage (having been forgotten) must not only be remembered, we must learn (again) how to pass through it. This chapter intends to weave rhetoric and the sacred into a *passing through* various forgotten passages and the passwords with which we gain entrance to "the answer itself. The one that was waiting for us" (78), even the one that is *secret*.

To overrule the secret, that is also sacred, was the project of philosophy and early Christianity. I take us on this passage back to lost passages, and passwords, in order to reassert a lost connection to the feminine that *is* the *within* of rhetoric's relation to the sacred. They are one and the same, though not the logic of the Same proposed and accomplished (for millennia) in Plato's "Allegory of the Cave" from *The Republic*. As Irigaray reads Plato's project in her essay "Plato's *Hystera*," she puts us in the shackles of a Platonic attack on the *hystera protera*. In Irigaray's allegory, "[Plato's] project prescribes and overdetermines, in silence, the whole system of metaphor. Shutting it in, like the 'prisoners' in Plato's cave. Chained up like ourselves—I might say—backs to the origin, staring forward. Chained up more specifically by the effects of a certain language, of certain norms of language that are sometimes called *concatenation*, or chain of propositions, for example" (259). Plato's project was accomplished with no sleight of hand; rather, it was fulfilled the moment he crafted a metaphorical chain of propositional logic. As Irigaray tells us, the cave, described like a womb, was the "representation of something always already there, of the original matrix/womb which these men cannot represent since they are held down by chains that prevent them from turning their heads toward what is more primary, toward the *proteron*, which is in fact the *hystera*" (244).

Our heads want/need/are re-turned toward the *hystera* and its sacred/secret relation to rhetoric and the feminine. To accomplish this turning, I first discuss the Eleusinian mystery religions of the Hellenistic era from 550 BCE to 170 CE, where we find not only the sacred worship of goddesses and female genitalia, but we hear the voices of initiates repeating the first passwords required to witness the secrets revealed therein. Next I examine the shift from the sacred feminine to masculine logic via Martin Heidegger's treatment of the Stoic vision of *logos spermatikos* (the dissemination of God's seed/Word). Alongside Heidegger's version of the history of logic (itself an alternative history), I draw on Andrea Nye's alternative feminist history of logic briefly. Finally, I navigate ancient/primary sacred passages with new rhetorical passwords found in both Cixous's and Irigaray's readings of philosophy and phallogocentrism. As a means of conducting rhetorical history, the primary method I have chosen, of naming passwords, also goes by another name: *philology*. However, *philos* (love) and *logos* (word, reason) are themselves fraught terms that were bound together inauspiciously. For if we are to understand the relation between rhetoric and the sacred, we must understand the stakes (and stakeholders) of that which subsumed the feminine precisely in order to usurp her powers and install itself as the only path to reason, which became *the* secular god (logic) that continues to this day to shackle (and mimic) the sacred feminine source of life (and love). What I hope to show is that when situated inside the sacred (and it always already is), rhetoric does its thing—it turns and re-turns, it offers up passwords to mark access points we would otherwise have missed. How to find these passwords, once we are attuned to doing so, is not actually that difficult.

ELUSIVE *ELEUSIS*

If we establish, through an etymological sleight of hand, a loose connection between secret (to separate) and sacred (to consecrate), we are already by necessity forging this association through the feminine (separated from the consecration by the church fathers). However, some pre-Christian pagan religions that worshipped goddesses, such as Demeter and Persephone in the Eleusinian mystery religions, did require a secret password before one became "initiated" into the mysteries, the sacred details of which were to be kept secret. According to Walter Burkert, "Clement of Alexandria [150 CE–215 CE] gives the password, *synthema*, of the Eleusinian *mystai*" (*Anthropology*, 285). Burkert correctly notes that the myths and activities surrounding the ceremonies were kept secret. We know, though, that they were profaned occasionally through revelations, such as when a drunken Alcibiades (likely) spilled the beans at the party recounted in Plato's *Symposium*.

Burkert's discussion of the mysteries is rather tame, suggesting that the point of the ritual was for the initiate to drink a concoction made of barley (*kykeon*) and to come forward to an altar on which a basket containing an ear of corn was placed (288). Merely to witness this amounted to a kind of rebirth. Burkert concludes that the password (*synthema*) "gives information on successive stages of the initiation rites, yet in veiled terms such as one initiate would use to another to let him know that he has fulfilled all that is prescribed: 'I fasted, I drank from the *kykeon*, I took out of the *kiste*, worked, placed back on the basket (*kalathos*) and from the basket into the *kiste*.' Clement himself apparently was unable to give further details, but intimated that this must be something obscene" (286). Burkert reminds us that even "Aristotle states . . . that the important thing was not to learn anything but to suffer or experience (*pathein*) and to be brought into the appropriate state of mind through the proceedings" (286). Generally speaking, Burkert's account suggests that the suffering concerned a ritual "experience of life overcoming death" (277). "In the background," he writes, "there appears once more the sacred deed in general, the encounter with death in sacrifice as such. Precisely for this reason mysteries do not constitute a separate religion outside the public one; they represent a special opportunity for dealing with gods within the multifarious framework of polytheistic polis religion" (277)—which is just another way of saying that "the certainty of life attained by intoxication and sexual arousal goes together with insight into the cycle of nature" (277). The problem with this assessment is that in its focus on death it ignores the cycle of nature that begins with birth, that begins in the first passage-way. But more about that soon.

George Mylonas gives a more nuanced account of how and why the *synthema* was necessary, not to mention spelling out the more "obscene" possible nature of the mysteries. According to Mylonas, the *synthema* was a password required upon first entering the Telesterion where the mystery rites would be performed. It was repeated by the *teletes*, those who were being initiated for the first time. After having drunk the barley potion, *kykeon*, they would repeat, "I fasted; I drank the kykeon." They would not have stated, as Clement of Alexandria (and Burkert) maintains, the second part of the *synthema*, "I took from the kiste; having done my task, I placed the basket and from the basket into the kiste" (*Eleusis*, 294). The reason for this, Mylonas argues, is that the *teletes* were not handling anything during the ritual. They were merely there to *see* the hierophant (high priest) show them what was inside the basket: "All the testimony regarding the Hiera refers to their *revelation*, and not their manipulation. The high priest of Eleusis is called the Hierophant because *he shows* the Hiera. . . . he *shows* the Mysteries. [And] according to Plutarch, Alkibiades' impeachment was 'for committing crime against the Goddess of Eleusis . . . by mimicking the mysteries and *showing* them forth to his companions in his house, wearing a robe such as the Hierophant wears when *he shows* the sacred secrets to the initiates'" (298). The manipulation theory, which involved the presence of a female pudenda (*kteis*) in the basket, varies from simply handling the *kteis* to rubbing it over one's body to actually taking a phallus and joining it with the *kteis* in an act of creation, or rebirth as a "child of Demeter" (296). Both Burkert and Mylonas reject these theories of what exactly was revealed in the ritual. It is, however, common knowledge that the *kykeon* potion contained ergot or mushrooms that in the mixture became a powerful hallucinogen.

In C. D. C. Reeve's article on Alcibiades in the *Symposium*, he not only connects Alcibiades's drunken proclamation of love for Socrates to his earlier alleged profanation of the mysteries, he also points the reader to how Plato's *Phaedrus* sets up a forgotten passage-way (to be explored in my next section). According to Reeve:

Next, based on the contrast [between farming and writing arguments], comes an equally telling analogy. The man who has "[seeds] of knowledge about what is just, and what is beautiful, and what is good" will have "no less sensible an attitude toward his seeds than the farmer" (276c3–5). Thus, when others "resort to other sorts of playful amusements (*paidiais*), watering themselves with symposia," he will amuse himself (*paidias*, 276d2) by writing "stories about justice and the other virtues," so as to "lay up a store of reminders both for himself, when "he reaches a forgetful old age," and for anyone who is following the same track, and he will be pleased as he watches their tender growth" (276d1–e3). But when "he is in earnest (*spoudê*) about them," he instead, "makes use of the craft of dialectic, and taking a fitting soul plants and sows in it arguments accompanied by knowledge (*met' epistêmês logous*), which are able to help themselves and the man who planted them, and are not without fruit but contain a seed, from which others grow in other soils, capable of rendering it forever immortal, and making the one who has it as happy as it is possible for a man to be" (276e5–277a4). Living arguments (*logoi*) are now explicitly likened to seeds (*spermata*)— something on which the Stoics, with their *spermatikoi logoi* (seminal principles) will capitalize. ("Study in Violets")[1]

We are now in the vicinity of analogy (ana-*logos*), metaphor, the masculine creation of logic out of its own twisted version of the passage from seed to plant, and by inference, the passage from the sacred to logic (without the rhetorical leap over the feminine such a passage involves). Before we hear from Irigaray about how Plato's "Allegory of the Cave" sup*plants* a more originary metaphor, indeed a move that Irigaray likens to the obliteration of the most originary forgotten passage (the vagina), it is helpful to hear what exactly is at stake in this forgetting. As we will learn soon, Plato's allegory, in which men are chained facing the back wall of a cave that is the likeness of a womb (*hystera*), obliterates not only the forgotten passage, but also *the very fact that it is forgotten.* Irigaray writes:

> It is within the project encircling, limiting the horizon in which the hystera is made metaphor, that this dance of difference is played out, whatever points of reference outside the system and the self are afforded for relating them one to another, bringing them together, making them metaphor. For metaphor—that transport, displacement of the fact that passage, neck, transition have been obliterated—is reinscribed in a matrix of resemblance, family

likeness. Inevitably so. Likeness of the cave, likeness(es) within the cave, likeness(es) of the transfer of the cave. Likeness(es) of copies and reflections that have a part to play in the cave. Where man, *ho anthropos*—sex unspecified, neuter if you will (*to genos?*) but turned to face only straight ahead—cannot escape a process of likeness, even though he re-presents or re-produces himself *as* like. He is always already a captive of repetition. Everything is acted out between rehearsal and performance, repetition and representation, or reproduction. ("Plato's *Hystera*," 247)

We turn now, as if chained ourselves (facing a wall), back to where Plato's obliteration took us, further and further away from the sacred forgotten passage into the hardening processes in which logic and reason sealed the passage away for all time—and in that hardening, cast away the pass-words with which it might have been possible to re-member the feminine, to re-live our own specificity with respect to every human passage from the womb *through* the vagina into "world," a password itself to be explored soon.

LOGOS CONCEIVED

> Reason, the mother, nurse, and guardian of knowledge, as well as of virtue, frequently conceives from speech, and by this same means bears more abundant and richer fruit.... Indeed, it is this delightful and fruitful copulation of reason and speech which has given birth to so many out-standing cities, has made friends and allies of so many kingdoms, and has unified and knit together in bonds of love so many peoples.
>
> —JOHN OF SALISBURY, *THE METALOGICON*

> Men armed with the authority of logic themselves completed the devas-tation, perfecting master languages insulated from criticism, ruthlessly pursuing Sophists, heretics, witches, scarlet women, unbelievers, Jews, extending the rule of law and truth over diversity.
>
> —ANDREA NYE, *WORDS OF POWER*

Again and again a call rings out for reason to be the standard for deeds and omissions. Yet what can reason do when, along with the irrational and the antirational all on the same level, it perseveres in the same neglect, forgetting to meditate on the essential origin of reason and to let itself into its advent?

—MARTIN HEIDEGGER, *EARLY GREEK THINKING*

In his interrogation of Being, Heidegger finds that *where* human beings dwell is a paradox. On more than one occasion, Heidegger claims "language is the house of Being" ("Letter on Humanism," 193; *On the Way to Language*, 5, 21–22). In other words, we are most at home, in our essential dwelling place (*ethos*), in language, but, paradoxically, the essence of language is unrepresentable and antithetical. Just as "the female revealer" of "The Thunder, Perfect Mind" reminds us by saying "I am the silence that is incomprehensible / and the idea whose remembrance is frequent. / I am the voice whose sound is manifold / and the word whose appearance is multiple. / I am the utterance of my name.... I am the hearing which is attainable to everyone / and the speech which cannot be grasped. / I am a mute who does not speak, / and great is my multitude of words" (MacRae, "Thunder," 272, 276). I would argue, then, that in his attempt to unveil the nature of Being and language, Heidegger had to turn to the pre-Socratic understandings of *logos*. After years of thinking, however, he could not grasp the essence of *logos*. In *On the Way to Language*, Heidegger explains that in fact, "it was a reflection on the *logos*, in which I was trying to find the nature of language. Yet it took nearly another ten years before I was able to say what I was thinking—the fitting word is still lacking even today" (8). In a bit of casuistic stretching, let us consider this one of our forgotten passages between rhetoric and the sacred, between being and language, between *ethos* and *logos* ... where the *synthema* is "between."[2]

In his search for the fitting word, Heidegger's encounter with Heraclitus is a search for the primordial point of tension (*relation*) between Being and *logos*. In *An Introduction to Metaphysics*, Heidegger claims that *logos* "does not let what it holds in its power dissolve into an empty freedom from opposition, but by uniting the opposites maintains the full sharpness of their tension" (134). The point of tension is in actuality not a fixed point so much as a point in motion. Within the sphere of motion there are conflicting forces that set up the possibility for destruction or harmony. Heidegger believes that Being is constituted *as such*, a process also described by Heraclitus. Taking the popular interpretation of Heraclitus to task, Heidegger argues that when we "sum up his philosophy in the dictum *panta rhei*, 'everything flows' . . . [these words] do not mean that everything is mere continuous . . . no, they mean that the essent as a whole, in its being, is hurled back and forth from one opposition to another; being is the gathering of this conflict and unrest" (133–34). In fragment 53, Heraclitus says, "Conflict [*polemos*] is for all (that is present) the creator that causes to emerge, but (also) for all the dominant preserver. For it makes some to appear as gods, others as men; it creates (shows) some as slaves, others as freemen" (qtd. in Heidegger, *Introduction to Metaphysics*, 62). As Heidegger understands it, Heraclitus uses *polemos* to name the conflict that first created opposites, such as gods and men, slaves and freemen. W. K. C. Guthrie provides a critical interpretation of this fragment in "Flux and *Logos* in Heraclitus," which generally supports Heidegger's thesis. Guthrie explains that Heraclitus disagreed with Pythagoras's doctrine of the harmony of opposites. The Pythagorean theory claimed that the order and beauty of the cosmos is achieved through the neutralization of opposites in which a limitation is placed on "chaotic *apeiron*" (198–99). As a result, he and his followers called this *good*; "their opposites—discord, disease, strife—were *evil*" (199). Guthrie suggests that Heraclitus rejects these value judgments. Using a familiar illustration, Heraclitus calls attention to *kykeon*, the aforementioned drink associated with the Eleusinian mysteries made by stirring barley and cheese into a cup of wine. Of importance to the illustration is that the "mixture had to be kept in motion until the moment it was drunk" (200). The point of Heraclitus's lesson is that "'the *kykeon* . . . falls apart if it is not being stirred'" (200).

LOGOS SPERMATIKOS AND THE DISSEMINATION OF LOGIC

To understand this analogy, it is helpful to situate the dissemination of *logos* as reason within the context of the history of rhetoric as "a fallen woman" in order to see how Heidegger's "fall" gets situated in similar (feminized) language (i.e., his "affair" with the Nazis).[3] It should not be surprising, then, to learn that philosophy and rhetoric have been classically divided along gender lines. That is, rhetoric has been depicted historically as feminine (and philosophy as masculine) in an effort to discredit its power and in an incipit plot to perpetuate its subordination to philosophy. According to Richard Lanham, rhetoric has usually been "depicted as a woman, especially an overdressed one—the harlot rhetoric" (*Motives*, 29). In my view, this explains many of the strident attempts to discredit Heidegger. He dared to reveal philosophy's repression of its rhetoricity—that is, its femininity. If we extend that relation further, we may apply a "counter-logic" to the relation between *logos* and *ethos* and actually name this relation the counterpart to rhetoric and the sacred. Moreover, I suggest that understanding this forgotten passage is critical to understanding the tragedy of violent *logos* and how it has played itself out in history. History, however, is often determined by "getting the story crooked" (Kellner, *Language*). Thus the following two sections recount two crooked tales, one from Heidegger and one from Andrea Nye's feminist perspective.

HEIDEGGER'S CRITIQUE OF LOGIC

Heraclitus and Sophocles understood the tragedy of *ethos*, and Heidegger points this out in his "Letter on Humanism":

> Along with "logic and "physics," "ethics" appeared for the first time in the school of Plato. These disciplines arose at a time when thinking was becoming "philosophy," philosophy, *episteme* (science), and science itself a matter for schools and academic pursuits. In the course of a philosophy so understood, science waxed and thinking waned. Thinkers prior to this period knew neither a "logic" nor an "ethics" nor "physics." Yet their thinking was neither illogical nor immoral. But they did think *physis* in a depth and breadth that no subsequent "physics" was ever again able to attain. The tragedies of Sophocles—provided such a comparison is at all permissible—preserve the *ethos* in their sagas more primordially than Aristotle's lectures on "ethics." A saying of Heraclitus which consists of only three words says something so simply that from it the essence of the *ethos* immediately comes to light. (232–33)

For example, Antigone's *ethos* obeys the divine *logos* (from the gods), not the human *logos* (reason) of Creon, who demeaned his own son, Haemon, for daring to side with a woman against the law (*nomos*) (cf. Heidegger, *Introduction to Metaphysics*, 146–65). The argument can only sustain itself by dissemination, by spreading its seed and engendering more power. And it must do so by seduction (*eros*), deception (*apate*), and force (*peitho*). (It is important here to remember Gorgias's defense of Helen.) It has no *legitimate* access to power otherwise. Why? Because the question of legitimation is an issue of *ethos*.

This may sound strange given that legitimation is mostly identified with reason, law, and the "proper" rights of man. But it is necessary to ask the question: Legitimate in the eyes of whom? Against whose standard? To use Heidegger's method of analysis, legitimation has the same root stem, *legein*, which forms the Heraclitean *logos* that gathers and assembles, that manifests who we are (*ethos*) in the *movement* between concealedness and unconcealedness. Thus the defiling of *logos* in this "irrational" sense was necessary, in order for *logic*, the ruling weapon of man, to be installed.

In preparation for examining its dissemination, however, Heidegger reminds us of two things. First, he claims that to "think against 'logic' does not mean to break a lance for the illogical but simply to trace in thought the *logos* and its essence which appeared in the dawn of thinking, that is, to exert ourselves for the first time in preparing for such reflection" ("Letter on Humanism," 227). Second, irrationalism may be a way out of rationalism, but it is "an escape which does not lead into the open but merely entangles us more in rationalism, because it gives rise to the opinion that we can overcome rationalism by merely saying no to it, whereas this only makes its machinations the more dangerous by hiding them from view" (*Introduction to Metaphysics*, 179). We can appreciate Heidegger's resistance to a simple reversal of the binary, and we respect the excruciating level of thinking that his excavation reveals. What is difficult to accept is that his search for origins *necessarily* entailed a synoptic point of view. That is, if his vision was limited by a task constructed so broadly as to exclude what was standing at his door, we may assume that his *ethos* was already damaged (perhaps irretrievably) by the very term he sought to understand. This is not to say that we should neglect to take his history of logic into account.

In a brief excursus on the history of logic (*Introduction to Metaphysics*, 119–40), Heidegger explains that logic emerged in the "curriculum of the Platonic-Aristotelian schools" and is, therefore, "an invention of school-teachers, not philosophers (121).[4] Irigaray, like Heidegger, also places much of the blame on teachers, although she equates teachers *with* philosophers. For in Plato's cave, "the tragedy is played out between him who holds the truth and him who holds the fantasy" ("Plato's *Hystera*," 270). None of the "scenographic . . . apparatus" is revealed to those chained in the cave: "It is only through some *new hocus-pocus*, of *reason* if you like, that the teacher forces him to see in those little 'statues' alone the cause—less disguised, truer, closer to being—of what had once captivated him. For, in making his demonstration, the teacher only lifts the veil in order that he may subsequently conceal the motives of desire, the different kinds of tropisms, even the effects of giddiness you get from swinging from the chandelier-Idea" (271).

What most concerns Heidegger about its history is how logic came to suppress the kind of thinking that allows being to become manifest. What we are most concerned with is how logic came to suppress the sacred feminine, which I have characterized as rhetorical insofar as rhetoric functions *within* the sacred and as revelatory insofar as her secret passages reveal our feminine origins. While rhetoric is not only associated with the sacred feminine, it does maintain historical affiliations (some not so positive) with the other tradition of truth, that being philosophy. Thus, like Heidegger, we are also concerned by the kind of logic he finds in the words of the philosopher Hegel: "The logical (is) the absolute form of truth and, what is more, it is also the pure truth itself (*Enzykl.* §19, WW, 6, 29)" (qtd. in Heidegger, *Introduction to Metaphysics*, 122).[5] Heidegger's brief history of logic is, however, only part of a section in which he examines being in relation to four concepts: being and becoming, being and appearance, being and thinking, and being and the ought. The discussion of logic falls within his exploration of the distinction *between* being and thinking. We begin to sense in this section that Heidegger is witnessing firsthand the dangers of these distinctions. And we now know the dangers of not using the *synthema* (password) *between*. Heidegger had forgotten this passage, not to mention the password. For instance, he claims that logic has produced the kind of intellectualism that "has become the feeding ground of political reaction" (122). Heidegger's response is that the "misinterpretation of thought and the abuse to which it leads can be overcome only by authentic thinking that goes back to the roots—and *by nothing else*" (122). In essence, Heidegger shows "how the initial separation between *logos* and *physis* led to the secession of the *logos*, which became the starting point for the domination of reason" (179). While Heidegger would like to investigate the consequences of this domination at another level, he seems hesitant. Alluding to the "slow end of this history, the slow end in which we have long been standing,"

Heidegger steers away from any overt references to the political climate outside his lecture hall at the University of Freiburg in the summer of 1935 (178). He writes, "In this lecture we do not propose to describe the interior history of this domination of thought (as the *ratio* of logic) over the being of the essent. Aside from the inherent difficulty of such an undertaking, such an account can have no historical cogency until we ourselves have awakened the energies of independent questioning from out of, and for the sake of, our own history in its present hour" (179).

The distinction between being and the "ought," which Heidegger says "belongs wholly to the modern era" (95), is given even less attention than his brief history of logic, roughly four pages (196–99). Even though he would later disclaim this remark as a rejection of "political science," Heidegger's *ethos* finally succumbs to his syn/opticism when he concludes that the "works that are being peddled about nowadays as the philosophy of National Socialism but have nothing whatever to do with the inner truth and greatness of this movement (namely the encounter between global technology and modern man)—have all been written by men fishing in the troubled waters of 'values' and 'totalities'" (199).[6] In short, what Heidegger does not seem to take into account is that *how* logic achieves its power has always interested those for whom its rule has been oppressive more so than those for whom it serves to empower. This should not surprise us, especially as we are engaged in the recovery of rhetoric *in* the sacred, and thus *of* the sacred feminine who proclaimed, "I am the one you have scattered, / and you have gathered me together" (MacRae, "Thunder," 274).

AN "OTHER" HISTORY OF LOGIC

Precisely for those whom logic/reason has oppressed, Andrea Nye's *Words of Power: A Feminist Reading of the History of Logic* traces the birth of autonomous reason from the perspective of those who were systematically excluded from its circle of power.[7] Nye initiates her project with a return to the trio of classical thinkers: the Presocratics, the Sophists, and the philosopher kings. Nye suspects the problem begins when Plato attempts to frame a new use for the term *logos*. When Gorgias rejects Parmenides's logic that "what is" and "what is not" are the same (thereby eliminating contradiction as a concept), he introduces the notion of *onto*-logical difference, but a difference that is not attached to morality. Gorgias believed that the rhetorician is not concerned with moral questions, but with understanding the *techné*, with teaching the linguistic strategies for defense against the external force of the *logos*. In other words, Nye claims, "the knot that reknits the conceptual relations torn by the Sophist is difference" (27). Plato, however, introduces a new twist on difference.

Nye explains that in the *Sophist*, Plato rejects the reduction of *logos* to a simple word for speech. She identifies the linchpin in Plato's attack on sophistry as follows: "*Logos* no longer can be the simple, ordinary 'what someone says,' but, as required by logical division, it must be restricted to statements that are either true or false and statements that reflect correct relations between formal objects. . . . Plato's division restores discussion, but this is a discussion from which reciprocity has been removed. . . . Logical division makes possible a conversation in which one party is in complete control of the discussion" (32, 33). At this point in the tale, Nye continues, Aristotle devised the syllogism to make logic produce new knowledge and bring it down to the level of real human interaction (41). This may sound like a more egalitarian model, but "real human interaction" is still confined to interaction between an elite group of participants. In Aristotle's theory of politics, "logic was a badge of office, a way to identify 'that one who can plan things with his mind' and is therefore 'the ruler by nature'" (*Politics* 1.1.1252a32–33; Nye, *Words of Power*, 48).[8] The exclusionary "nature" of his system meant that "women, slaves, workers, and conquered people, all those who did not participate in dialectical contests, were expected to accept the superior reasoning of their masters" (48). Thus, according to Nye, the "purpose of logic was not to open the discussion to all viewpoints with the purpose of establishing a consensus, but to establish a model of discourse that excluded what was contradictory or irrational" (49–50).

Beyond Plato and Aristotle, logic takes several interesting turns. Samuel IJsseling pinpoints another shifting of gears in his discussion of Isocrates's eulogy to *logos*, the *Nicocles*.[9] In the treatise, Isocrates characterized the distinguishing feature of human beings as the ability to speak, as "having *logos* at one's disposal" (IJsseling, *Rhetoric and Philosophy*, 19). What is significant about Isocrates's distinction, according to IJsseling, is that it signals the connection to community and assigns to *logos* even more power. *Logos*, it turns out, is that which directs (*hegemoon*) all thought and action (19)— *including the sacred*.

Later, the Stoics (e.g., Zeno) *seem* to revert back to the Presocratic notion of *logos* as "the grammar of the cosmos" (Nye, *Words of Power*, 66). Nye explains, however, that although the Stoics replaced Platonic Ideal forms and Aristotelian substance, their notion of *logos spermatikos* reinjects logic with yet another transcendental form. They believed that God's sperm disseminated logic throughout the universe (66). Thus, by being turned away from essence and form, Nye suggests, language is finally accorded the status needed to perform as the "actual instrument of rationality" (66). The Stoics perfected the syllogism, though they compressed it into a conditional expression of "if/then" logic (propositional logic). Unlike Aristotle's model, questions of *ethos* were not relevant in a dialectical debate because witnesses could not be trusted and the truth could be distorted (68). The purpose of speaking was no longer to give an account of events through intersubjective dialogue, but "success in a competition with fixed rules" (71). Truth becomes, then, merely "the avoidance of contradiction" (71).

At this point, Nye claims, logic begins to function autonomously, "a distance has to be created between our experience and what we say" (73). Propositions are true insofar as they fit the facts, which are not perceptions or relations, but "the structures and the objects that correspond to logical form" (73). The Stoics invent "a language insulated from what people say and what they say it about, a realm of logical objects not dependent on any reality" (73). Logic had finally freed itself from conceptual content. In their logic, the logician "has the ability to shape and control his instincts and so bring instinct into harmony with right reason" (76). In essence, as the dissemination of *logos spermatikos* spreads logic over a passive crowd, they are suddenly capable of bringing order to thought and of administering the possessions of those less fortunate—that is, those not in possession of logic. Nye finds further evidence that logic is used to strengthen the power of the few—namely, the men who have achieved a "state of Stoic a-pathy . . . [who have] driven passion from [their] life" (76). In the Stoic cosmology, the active is the divine *logos*, the passive is the physical substance in the world. Nye reveals that this logic kept women out of the affairs of state because the feminine principle was passive (78). In addition, logic helped to quell rebellious cultures, silencing others and rendering subjects speechless, "unable to voice their reservations" (79). In short, Nye argues, "language is now capable of generating its own cosmos, the cosmos of sexist, racist, ethnocentristic culture" (79).

So many women can attest to the bulldozing of the feminine principle into a passive, secret, forgotten passage where the guardians/logicians keep vigilant watch over the real prisoners in chains. And we are not only shackled, we are invisible. No sacred passwords can penetrate their fortified walls, their denials, their dichotomies, their "hocus-pocus" peep show of self-stimulating performances. Forget the apparatus of transitions. I am going to play the ghost. Irigaray knows that "a ghost has never been stopped by a wall, or even a door, much less by a curtain or a veil. . . . The ghost transgresses these established borders" ("Plato's *Hystera*," 282). For the "path within the cave. . . . like *trakheias*. . . . [are] full of sharp edges and points. . . . For her company is represented to him, here, as thorny, pregnant with danger" (283).

SECRET PASSAGES

It is going to take every ounce of rhetorical courage for me to tell the secret/ sacred story hidden behind Irigaray's and Cixous's readings of Plato and phallogocentrism. The words on the pages of their respective, and dis/ respectful, treatments of philosophy's abduction of the sacred, of the forgotten passage, are as full of "woman" as a page can be (though we all know that the boundaries of this fully justified print format lose sight of her, of her passage, of *all* our passages, as soon as it is bound). The courage of rhetoric's capacity to unconceal is its sacred bond with the feminine. But to name this bond sacred is still an attempt by the masculine language/ grammar we have inherited . . . an attempt to name a hidden space, a forgotten passage, in order to (to order them) move across a sacred path by ignoring, pushing aside, the soft, pulsating rhythms that set us all on the way to "world." I am not trying to be cryptic. I am trying to tell a very secret story set within a rhetorically amniotic, and hence messy, event.

Let us go back to the cave/*hystera* that Irigaray staged for us earlier. It is a long passage in more ways than one:

In that cave, inside that cave, burns *a* fire "in the image of" *a* sun. But there is also a path, no doubt made in the image of the conduit, neck, passage, corridor which goes up (or rather would go down) out of the cave toward the light of day, toward the sight of day. . . . A conduit which is taken up and reproduced inside the cave. A repetition, representation, figuration re-enacted within the cave of that passage which we are told leads in and out of it. Of the path *in between*. Of the "go-between" path that links two "worlds," two modes, two methods, two measures of replicating, representing, viewing, in particular the sun, the fire, the light, the "objects," and the cave. Of this passage that is neither outside nor inside, that is between the way out and the way in, between access and egress. This is a key passage, even when it is neglected, or even especially when it is neglected, for when the passage is forgotten, by the very fact of its being reenacted *in* the cave, it will found, subtend, sustain the hardening of all dichotomies, categorical differences, clear-cut distinctions, absolute discontinuities, all the confrontations of irreconcilable representations. Between the "world outside" and the "world inside," between the "world above" and the "world below." Between the light of the sky and the fire of the earth. Between the gaze of the man who has left the cave and that of the prisoner. Between truth and shadow, between truth and fantasy, between "truth" and whatever "veils" the truth. Between reality and dream. Between.... Between.... Between the intelligible and the sensible. Between good and evil. The One and the many. Between anything you like. All oppositions that assume the leap from a worse to a better. An ascent, a displacement (?) upward, a progression along a line. Vertical. Phallic even? But what has been forgotten in all these oppositions, and with good reason, is how to pass through the passage, how to negotiate it—the forgotten transition. The corridor, the narrow pass, the neck. ("Plato's *Hystera*," 246–47)

Here the *synthema* "between" must be spoken woman to woman. That is the twin to the "between" we revealed was lost on Heidegger. Is it no wonder—given the through line from the Eleusinian mysteries to Plato to the Stoics to Heidegger to Nye to Irigaray—it is *no* wonder? Irigaray says, "There is no end to it. This cave produces more ghosts than any other, even if they are sometimes clean, clear, even sunlit ghosts. Washed of their uterine contaminants and their graveyard corruption" (282). We could go on, but my story has waited long enough, too long, it is beyond my *trakheia* now.

RHETORICAL PASSWORDS

"Language's tricks are the allies of the artist who goes into resistance or exile. . . . Every language artist is an artist of the struggle against the condemnation to death. Sentences and their words always lead elsewhere than the place we were expecting them" (Cixous, "Preface," xii). Thus did I begin this essay with "I begin with an anonymous 'female revealer'" only to discover in the passage from there to here that she is me.[10] Cixous is with me, whispering in my ear, "Why is it so difficult to write? The most difficult 'border passage,' the most tortuous, we cannot make it on purpose, not wittingly. It's a dream. It doesn't obey us. It's a dream: it's a wind. The wind blows at its hour" ("What Is It O'Clock?" 82).

That being said (and the saying is not nothing), she sets up the password (where I am headed) with this passage:

> Now I'm going to make my (silent) declaration of love to a person I've loved since birth; double birth, ours, like the mother is born of the child's birth:
>
> "Go away. I love your departures. I give you compete freedom. This is the condition for my being able to hope for your comings, hope, heart beating, hope spiced with fear, fear that this is never without hope's *élan*, contraction and dilatation, this is the rhythm of my organism in love. And the freedom I give you takes nothing from you.
>
> "The first gesture that links us was to have cut the umbilical cord. Each one for herself: you can go, I'll wait for you. I'm not waiting for you: you can come. I'm not (like) you. You're not like me. I don't mistake you for me. I don't think I know you. Leave, my love, you who's just left (me)." Say I. ("What Is It O'Clock?" 80)

The first password is "I."[11] ("I have fasted. I have drunk the *kykeon*.") Or: *I had a baby in secret*. The father was a preacher's son who later became a preacher himself (*logos spermatikos*). He denied the child was his. But I knew. The fetus knew. I was seventeen. It was 1970. And like four million other girls and young women between 1950 and 1973 ("Adoption"), I made a decision to surrender my child for adoption. I lived in a home for "unwed" mothers for four months. I paid the $250 total rent from my earnings that previous summer as a tennis instructor. I bore a daughter in secret, without my family present (though they were loving and supportive and nearby). The delivery room was dark. I was given no anesthetic. I was told to push. I pushed. Then I was told to stop pushing. I said, "I can't." They covered my nose with a rubber cup and told me to breathe, and during my dream I was separated from her, she from me.

I need Cixous to bear witness to what happened next: "The first gesture was to have cut the umbilical cord. Each one for herself: you can go, I'll wait for you" ("What Is It O'Clock?" 80). But after she left, I had to wait eighteen years before I would see her for the first time. She was taken down the hall to the nursery in the hospital. I was told to walk the halls for exercise after I gave birth. I would drift toward the nursery. There was one room beside the visible babies that had its curtain drawn. She was there, alone. I was on the outside, alone. It was like a dream, but not a dream. Cixous likens it to "the story of the hen who doesn't recognize her egg. . . . With the child it's the same, the work of art is the same" (80). And so she was taken, to a family who loved her very much from that day forward.

I had to deal with my "abandonment" of her for many years. But then after this long fast, I drank the *kykeon*. Cixous understands (she stands under me):

> This is love. I will never know how I love you. I love you I don't even know it. You will never know how I love you. . . . Not understanding is a way of holding myself in front and of letting come. Transverbal, transintellectual relationship [sacred], this loving the other in sub-mission to the mystery. (It's accepting, not knowing, forefeeling, feeling with the heart.) . . . I'm speaking in favor of closeness, *without any familiarity*. How good it is not to understand you. I don't understand you with an incomprehension so vast it surpasses all my great understanding of you. But I pass through an incomprehension of you towards you, one that doesn't abandon you. It's a great activity of feeling and not translating. I say to you: world. (81)

The second password is "world." She, my daughter, was/is of the world. I moved about in the world wondering, wandering, searching for her in my heart. Finally searching for her in the databases until she was found. We were joyfully reunited. Eighteen years of "world" between us, the password called "world" is not secret, it is the passage that is secret. Cixous admits that of "world": "The password? No password. But there is the sign that says natal, fatal, destinal country: heart beating" (81). So, even the world, which we know is fatal, cannot be only a password, for it passes—eventually— without us. Into an unknown passage we pass through with every-one. Yet we do have one more password that I have saved for last, one that Cixous renders with a rhetorical if/then argument (not one born of the masculine if/then logic):

> If there were a word, [then] it would be the most ordinary, immense word, synonym of infinity, distracted word, unnoticed, word that passes, so humbly, almost useless, a word that could just as well fall silent, it would be, yes, you have recognized it, yes, it would be yes, the raw word, the believable, the unbelievably vast, the open door to all that will come, a courageous word, open-handed, yes, I receive, I let go.
>
> But in the region under the Passat [Celan's word for wind], all the words without exception are easily worth a yes, they all say yes too. No too.
>
> I tell you yes. I begin us with a Yes. Yes begins us. (81)

I am persuaded, it is believable because I have lived this "Yes" and "World" and "I" in the surrender of my daughter, in my nonrecognition of her, in my finding her for the first time—seeing her for the first time sitting on a sacred horse, the Yes of the natural world. The *kykeon* that must be drunk while it swirls in motion, always in motion. Not conceived via the *logos spermatikos*. I end with a female revealer, intoxicated from the sacred with/in rhetoric that took forty-eight years to reveal itself as neither inside nor outside, but as a sacred passage begun with the words "stop pushing." I do not say, "I can't." I say Yes. I say I. My daughter *is*. This is why I can say to the "world," "I am the whore *and* the holy one." There is nothing more sacred.

Notes

1. Reeve refers here to SVF (*Stoicorum Veterum Fragmenta*) 1.497, 2.780, 1027, 1074, 3.141.

2. According to Kenneth Burke, "By casuistic stretching, one introduces new principles while theoretically remaining faithful to old principles" (*Attitudes Toward History*, 229). Burke advocates a "liquid attitude toward speech" (231), which is how I view the juxtaposition of opposites in "The Thunder, Perfect Mind," as well as in the interstices, the between, that these forgotten passages reveal. I

would like to thank Kyle Jensen for reminding me of Burke's definition of casuistry.

3. Much of the scholarship lays the blame for his discreditation at the feet of his philosophy, but often feminizes him in the process. In one example, *Heidegger and Modernity*, Luc Ferry and Alain Renaut argue that Heidegger is guilty of fascist/racist theory and practice. There are, however, serious problems with their study. First, Ferry and Renaut base their claim solely on brief explications of still briefer passages in *Being and Time*. This is not in and of itself problematic unless (and especially) one is grounded in a humanist theory of the subject that bases its critique on objectivist rationalist logic (as described by Andrea Nye). Basically, Ferry and Renaut launch a discourse of counter-outrage without being self-conscious of their own ideological complicity. In addition, their attack is laced with highly charged language. In a direct feminization of the French Heideggerian response (i.e., that of Heidegger's "disciples") to Victor Farías's revelations, Ferry and Renaut have this to say: "In short, according to a superb witches' brew, everything was known and there wasn't anything there to know. Therefore, one will go on unruffledly managing the inheritance: nothing happened, nothing could have happened, and that is why your daughter can't talk" (27). By using the "witches brew" analogy and by implying that these critics are "unruffledly managing the inheritance," Ferry and Renaut not only mix their metaphors (the witch and the father), they unwittingly reveal their own desires to "manage the inheritance" of Holocaust narratives. Either way, it becomes a matter of competing motivations. Ferry and Renaut would have us believe *they* are the "proper" fathers acting on behalf of their daughters who cannot talk. Thus their *ethos* supposedly stakes a greater moral and familial claim. This is not said to diminish in any way the horrific nature of suffering by the victims of the Holocaust; rather, it is said in order to reveal (perhaps) what is at stake in advancing their attack on Heidegger.

4. Thomas Fay makes this his focus in *Heidegger: The Critique of Logic*. Fay skillfully

explicates Heidegger's critique while arguing that he did not reject logic so much as suggest that "there is more than one path to Being" (115). According to Fay, we should not presume that "going back to the original sense of *logos*, does not necessarily entail giving oneself up to irrationalism" (115).

5. See David Farrell Krell's "Hegel, Heidegger, Heraclitus" for an excellent article that brings together all three thinkers on the problem of metaphysics.

6. We should point out here that Heidegger does seem to recant this position (if only by clarifying) in his "Facts and Thoughts" essay ("Self-Assertion"), which attempts to explain his Rectorate Address of 1933.

7. Although I do not believe that Nye's counterproposal of critical (careful) reading is as effective as it could be, it is necessary to consider a history of logic written "against the grain," so to speak. (Reading is crucial, but surely it requires other tactics, such as the construction of a different *symbolic*.) In other words, her account reminds us that we must be suspicious of histories or interrogations that rely solely on philology (as Heidegger is *prone* to do). The problem is that philology, as John of Salisbury reminds us, means "love of reason" (McGarry *Metalogicon*, 266).

8. Aristotle also believed that humans are "political animals" (i.e., communal) because they have the power of *logos* (*Politics* 1.1.1253a15–18, qtd. throughout Schiappa, *Protagoras and Logos*).

9. IJsseling develops his own account of the shift from *logos* as speech to reason that corresponds to Nye's only in its treatment of Plato and Aristotle. In IJsseling's view, the shift occurs for several reasons: (1) Plato's hostile rejection of rhetoric, (2) the different meanings of *logos* of old (e.g., number, account, connection, discourse, significance), and (3) the theological association of *logos* with the divine (e.g., divine word, divine fate, order of the cosmos, personal thought of God, the *ratio essendi*) (*Rhetoric and Philosophy*, 20–21). See also Gerhard Kittel for a comprehensive tracing of the term *logos* from its Presocratic roots through its shift to Stoic logic (*Theological Dictionary*, 69–91).

10. It was truly not until this moment in the writing of this essay that I realized what wanted to be written, that had to be revealed.

11. Thanks to Kyle Jensen, who pointed me to Richard M. Doyle's essay, "Abducted by Nada: Ego Death, Open Source, and the Importance of Doing Nothing in the Infoquake," in which Doyle offers another (connected) version of the "I" in the spiritual teachings of Gnosticism. An important difference between our readings of the Gnostic Gospels, however, is in his focus on how their vision of the self leads to "ego death" (265). I am following Cixous's exhortation to her daughter at the moment of birth, "Say 'I.'"

Bibliography

Buerkert, Walter. *The Anthropology of Ancient Greek Sacrificial Ritual and Myth*. Translated by Peter Bing. Berkeley: University of California Press, 1983.

Burke, Kenneth. *Attitudes Toward History*. 3rd ed. Berkeley: University of California Press, 1984.

———. *Greek Religion*. Cambridge, MA: Harvard University Press, 1985.

Cixous, Hélène. "Preface." In *Stigmata: Escaping Texts*, xi–xvi. Translated by Catherine A. F. MacGillivray. 2nd ed. London: Routledge, 2005.

———. "What Is It O'Clock? or The Door (We Never Enter)." In *Stigmata: Escaping Texts*, 57–83. Translated by Catherine A. F. MacGillivray. London: Routledge, 1998.

Doyle, Richard M. "Abducted by Nada: Ego Death, Open Source, and the Importance of Doing Nothing in the Infoquake." In *Abducting Writing Studies*, edited by Sidney I. Dobrin and Kyle Jensen, 255–69. Carbondale: Southern Illinois University Press, 2017.

Fay, Thomas A. *Heidegger: The Critique of Logic*. The Hague: Martinus Nijhoff, 1977.

Ferry, Luc, and Alain Renaut. *Heidegger and Modernity*. Translated by Franklin Philip. Chicago: University of Chicago Press, 1990.

Guthrie, W. K. C. "Flux and *Logos* in Heraclitus." In *The Pre-Socratics*, edited by Alexander P. D. Mourelatos, 197–213. New York: Anchor Press, 1974.

Heidegger, Martin. *Early Greek Thinking*. Translated by David Farrell Krell and Frank A. Capuzzi. San Francisco: Harper & Row, 1984.

———. *An Introduction to Metaphysics*. Translated by Ralph Manheim. New Haven, CT: Yale University Press, 1959.

———. "Letter on Humanism." In *Martin Heidegger: Basic Writings*, edited by David Farrell Krell, 189–242. New York: Harper & Row, 1977.

———. *On the Way to Language*. Translated by Peter D. Hertz. New York: Harper & Row, 1971.

———. "The Self-Assertion of the German University: Address, Delivered on the Solemn Assumption of the Rectorate of the University Freiburg; the Rectorate, 1933/34: Facts and Thoughts." Translated by Karsten Harries. *Review of Metaphysics* 38 (March 1985): 467–502.

IJsseling, Samuel. *Rhetoric and Philosophy in Conflict: An Historical Survey*. Translated by Paul Dunphy. The Hague: Martinus Nijhoff, 1976.

Irigaray, Luce. "Plato's *Hystera*." In *Speculum of the Other Woman*, 243–364. Translated by Gillian C. Gill. Ithaca, NY: Cornell University Press, 1985.

Kellner, Hans. *Language and Historical Representation: Getting the Story Crooked*. Madison: University of Wisconsin Press, 1989.

Kittel, Gerhard, ed. *Theological Dictionary of the New Testament*. Vol. 4. Translated by Geoffrey W. Bromiley. Grand Rapids, MI: Eerdmans, 1967.

Krell, David Farrell. "Hegel Heidegger Heraclitus." In *Heraclitean Fragments*, edited by John Sallis and Kenneth

Maly, 22–42. Tuscaloosa: University of Alabama Press, 1980.

Lanham, Richard. *Motives of Eloquence.* New Haven, CT: Yale University Press, 1976.

MacRae, George W., trans. "The Thunder, Perfect Mind." In *The Nag Hammadi Library in English*, ed. James M. Robinson, 271–77. San Francisco: Harper & Row, 1978.

McGarry, Daniel D., trans. *The Metalogicon of John of Salisbury.* Gloucester, MA: Peter Smith, 1971.

Mylonas, George E. *Eleusis and the Eleusinian Mysteries.* Princeton, NJ: Princeton University Press, 1961.

Reeve, C. D. C. "A Study in Violets: Alcibiades in the Symposium." In *Plato's Symposium: Issues in Interpretation and Reception*, edited by James Lesher, Debra Nails, and Frisbee Sheffield. Washington, DC: Center for Hellenic Studies, 2007. https://chs.harvard.edu/CHS/article/display/6261.

Nye, Andrea. *Words of Power: A Feminist Reading of the History of Logic.* New York: Routledge, 1990.

Schiappa, Edward. *Protagoras and Logos: A Study in Greek Philosophy and Rhetoric.* Columbia: University of South Carolina Press, 1991.

CHAPTER 2

Engaging a Rhetorical God

Developing the Capacities of Mercy and Justice

DAVID FRANK

> At the beginning God created the heavens and the earth. The earth was
> without form and void, desolate of people and empty of all animals; dark-
> ness was upon the surface of the deep and a merciful wind [or spirit of
> mercy] from before God was blowing over the surface of the water.
>
> —*TARGUM PSEUDO-JONATHAN: GENESIS*
> (TRANS. MICHAEL MAHER)

> For three years the [the rabbinical schools] of Beth Shammai and Beth
> Hillel disagreed. . . . Ultimately, a heavenly voice emerged and said,
> "[Both schools] expressed the words of the living God." However, *hal-
> akha* [Jewish law and tradition] preferred the opinion of Beth Hillel
> because [the school] was "agreeable and forbearing, showing restraint
> when affronted, and when they taught *halakha*, the school would teach
> both their own statements and the statements of Beth Shammai. More-
> over, when they formulated their teachings and cited a dispute, they
> prioritized the statements of Beth Shammai to their own statements, in
> deference to Beth Shammai."
>
> —*THE BABYLONIAN TALMUD* (TRANS. ISADORE EPSTEIN)

The primary characteristic of the divine, Michael Bernard-Donals argues,
is its violent displacement of the human being. This violent displacement

takes place in two phases. First, the divine is defined as an "altogether other" ("'Difficult Freedom,'" 408) by the human. Drawing from the work of modern thinkers, including Emmanuel Lévinas, Jean-François Lyotard, Walter Benjamin, and a host of others, Bernard-Donals contends that the human subject, when addressing the divine, "is compelled to speak in the face of that which radically exceeds it" (400). The essence of the divine is so far beyond that of the human as to make communion impossible, creating an unbridgeable displacement.

This first displacement is joined to a second. As Bernard-Donals writes, rhetoric is displaced from any referent as language itself is "foiled by temporality" (402)—the relationship between the symbol and reality is disrupted by the continual displacement of the symbol's referent by the passage of time. The nature of the divine "exceeds language's ability to denote it," creating displacement, rupture, and in Bernard-Donals's subtle reading, there is present a "rhetorical violence" (405) when humans and the divine engage in communication. The divine is "set apart" (406) from the human. As Bernard-Donals summarizes, "The divine marks the subject's separateness from community, defying the subject's ability to forge a knowledge of that singularity and undermining the subject's certainty about the ground on which she stands and the name that she provides for herself as a resident of that community or territory. The divine, in other words, puts into question the subject's capacity to establish a community, a 'we,' and unmoors the human subject from himself and from the location of utterance. And it is this displacement that is, in fact, the only home we have" (408). The divine, in this reading, is beyond the pale of rhetoric, for God is impervious to the reasoning and speech of the human.

I honor these insights but offer an argument of contrast and disagreement. I concede the very real existence of divine cruelty, rhetorical violence, and displacement. I pair this concession with an understanding of the divine that develops (and continues to develop) the capacity for mercy and justice. Bernard-Donals denies the very possibility that the divine might understand, love, or achieve communion with the human. The divine, which is captured for my purposes in the figure of God as it is displayed in the Hebrew scriptures, develops the capacities for mercy and justice as a function of engagements with and confrontations by humans who protest against God's injustice and divine violence. While rhetoric can produce displacement, I suggest that it also offers God and humans the capacity to participate in communication that crosses and bridges the chasm between the divine and human.

Chaïm Perelman and Lucie Olbrechts-Tyteca call the moment of meaningful rhetorical communication "le contact des esprits" (*New Rhetoric*, 15–17), which James Crosswhite suggests should be understood as the "meeting of lives" (*Rhetoric of Reason*, 21). My review of the Jewish thought that wrestles with the human-divine relationship suggests that the lives of God and the human can meet and engage rhetorically by working through disagreements with reason and speech. As they do so, both develop the capacities for moral judgment and mercy. There is a rhetorical god and a sense of the divine nested in a rhetorical cosmos. In the spirit of the argumentative approach taken by the rabbinical school Beth Hillel, I will prioritize and treat with charity the claims opposing those I make in this chapter.

These claims are developed in two important statements on the relationship between rhetoric and divine in the contemporary literature: Allen Scult, Michael Calvin McGee, and J. Kenneth Kuntz's analysis of the book of Genesis and Michael Bernard-Donals's essay on divine cruelty and rhetorical violence, which I summarized at the outset of this essay. Drawing from an interdisciplinary analysis of Genesis 1–3, Scult, McGee, and Kuntz display, in a sophisticated rhetorical analysis, how the first book of the Hebrew Bible has come to command such power in Western culture. There are, the authors observe, two accounts of creation in Genesis 1–3: one authored by "P" that depicts a God "with the absolute power of a creator" ("Genesis and Power," 123); and a second, composed by "J," that tells the story of a "conflict between God's authority . . . and human free will" (123). Ultimately, the authors write, human free will yields to the power and authority of God.

"As human beings live through the story of their relationship with God," the authors continue, "their participation in creation is circumscribed by God's authorship." God has "absolute power." This is a "kind of power that does not recognize human choice and does not brook, or even tolerate, the possibility of resistance, dissent, or conflict. It is self-willful, existing without equal or opposite will and with no notion even of the desirability of negotiation. It is perfect and permanent" (124–25). In his essay, Bernard-Donals develops the implications of the divine's absolute power for rhetoric.

Scult, McGee, and Kuntz's interpretation of the deity they discover in Genesis and Bernard-Donals's depiction of the divine features a God and a sense of the divine that is unitary, all powerful, capable of abuse and violence, with rhetoric serving the ends of displacement. In their accounts, God and the divine are framed as immutable and unchanging. Rabbinic commentary in the early tannaitic period (10 CE–220 CE) supports their interpretations, directly confronting the one I offer. The rabbis held that "God should not be critiqued, controverted, or challenged, but submissively encountered," suggesting that my interpretation can and should be challenged (Weiss, *Pious Irreverence*, 22). God is a "rock," proclaims the Sifre Devarim midrashim: "His work is perfect: His actions in regard to all creatures of the world are perfect; there can be no complaint whatsoever about His work" (Hammer, *Sifre*, 310). These "anti-protest" rabbis did not brook dissent against a divine commanding the qualities of a rock and perfection.

The rhetorical god I portray has a biography and a life, is capable of mercy, justice fueled violence and abuse, joy, laughter, surprise, and change (Miles, *God*; Waisanen, Friedman, and Friedman, "What's So Funny"). This is the sense of the divine developed by the "pro-protest" rabbis during and after amoraic era (230 CE). According to the pro-protest rabbis, God was not morally or essentially perfect, nor was the divine moored in an unchanging, immutable essence (Weiss, *Pious Irreverence*). God would develop the capacity to share language and conversation, and then to argue and debate with humans. Through conversation, argument, and debate, God develops, between his initial exchange with Adam in Genesis to his last argument with a human in Job, the capacities of mercy and justice. This god has a multitude of names reflecting the diachronic development of moral faculties.

In Genesis 1 the deity is called "Elohim," or God creating and judging (Dahl and Segal, "Philo"). Rashi, who is responsible for the "most authoritative" commentary on the Torah, alerts us to a tension God faced, at the beginning of creation, between justice and mercy (Levy and Levy, *JPS Rashi*, xvi). God, Rashi teaches, intended to create the world with the divine standard of justice, but "perceived that the world would not endure, so He preceded it with the Divine Standard of Mercy, allying it with the Divine Standard of Justice" (Pearl, *Rashi*, xv). Divine justice, without mercy, as the Zohar would highlight, could be violent and abusive. This is a foundational tension central to formation and evolution of a rhetorical cosmos, one driving the moral development of the divine and human.

When the creator-God endows humans with reason and speech in Genesis 2, and seeks conversation with them in Genesis 3, the creator's name changes to "YHWH Elohim." YHWH is "equated with the attribute of mercy" and becomes justice's predicate (Dahl and Segal, "Philo," 14). Given the events in Genesis 4, which include the first recorded murder following from the first recorded argument, the name used in this chapter is "YHWH," which interpreters suggest captures the deity's aspirations to, in Rashi's words, ally mercy with justice. Yet Hebrew scripture documents an angry and violent YHWH, displacing rhetoric and abusing humans, offering proof of Bernard-Donals's claim. David Blumenthal, in his *Facing the Abusive God*, writes, "We must begin, under the seal of truth, by admitting that Scripture does indeed portray God as an abusive person; that God, as agent in . . . sacred scripts, does indeed act abusively; that God, as described in the Bible, acts like an abusing male, husband, father and lord" (242). Blumenthal concludes with a qualification: "*God is abusive, but not always*" (247). Acknowledging "abusive behavior is *inexcusable in all circumstances*," Blumenthal pivots to recognize that God "is often loving and fair, even kind and merciful" (247). The divine, Blumenthal writes, hosts a range of attributes with the good pitted against the bad. The capacities of the divine and human unfold in Hebrew scripture and its interpretation in the sixty-six books of the Hebrew Bible, from the first exchange between God and Adam in Genesis to the last exchange between God and humans in Job.

Hebrew scripture, as Erich Auerbach has explained, calls for a different mode of interpretation than that used to understand ancient Greek texts. The texts I consider here are, in Auerbach's words, "fraught with background" that is incomplete, unexpressed, and "require subtle investigation and interpretation" (*Mimesis*, 15). The divine as revealed in the Hebrew Bible and the Torah (the first five books of the Hebrew scriptures) need the interpretations offered by Rashi, the Talmud, the Zohar (the teachings of the Kabbalah), the Targum (Aramaic translations and interpretations of the Hebrew Bible), and Jewish folklore (Berlin, Brettler, and Fishbane, *Jewish Study Bible*; Levy and Levy, *JPS Rashi*, v; Neusner, *Talmud*, viii; Epstein, *Babylonian Talmud*; Lachower and Tishby, *Wisdom of the Zohar*; McNamara, Cathcart, and Maher, *Aramaic Bible*; Stern, "Introduction"). The Talmud establishes the principles of "normative Judaism," the Zohar is "a source of doctrine and revelation equal in authority to the Bible and Talmud," the Targum are considered "sacred writings along with Scripture and other religious texts," and the Jewish folklore collected in Louis Ginzberg's *Legends* is the first book "to which a student or scholar turns to learn the main lines of the postbiblical understanding of a biblical episode and its sources" (Scholem, *Zohar*, vii; Neusner, *Talmud*, 1; McNamara, Cathcart, and Maher, *Aramaic Bible*, 319; Stern, "Introduction," xxxii). Taken collectively, these texts that interpret the Hebrew Bible make up the Aggadah, or the body of work designed to translate sacred texts into practice.

To illustrate Auerbach's thesis and the need for texts that interpret Hebrew scripture, consider the "fraught background" and elliptical expression that makes up the prelude to the argument between Cain and Abel: "Cain said to his brother Abel . . . and when they were in the field, Cain set upon his brother Abel and killed him." The Hebrew text, with the ellipsis (absent in most English translations), does not tell the reader what Cain said to his brother. Filling the textual void, the Targum provide the argument that takes place between the brothers, revealing the motive for the murder and a central touchstone for the interpretation of merciful argumentation I offer below.

The texts seeking to tease out the meaning of the Hebrew scripture portray a God capable of collective punishment and open to the possibility of individual innocence (Gen. 18:23–32); anger and a willingness to let emotions cool (Exod. 32); a casual cruelty and recognition of divine wrongdoing (Job); surprise and the acknowledgment, with joy, that humans might win an argument with the divine (Babylonian Talmud Seder Nezikin 353); affirming singular and multiple truths (Babylonian Talmud Seder Moed 85–86). These interpretations reveal a God that acts on and is reactive to creation, that is abusive and merciful, and that is capable of disruptive and authentic communication. The Targum, relative to the Hebrew scripture, stresses the value of mercy. Consistent with Blumenthal's conclusions, the Zohar reads the Hebrew scripture and finds a God that acts out in violence in the name of justice if mercy is absent.

These texts, which interpret Hebrew scripture, set forth a profoundly rhetorical cosmos, one that gives creation agency and establishes a "rhetorical wedge" (Johnstone, "Rhetoric") between the divine and creation. To illustrate, the spirit and winds of mercy appear, during the ongoing act of creation, "before God": "This gives the spirit a character independent of

God; it is the 'Spirit of mercy,' not directly the 'Spirit of God,' in the same way that a human being may be said to have spirit. . . . It is not God's own Spirit of mercy but a spirit that was 'before' him, that is, in front of [God]" (McNamara, Cathcart, and Maher, *Aramaic Bible*, 21–22). The spirit and wind of mercy operates almost independently of God, and as scholars with a strong command of Hebrew and Hebrew scripture have explained, the earth and sky were persuaded, not commanded, by God in Genesis 1 to collaborate in the act of creation (Brown, "Divine Act"). Underscoring the centrality of rhetoric in creation, God speaks his contributions to creation into existence. And in Genesis 4, the earth cries out in moral anguish in response to the murder of Abel, revealing an independence from the divine and a moral commitment to human life (Jørstad, "Ground That Opened"). The cosmos itself is steeped in rhetoric. While acknowledging the truths in Bernard-Donals's depiction of displacement as a primary characteristic of the divine-human relationship, these truths should be joined to a recognition that this relationship is also infused with reason, speech, language, conversation, argument, and debate that cultivate the capacities of divine and human understanding as well as the expansion of merciful and just action.

A RHETORICAL CREATION

Scult, McGee, and Kuntz portray a God creating the cosmos "through the active power of his word," exercising "full control over primordial chaos," ensuring that the "sun, moon, and stars . . . [are] made vassals responsible to one sovereign deity," with human beings "confined always to grammatical objectivity" ("Genesis and Power," 120). This God, they believe, "acts without reason, passion, or purpose in a scene specifically described as a void and formless waste of water and darkness. . . . There is no conflict in creation" (120). The interpretation of Genesis 1–4 I offer seeks to identify the rhetorical foundation of a cosmos that is a result of conflict, deliberation, and persuasion (Genesis 1); in which humans are endowed with reason and speech (Genesis 2); humans and the divine engage through questioning (Genesis 3); and, guided by the polar stars of mercy and justice, both humans and God struggle with their flaws (Genesis 4). In the wake of Genesis 1–4, God and humans develop a protest theology designed to confront failures and injustice and to enact mercy.

Genesis 1: A God of Persuasion and Deliberation

William P. Brown and Michael Welker, in separate works making use of a careful study of the Hebrew in Genesis 1, reach the same conclusions: God collaborates with the earth, the waters, and humans in the ongoing construction of the physical and symbolic cosmos. Creation is a result of deliberation, involving conversation, debate, and persuasion. Jewish folklore reports that God consulted with Torah (God's wisdom) before collaborating in the act of creation, and Rashi tells us God consulted with the angels before creating the human (Pearl, *Rashi*). God had faith that humans would, as a result of the nudges of hell and paradise, serve the causes of mercy and justice.

As God enters the scene of a creation in process, the winds of mercy are blowing across waters that seem to preexist God's arrival. God does issue "divine commands" (e.g., "Let the earth sprout vegetation," "Let the waters swarm a swarming of living creatures"), though these commands should be read, Brown and Welker explain, more as divine invitations than dictates. As Brown observes, the Hebrew indicates that "the commands to the earth and the waters are invitations to enter into the grand creative sweep of God's designs" ("Divine Act," 29). Brown continues, "God is not set over and against creation but rather with creation, exhorting certain elements to yield their appropriate products (vegetation, sea creatures, etc.). Such a creative process does not thereby imply a God who simply impose order on unruly matter or creates everything ex nihilo" (29). The earth and waters are active participants in the creation of the nature. Jewish folklore recounts that the waters resisted God's efforts: "When God commanded, 'Let the waters be gathered together, unto one place, and let the dry land appear,' certain parts refused to obey. They embraced each other all the more closely. In His wrath at the waters, God determined to let the whole of creation resolve itself into chaos again" (Ginzberg, *Legends*, 12). The waters would repent.

After the creation of the physical cosmos and nonhuman living things, God made a declaration that became a debate resolution: "And God said to the angels who minister before him 'Let us make man in our image [*imitatio dei*], in our likeness'" (Maher, *Targum Pseudo-Jonathan: Genesis*, 20–21). Rashi teaches that God sought to consult with the angels about the desirability of creating the human knowing that God would need their support. After vigorous debate, the angels were equally divided on the question. The

Angel of Truth opposed the resolution because humans would lie, the Angel of Peace did as well because humans would be quarrelsome. The Angels of Justice and Love supported the resolution, arguing that humans would practice justice and affection. Although the angels were equally divided, God, who remained in support of the resolution, used His power to secure their assent through manipulation and the withholding of evidence (Ginzberg, *Legends*, 51–53). When God sent the angel Gabriel to earth for the materials to make the human, the earth resisted, claiming that the earth would "become a curse" because of the human. God ignored the complaint, seized the dust from the ground, and created the human (53). Genesis 1 ends with the human embedded, like the earth and wind, within the realm of the physical universe; in Genesis 2 the human is endowed with the capacities of the rhetor, ready to complement the physical universe with culture.

Genesis 2: A God That Endows Humans with Reason, Speech, and Two Inclinations

Over a six-day period, recounted in Genesis 1, God and creation collaborated to make significant progress in the formation of the physical universe. In Genesis 2, the cultural universe is the subject of creation. God breathes into the nostrils of the human and the human becomes a living soul. Rashi teaches us that God endowed the human with "reason and speech," capacities not granted to the cattle and beasts (Ben-Isaiah and Sharfman, *Pentateuch and Rashi's Commentary*, 1:21). This yoking of reason and speech, Perelman and Olbrechts-Tyteca suggest, is the very definition of rhetoric. God then vested the human with the responsibility to name the animals, giving the human control over the symbols and representations needed to create culture.

Humans and God use the endowment of rhetoric to develop the capacities of conversation, argument, and debate. Although this is another step in the unfolding of creation, it is noticeable that after Genesis 1, in which all the acts of creation are declared "good" by God, the acts of invention in Genesis 2, including the endowment of the human with the powers of reason and speech, are not celebrated or judged as good by God. This silence might allow us to conclude, with Aristotle, that rhetoric, as defined in Hebrew scripture, is a neutral art that can be used for good or evil.

Along with the endowment of reason and speech, the human is created with two inclinations (*yetzer*): one good (*yetzer hatov*), the other evil (*yetzer hara*) (Maher, *Targum Pseudo-Jonathan: Genesis*, 22). Based on the stories recorded in Genesis and subsequent books, the consensus of the rabbinical interpretation is that humans are in a constant struggle with these two inclinations. The history recorded in the Bible reveals that reason and speech can produce both good and evil. The rabbis identified a rhetorical polylactic to prevent the evil *yetzer* from winning the struggle: "Since both obeying the law and engaging in study are called 'Torah,' it is at the same time the therapeutic tool for tackling the *yetzer* and the central object of its attacks" (Rosen-Zvi, *Demonic Desires*, 24). The goal of Torah study is to prevent the victory of the evil *yetzer* by impressing the very words of the Torah on the heart.

As a therapeutic tool, the Torah study is oral and essentially argumentative. David Kraemer has thoroughly documented how reason and speech expressed in argumentation are at the center of the Torah study (*Mind of the Talmud*). Prominently citing the work of Perelman and Olbrechts-Tyteca, Kraemer identifies how the active argumentative engagement involved in the study of Torah fosters moral reasoning, a humility in the face of multiple truths, and can inspire mercy and resistance to evil. Similarly, God is conflicted, needing argumentation to sustain a rapprochement between mercy and justice.

The Zohar explains the conflicted nature of the divine and depicts God as having two sides: *Sitra D'Kedushah* (the side of holiness) and the *Sitra Achra* (the side of evil). "Evil," Isaiah Tishby tells us, is "portrayed as an organic process . . . something that is implanted . . . in the natural life of the Godhead" (Lachower and Tishby, *Wisdom of the Zohar*, 460). In dealing with the conflicted nature of the divine, God needs—according to Michael Hyde's review of the Kabbalah and the writings of Isaac Luria, Marc-Alain Quaknin, and Abraham Heschel—the assistance of humans to achieve mercy and justice. Blumenthal's conclusion is that "God is corroborated in zoharic Judaism, which teaches that God has an 'irrational side' and that he 'did not step over a boundary calling God abusive; although it is not a doctrine we teach in public'" ("What Are the Limits," 625). Tishby continues that among the ten attributes of God outlined in the Zohar, "the main view [expressed in the Zohar] is that evil has its origins in the divine attribute of

Judgment" (Lachower and Tishby, *Wisdom of the Zohar*, 461). Evil erupts
out of judgment when it is out of alignment with mercy.

"When there is harmony and reciprocity among the powers and attributes within the divine system," writes Tishby, "Judgment is one of the
foundations of the divine world and of creation, for their survival depends
on the correct tension and balancing of opposites" (Lachower and Tishby,
Wisdom of the Zohar, 459). To achieve this "correct tension" and "the balancing of opposites," it is imperative that "Love and Judgment (*Hesed* and
Din), which are by nature extreme opposites, are mingled together in mercy
(*Rahamim*)" (Lachower and Tishby, *Wisdom of the Zohar*, 461). Without
the check that love serves on the powers of judgment, then "the fire of
Judgment becomes a destructive and murderous conflagration, burning and
consuming with great cruelty, heeding neither law nor justice, and it is in
this condition that it engenders and sustains the power of evil" (Levy and
Levy, *JPS Rashi*). Unbridled, justice draws its fuel from "furious anger,"
which destroys the correct tension and the balancing of opposites offered
by mercy. Foreshadowing a theme I intend to develop, it is with a protest
theology based on argument that divine judgment can be brought into correct tension and the balancing of opposites. To accomplish these aspirations,
it must be possible for the divine and the human to communicate, which is
the topic of Genesis 3.

Genesis 3: A God That Engages with Language, Conversation, and Questions

God places Adam in the Garden of Eden and draws from him a companion
named Eve. As God is walking in the garden in the direction of the sun, He
engages Adam with a question: "Where are you?" Avivah Zornberg translates Rashi's interpretation in this manner: "God knew where he was, but
asked [Adam] in order to *enter into language with him*" ("Seduced into
Eden," 207). Zornberg's translation allows her to feature the role played by
language as a mediating bridge between the divine and human. "One might
almost say," writes Zornberg, "that God's main wish is not for a particular
content or truth to be spoken, but for a world of language to be entered in
which, for the first time, man can express himself to God" (207). Adam has
named the animals and himself; his use of symbols is competent. But here
he must move beyond taxonomy to an engagement with the divine. More

traditional interpretations of Rashi have him declaring that "God knew where he was but asked [Adam] in order to enter *conversation* with him" (Ben-Isaiah and Sharfman, *Pentateuch and Rashi's Commentary*, 21). At this point, God and humans have, because of an initial question, exercised and developed the capacities of a shared language and then conversation.

Adam responds to the question by telling God that he has heard the divine, that he hid from God because he was naked and afraid. God responds with a second and third question: "Who told you that you are naked? Did you eat from the fruit of the from the tree of which I commanded you not to eat?" Adam responds, "I heard the voice of your Memra [speech] in the garden and I was afraid, for I was naked, because I neglected the commandment you gave me, and I hid myself for shame" (Maher, *Targum Pseudo-Jonathan: Genesis*, 27). In this episode, the divine and human have communicated, the human has heard and understood the voice of the divine, so there is no "excess" preventing "le contact des esprits." God's first question "will unlock the new that language, after the unequivocal competence of Adam's naming of all things, will liberate the conflicting voices within him. This, paradoxically, is the discourse that God desires: the incisive, imperious wisdom of naming by the free associations of a self newly uncanny to itself" (Zornberg, "Seduced into Eden," 207). Adam cannot return to the "language of pure naming. . . . [He] must learn to use a flexibly tensed speech in which meaning in continually transformed" (208–9). God unleashes Adam's linguistic capacities with God's question, forcing him into "painful confrontation with confusing truths" (209).

God did not engage the earth, waters, and the physical elements of creation with commands, but with divine invitations. With humans, God in Genesis and subsequent encounters uses questions, not dictates, to develop a relationship. The question, as Michel Meyer has explained, is foundational to the development and evolution of understanding (*What Is Rhetoric?*). God poses questions, seeking insight and communion with the human. Rather than asserting and imposing answers in God's engagement with Adam, the form of the conversations begins with and revolves around the question.

Genesis 2 teaches that the divine and human can communicate with language, achieving the goal of shared meaning. This same language can betray efforts to secure understanding. Rashi offers an interpretation of the "binding of Isaac" (Genesis 22) suggesting that Abraham misheard God.

The divine did not mean for Abraham to kill his son. Rather, God simply wanted Abraham to take his son up the hill. Understanding and misunderstanding are both linguistic capacities.

Adam moved from naming to conversation as a result of God's questions. Adam and Eve's "painful confrontations" with the truths that were confusing revealed a "deficit of a moral center" (Shulman, *Genius of Genesis*, 48). Adam admitted to defying God's command and eating the apple but deflected blame for his action, as did Eve. As a result, they found themselves outside the Garden of Eden, but were granted the joys and tribulations of parenthood. In Genesis 4, humans, having gained command of naming and conversation, develop the capacity for argument.

Genesis 4: God's Face and the First Argument

Adam and Eve's children, Cain and Abel, make offerings to God. Cain gave God the seed of flax, Abel brought the youngest members of his flock and their fat parts. God "turned a friendly face" toward Abel and his offering, "but to Cain and his offering he did not turn a friendly face." Cain was angry, "his face was downcast." This is the first moment in the Jewish texts that God's face is revealed and comes face to face with humans. God then asks Cain, "Why are you angry . . . ?" "Control your emotions," God insists, recognizing the two inclinations that do battle within the human soul. "If you do well" Cain, and avoid sin, "you will be fine." Cain then shifts the conversation to his brother and tells him to meet him in the fields. An argument takes place concerning God's preference for Abel's offering, one the Hebrew text does not recount, leaving it in the realm of ellipsis. The Targum Pseudo-Jonathan fills in the ellipsis, presenting Cain as launching the argument with these lines of reasoning: "I know that the world is created with mercies, but it is not led according to fruits of good deeds, and there is favoritism of persons in judgment: for what reason was your offering received and my offering not received from me with favor?" (Chilton, "Comparative Study," 556). Cain establishes the criterion for judging the dispute: the world is created with mercies, anchoring his claim in Genesis 1, which portrays the spirit and wind of mercy helping to create the world before God appeared. That God's judgment on the two offerings did not meet this standard is the core of Cain's argument—he and his offering have not been treated with mercy.

Abel answers, "The world is created with mercies, and it is led according to fruits of good deeds, and there is no favoritism of persons in judgment:

and because the fruits of my deeds surpassed yours—and were more timely than yours—my offering was received with favor" (556). Abel agrees with the criterion of mercy and claims that God's judgment is fair—that Abel's offerings were better than Cain's and that he was on time.

Cain provides a rebuttal: "There is no judgment and there is no judge, and there is no other world, and there is no giving of good reward to the righteous and there is no repaying from the wicked" (556). Here, Cain abandons a commitment to the criterion of mercy he introduces at the beginning, denies the existence of heaven and God, and portrays a universe absent a moral center. Abel answers, "There is judgment and there is a judge, and there is another world, and there is giving good reward to the righteous and there is repaying from the wicked" (556). Abel mimics his brother by abandoning the criterion of mercy, then justifies God's decision to favor Abel's offering by declaring the existence of heaven, God, and a universe that rewards good and punishes evil. The argument concludes with Cain driving a stone into his brother's forehead, ending the first recorded argument with the first recorded murder.

Cain's initial argument, and Abel's response, exhibit the signs of a genuine disagreement in which the criterion of judgment (mercy) is shared. By the third exchange, the criterion of mercy is discarded by both brothers, and their arguments become mutually exclusive, without a moral center to judge them. Cain's move to murder is unjustified. However, Abel shows no mercy to his brother, does not seek to understand his brother's anger, appreciate Cain's claims, or use lines of reasoning that acknowledge he is arguing with his only brother. Had both brothers agreed to moor their argument to the value of mercy, the trajectory to a reasonable conclusion might have evolved. If Abel failed in his argumentative responsibilities, Cain, in the wake of the murder, learned that there is judgment, there are judges in this and other worlds, and there is mercy.

God then comes on the scene and asks Cain, "Where is your brother Abel?" Cain responds, "I do not know, am I my brother's keeper?" Emmanuel Lévinas does not see Cain's response "as a case of simple insolence. Instead, it comes from someone who has not yet experienced human solidarity and who thinks (like many modern philosophers) that each exists for oneself and that everything is permitted" (Lévinas, *Difficult Freedom*, 20). Cain, Lévinas suggests, had not developed the moral capacity to care for his brother or for beings beyond himself. Yet Lévinas holds that Cain's murder of his brother has "disturbed the natural order." This is an order demanding an ethical commitment to others before all else (ethics before ontology). Cain seemed incapable of recognizing this demand because he did not look his brother in the face; had he done so he might not have murdered his sibling (Batnitzky, *Leo Strauss*, 25–26). The human face, Lévinas insists, is "the medium through which the invisible in him becomes visible and enters into commerce with us" (*Difficult Freedom*, 140). By not looking into his brother's face, Cain was guilty of a "sober coldness" and failing to see that the "trace" of God is in the face of the other. Could it be that Abel did not look his brother in the face during their argument, missing the suffering Cain experienced in the wake of God's rejection of his offering? Could it be Cain was mimicking his brother's emotionless response to Cain's pain?

Cain was cold to his brother, according to Lévinas, because his "pre-original" ethical responsibility for the other has yet to be awakened (Atterton, Calarco, and Friedman, *Levinas and Buber*, 45). "Is this not," Lévinas asks, "through the face of others, the very significance of the word of God, the unheard-of significance of the Transcendent that immediately concerns and awakens me?" (*In the Time*, 111). Because of the face and speech, Lévinas contends, it is possible to bridge the divide between the human and divine with an ethic of responsibility. Human morality is "awakened" through reason, speech, questioning, the confrontation of argument, and the face of the other.

The earth exercises moral agency in this story and is the first to judge Cain as "the land . . . becomes the source of testimony and indictment against him" (Jørstad, "Ground That Opened," 706). God tells Cain, "Your brother's blood is crying out to me from the ground." To his credit, Cain asks for forgiveness. Yet unlike the brothers, God is merciful. God does not murder Cain in response to the death of his brother, but does mark him as a murderer, and mandates that anyone who kills Cain will suffer vengeance. René Girard's theory of mimesis explains how God's decision to both punish Cain and seek his redemption "discourage[d] mimetic rivalry and generalized conflict," which ritualized an end to the violence and helped prevent the possibility of endless retributions (Girard, *Things Hidden*, 146).

In the aftermath of Genesis 1–4, a rhetorical universe is in play, comprising a God and humans with the capacities to reason and speak, use language to name things, engage in conversation, and argue. After repeated halting starts to engaging in conversation (Gen. 3) and argument (Gen. 4), God and humans develop their powers of communication. A key topic of discourse and frequent disagreement concerned the mercy-justice relationship. In facing a God that was abusive in the name of justice (but not always), rabbis and members of the Jewish community, beginning in the rabbinic age (70 CE–800 CE), developed a theology of protest that justified, and maybe even demanded, that they confront the abuse and injustice caused by the divine. Weiss had identified over 150 illustrations in Hebrew sacred texts of rabbis and important Jewish historical figures confronting and arguing with God (Weiss, *Pious Irreverence*, 11). The "arguing with God" theme is prominent in the history of Jewish rhetoric (Laytner, *Arguing with God*; Frank, "Arguing with God").

ALLYING MERCY AND JUSTICE: ABRAHAM, MOSES, AND JOB'S ARGUMENTS WITH GOD

Significant among the 150 illustrations of humans confronting God with argument are Abraham's argument with God about the fate of Sodom and Gomorrah (Gen. 18:16–33), Moses's engagement with the divine about the behavior of the Israelites (Exod. 32–33), Job's resistance to the violence visited on him by the divine (Job), and Rachel's success in triggering God's mercy (Lam.). I highlight these four illustrations to underscore the importance of argument in creating the pressure necessary for humans and God to develop the capacities of mercy and justice. In the illustrations I discuss below, humans mimic the argumentative approach used by God in Genesis 4. They all lead with and use questions in their arguments with God. They all seek to hold God to the principle of mercy, one that God has committed to at the beginning of creation. They all call on God to control His own anger. In these argumentative exchanges, God acknowledges the world and emotions of the human, the irreducible plurality of the cosmos, the possibility that the divine might be wrong, and the idea that God should pair mercy with justice.

Abraham's Argument with God

Before destroying Sodom, Gomorrah, Admah, Zeboiim, and Zoar, God declares that He will not act until Abraham has been informed, a pattern of consultation with others that God initiated at the beginning of creation.

Targum Pseudo-Jonathan, unlike the Hebrew Bible, explains why God seeks the destruction of the two cities: "because they oppress the poor and decree that whoever gives a morsel of bread to the needy shall be burned by fire." Unlike the text in the Hebrew Bible, Targum Pseudo-Jonathan has God state quite explicitly (a recurring theme in this targum) that he would "not take revenge" against the cities if they repent. Moses contests God's intent to destroy the cities and begins the first recorded argument with God with this question: "Shall your anger wipe out the innocent with the guilty?" The use of the question, which mimics the approach used by God in his exchanges with Adam and Cain, identifies anger as the source of God's judgment: "Will *your anger* wipe (them) out and not forgive the place for the sake of the merits of the fifty innocent people who are in it?" Unlike the text in the Hebrew Bible, Targum Pseudo-Jonathan identifies anger at four different moments as God's motivating reason to destroy the cities. Abraham argues that the innocent should not be victims of God's anger. God agrees.

Abraham then pairs his argument against anger with the more positive claim that God is merciful, one he makes eight times in Targum Pseudo-Jonathan, threading the value of mercy into the core of the dispute. If there are fifty innocent people in the cities, Abraham contends, "is it possible that he who judges the whole earth should not do justice?" God answers positively: "If in Sodom I find fifty innocent people . . . I will forgive the whole place for their sake." Abraham then joins justice to mercy, "*I beseech, by (your) mercy!* . . . What if five of the fifty innocent are lacking?" God responds, "I will not destroy if I find forty-five there." Abraham: "What if forty [innocents] are found? . . . *For the sake of your mercy*" please forgive the small city of Zoar. God agrees to this standard and request. Abraham responds, "What if thirty are found? . . . [for the] *sake of your mercy forgive [the cities] of Zeboiim and Zoar.*" God responds that He will not destroy the cities if thirty are found. Abraham responds, "What if twenty . . . are found? . . . *For the sake of your mercy*" will God forgive three of the cities that have not been listed to this point? God agrees. Abraham responds, "*I beseech by the mercy before you,* let not the anger of the Master of all the worlds, the Lord, be enkindled, and I will speak this last time. What if ten are found there, *and they and I beseech mercy for the whole place and you forgive them?*" God replies, "I will not destroy for the sake of the merits of ten." Unlike the Hebrew Bible, Targum Pseudo-Jonathan has God yielding to Abraham and committing to blanket mercy for all five cities if ten innocents are found.

In a reversal of the role played by God in Genesis 4, it is the human, not God, who leads the arguments with questions. It is the human who calls God to resist the influence of anger on judgment. Anger-fueled judgment, according to the Zohar, is the source of God's abuse, violence, and evil. Abraham smothers the fire of God's anger with the many reminders of God's essential mercy. Using the power of argument, Abraham brings into alignment the values of justice and mercy. Here, humans develop the capacity to persuade through reason, speech, and questioning, and God develops the capacity to change an initial judgment in the face of compelling arguments. Moses accomplishes the same goal in his dispute with God.

Moses's Argument and Engagement with God

The pattern of argumentation developed in Exodus 32 is similar to the one on display in the exchange between Abraham and God. Moses, who has traveled to the top of Mount Sinai, is confronted with an angry God. The people of Israel have done wrong. According to Targum Pseudo-Jonathan, God does not want to hear Moses defend his people: "*Do not entreat on their behalf* before me; *I will arouse a mighty burning anger* against them, and I will wipe them out, and make of you a great nation." Targum Neofiti, in its interpretation, highlights God's attempt to inoculate against the predictable attempt by Moses to call for mercy: "Now restrain yourself [Moses] *from beseeching mercy for them before me* that my anger may be enkindled against them and that I may blot them out." The anger-mercy pairing recurs.

Following the pattern introduced by God in His argument with Cain and Abraham's argument with God, Moses leads with a question: "Why, O Lord, is your anger kindled against your people, whom you brought out from the land of Egypt with great power, and with a mighty hand? . . . Turn from your blazing anger and let there be regret before you concerning the evil which you threatened to bring upon your people." Moses pointed out that God had made a commitment to people of Israel and that God would lose face if He betrayed that commitment. Moses was persuasive: "And the Lord repented about the evil which he had spoken (thought) to do to his people." That God "repented" reveals the power of argument to affect the divine. The appeal to mercy was effective.

Exodus 33 describes the communicative relationship between God and Moses moving from argument to an expression of Perelman and Olbrechts-Tyteca's "le contact des esprits." In the wake of Moses's successful argument with God recorded in Exodus 32, Moses sets up a "tent of meeting" designed to host conversations with the divine. God would visit the tent to engage Moses. The engagement is direct. The Hebrew text reports that the "Lord would speak to Moses face to face, as one man speaks to another." According to the Revised Standard Version, Moses would speak "face to face" with the divine as "a man speaks to his friend." Targum Neofiti interprets this passage as follows: "And the Lord spoke with Moses, *speech to speech*, as one speaks to his companion." At this time and place, the communication between the divine and human was in concert. Yet the book of Job, which marks the last argument and engagement between humans and the divine, substantiates Bernard-Donals's claim that the divine-human relationship is marred by violence and abuse.

The Book of Job

Scult, McGee, and Kuntz as well as Bernard-Donals can point to the divine's treatment of Job as substantial proof for their arguments: God does not negotiate with humans, but exercises raw power, inflicting misery on the human without good cause. Job is a good person, a man of mercy and justice. God showers violence and abuse on him, murdering his family, inflicting punishment on him "for no reason other than to prove to the devil that Job will indeed 'fear God for nought'" (Miles, *God*, 558). He is suffering: "My skin, blackened, is peeling off me; / My bones are charred by the heat." Job's three "friends" do not show him mercy, and instead blame him for his condition. The God who is willing to argue with Abraham and Moses earlier in the Hebrew scripture remains silent as Job calls out to the divine: "I cry out to You, but You do not answer me."

God does not share language, conversation, or argument with Job, displacing him with a gratuitous silence. But then God does answer, in anger, speaking out of a tempest rather than a gentle wind of mercy, marshaling an argument claiming a power and knowledge far beyond the pale of humans: "Where were you when I laid the earth's foundations?" Job, of course, was not there. Here, the reader finds the two phases of displacement Bernard-Donals describes. In the first phase, Job is displaced by God's refusal to answer his pleas, and when God does reply, it is not to the questions Job poses about the unjustified suffering he is experiencing. In the second phase, God displaces Job defining the divine as an excess surpassing and displacing that of the human. In the tradition, Job's final

response to God has been read as an acknowledgment of this double
displacement:

> You know you can do anything
> Nothing can stop you.
> . . .
> But now I see You with my eyes;
> Therefore, I recant and relent,
> Being but dust and ashes.

Job seems to concede—but does he?

Earlier in the chapter, Job understands that God may kill him, but that
he will continue to argue with God. The argument from power and superior
knowledge that God presents is not novel—Job's friends allude to it, and it
is a claim Job acknowledges before God is moved to speak. Job sees and
concedes that God is powerful, but is God merciful and just? Miles and
others suggest the word "repent" can be translated as "despise myself" and
that the final passage can be cast as follows: "Now that my eyes have seen
you, / I shudder with sorrow for mortal clay." Apparently moved by mercy
and compassion for Job, God "abandons his wager with the devil, and after
a vain attempt to shout Job down, atones for his wrongdoing by doubling
Job's initial fortune." God recognizes the abuse and violence God has visited
on a just man.

The last words in the Hebrew Bible spoken by God are to the suffering
Job, words of great insensitivity and callousness, which are then followed
by a form of restorative justice: Job regains his health, forms a new family,
and recovers his wealth. Miles explains the significance of the final exchange
between the divine and the human in the Hebrew scripture: "To be sure,
Job has brought his own all too simpleminded trust in God into accord with
a far more nuanced and mature Jewish wisdom—into accord, in other
words, with a realistic vision of the world in which justice is both guaranteed by the good God and occasionally threatened by the bad God. But the
God who is seen in this vision is new not just for Job but also for God
himself" (*God*, 327). Job experiences both the good God and the bad God;
however, "with Job's assistance, '[God's] just, kind self has won out over
[God's] cruel, capricious self.'"

This God of the good and bad, after the book of Job, does not speak again, withdrawing from direct contact with humans. The books in the Hebrew Bible following Job do not portray a God seeking conversation with humans, nor are there accounts of arguments between the divine and humans. The rabbis then take it upon themselves to represent God and the arguments that they imagined God would make. In so doing, they make the divine more human. Jacob Neusner and others have traced this transformation, describing the emergence of anthropomorphic expression of the divine. Suzanne Stone's midrash on rabbinic commentaries on Lamentations captures this trajectory and describes the "transformation of God from an impersonal, affectless, and unrelenting—almost ministerial—judicial figure to a judge who is capable of empathy . . . [which] is effected . . . through human persuasion and argument" ("Justice," 151). Her midrash reveals the development of a deep rhetoric shared by the divine and human, anchored in mercy and justice.

Stone's Midrash and Merciful Argumentation

The rabbinic commentary on Lamentations rehearses the same issues addressed by Abraham and Moses in their arguments with God. Because the people of Israel have not been faithful or good, they are sentenced with exile, threatened with death, and their sacred temple is destroyed. God holds a trial to see if this see if this sentence is just. Abraham and Moses reprise their roles as the defense council for the people of Israel, and God serves as the judge. Abraham interrogates the witnesses against the people of Israel. He is able to persuade them that, with their deeds, the people have been just; the witnesses did not testify, and so the case against the people collapses. God remains silent. Moses then defends the people by pointing out logical inconsistencies in God's behavior, ending his appeal with an implicit claim that God is a hypocrite because He had been inconsistent in applying the standards of justice in this case.

At the end of Moses's defense, God does not answer, and may have ruled against the people but for Rachel's intervention. As Moses was concluding, Rachel "leapt up" to defend the people. Rather than claim that the people had been just or that God was a hypocrite, Rachel appealed for mercy, citing the compassion and mercy she had shown to her sister Leah. If Rachel was capable of mercy, God should be as well. "Immediately, the compassion of

[God] was aroused. . . . 'For your sake, Rachel, I will restore Israel to its place.'" Stone's midrash seeks to identify "what triggers divine mercy" in this story and to detail "its quality and the emotional attitudes that underlie it" (152).

Stone suggests that her midrash "should be read as an exploration of the normative ethical categories of justice and mercy as applied to God" (147). One major purpose she accomplishes in the midrash is to prove that the qualities of justice and mercy were not, in the rabbinic tradition, tied inextricably to gender stereotypes. Justice was not a capacity assigned to males, with mercy relegated to females. Rather, these were fluid qualities both genders exercised. The quality of mercy, Stone contends, is not a function of gender; instead, it is "effected within our midrash through human persuasion and argument" (152). This point is underdeveloped in her midrash.

Justice and mercy emerge from the story in rapprochement because of Rachel's merciful argumentation and persuasion. Her argumentation assumes but transcends the basic principles of logic. Abraham and Moses make arguments to justice, principle, and the law of noncontradiction, but God is unmoved. God has and displays an understanding of unmediated justice, which often unleashes His anger. Moses, for example, does not call God to pity "the afflicted, suffering Jews" (152). Instead, Moses "lodges a legal complaint against God, a common Midrashic argument that is based on the view that God, too, is bound by the law" (152). Moses's vision of reason is limited to "rational arguments based on analogy and the need for consistency with prior norms" (153).

Rachel complements the appeals to strict justice made by Abraham and Moses when she puts pressure on God to honor mercy. This pressure, in Stone's words, "evoke[d] the attribute of mercy" in God (157). This quality had remained dormant until Rachel seized the stage. Mercy, this case, restrained the impulse of an anger-inflected justice. Stone makes the case that mercy is an independent attribute turning on a preexisting love of creation and humans. As the story indicates, arguments designed to induce mercy can bring justice into alignment with love. The power of Rachel's argument, according to Stone, leads to "an ironic reversal of *imitatio dei* that we might call *imitation hominis*, it is the model of behavior to which God now turns in submitting to Rachel's example" ("Justice," 163). God mimics

Rachel in drawing from the attribute of mercy to show compassion for the people of Israel. This attribute has a form and a shape that affects the expression of argument, an implication of this midrash I will briefly develop.

The rabbinic commentary on Lamentations illustrates an evolution in the interpretation of Hebrew scripture: the rabbis developed a system of merciful argument that recognizes the irreducible plurality of the universe, acknowledges and honors opposing arguments, allows for those who argue to acknowledge defeat in argument—doing so with gratitude that the stronger truth has prevailed—and seeks to join mercy to justice. This system, well articulated in the Babylonian Talmud, assumes that disagreement, merciful argumentation, and rhetoric are the best fulcrums for the development of values and right action. Humans and God can participate within this framework of engagement. This system seeks an "unending conversation" and refuses to acknowledge an absolute truth, but it is not relativistic. Mercy and justice serve as the system's polar stars.

As David Kraemer notes, Talmudic argumentation "is posited on the ultimate indeterminability of a single, definable truth" (*Mind of the Talmud*, 100). One keystone story in the Talmud captures this truth. The rabbinical schools of Beth Shammai and Beth Hillel are in a long-running disagreement. A representative of God offers a judgment: both schools are right—"These and these are the words of the living God." Yet Beth Hillel's argumentation was privileged by the representative for three reasons: (1) It responded with a positive forbearance when confronted with reasoning of Beth Shammai that challenged Beth Hillel's claims; Beth Hillel did not demonize the opposition. (2) When teaching the dispute between the two schools, Beth Hillel included in the curriculum all the arguments included in the debate. (3) When teaching and writing about the dispute, Beth Hillel prioritized the arguments of Beth Shammai to honor its reasoning. These are the essential characteristics of merciful argumentation designed to recognize the face of the other in the context of disagreement.

Genuine argument with the divine is possible because God can yield to the stronger argument. Moses, Abraham, and Job were successful in their arguments with God, as was Rachel. The Talmud tells the story of a dispute that ended with God admitting, with laugher and joy, "My children have defeated me, my children have defeated me!" (Babylonian Talmud 59B Bava Metzia). The divine becomes, through argument, capable of disagreeing with the human via argument and is thereby willing to cede power to reason. Argument, which requires an attempt to understand others and to honor their reasoning, helps to foster compassion, empathy, and the capacity of mercy.

THE LIMITS OF A RHETORICAL GOD

Scult, McGee, and Kuntz as well as Bernard-Donals depict a God and a sense of the divine that resonates with many. The God in Genesis 1–3, Scult, McGee, and Kuntz argue, is an omniscient, all-powerful force that does not brook dissent. Taking a broader view, one rooted in the thinkers of modernity and postmodernity, Bernard-Donals details the violent rhetorical and material displacement of the human subject affected by the divine. There is as well a "fierce anti-protest" tradition in Judaism, one that earned a "near unanimous antipathy to the notion of challenging or critiquing God" in the ancient period (Weiss, *Pious Irreverence*, 22). God, in this tradition, is perfect.

In contrast, I describe a rhetorical relationship between the divine and human that is rooted in human time and space. This relationship evolves out of God's use of persuasion and deliberation to create physical reality, the endowment of the human with reason and speech, and the development of the rhetorical capacities of the human that included naming, conversation, argument, and debate. There are, of course, significant limits to a rhetorical perspective on the divine-human relationship.

There is a good and bad God, writes Miles; God has abusive and loving attributes, as Blumenthal has noted. Both the human and the divine are flawed, the human with evil inclinations and God quick to enforce an anger-driven definition of justice. The rhetorical engagement of the divine and of humans is a profoundly risky endeavor. I agree with Bernard-Donals: "to approach the other is to become vulnerable, and to do so exposes the individual to the possibility that she will be rebuffed, in some cases violently" ("'Difficult Freedom,'" 72). Both the human and the divine, then, are vulnerable, with capacities that can be evoked or called on to visit abuse and violence, or mercy and justice, on creation. The Jewish-inflected rhetoric I have surveyed can serve as a vehicle to inoculate against this vulnerability and be used to repair the world.

Bibliography

Atterton, Peter, Matthew Calarco, and Maurice S. Friedman. *Levinas and Buber: Dialogue and Difference*. Pittsburgh: Duquesne University Press, 2004.

Auerbach, Erich. *Mimesis: The Representation of Reality in Western Literature*. Garden City, NY: Doubleday, 1957.

Batnitzky, Leora Faye. *Leo Strauss and Emmanuel Levinas: Philosophy and the Politics of Revelation*. Cambridge, UK: Cambridge University Press, 2006.

Ben-Isaiah, Abraham, and Benjamin Sharfman, trans. *The Pentateuch and Rashi's Commentary: A Linear Translation into English*. 5 vols. Brooklyn: S. S. & R., 1949.

Berlin, Adele, Marc Zvi Brettler, and Michael A. Fishbane, trans. *The Jewish Study Bible*. Oxford, UK: Oxford University Press, 2004.

Bernard-Donals, Michael F. "'Difficult Freedom': Levinas, Language, and Politics." *Philosophy and Rhetoric* 35, no. 3 (2005): 62–77.

Blumenthal, David R. *Facing the Abusing God: A Theology of Protest*. Louisville, KY: Westminster / John Knox Press, 1993.

———. "What Are the Limits of Protest Theology? A Review Essay." *Reviews in Religion and Theology* 24, no. 4 (2017): 620–25.

Brown, William P. "Divine Act and the Art of Persuasion in Genesis 1." In *History and Interpretation: Essays in Honour of John H. Hayes*, edited by Graham, M. Patrick, William P. Brown, and Jeffrey K. Kuan, 21–32. Sheffield, UK: JSOT Press, 1993.

Chilton, Bruce. "A Comparative Study of Synoptic Development: The Dispute Between Cain and Abel in the Palestinian Targums and the Beelzebul Controversy in the Gospels." *Journal of Biblical Literature* 101, no. 4 (1982): 553–62.

Crosswhite, James. *The Rhetoric of Reason*. Madison: University of Wisconsin Press, 1996.

Dahl, Nils A., and Alan F. Segal. "Philo and the Rabbis on the Names of God." *Journal for the Study of Judaism in the Persian, Hellenistic, and Roman Period* 9, no. 1 (1978): 1–28.

Epstein, Isadore, trans. *The Babylonian Talmud*. London: Soncino, 1948.

Frank, David A. "Arguing with God, Talmudic Discourse, and the Jewish Counter-model: Implications for the Study of Argumentation." *Argumentation and Advocacy* 41, no. 2 (2004): 71–86.

Ginzberg, Louis. *The Legends of the Jews*. Translated by Henrietta Szold and Paul Radin. 7 vols. Baltimore: Johns Hopkins University Press, 2003.

Girard, René. *Things Hidden Since the Foundation of the World*. Stanford, CA: Stanford University Press, 1987.

Hammer, Reuven, trans. *Sifre: A Tannaitic Commentary on the Book of Deuteronomy*. New Haven, CT: Yale University Press, 1986.

Hyde, M. J. *The Interruption That We Are: The Health of the Lived Body, Narrative, and Public Moral Argument*. Columbia: University of South Carolina Press, 2018.

Johnstone, Henry W., Jr. "Rhetoric as a Wedge: A Reformulation." *Rhetoric Society Quarterly* 20, no. 4 (1990): 333–38.

Jørstad, Mari. "The Ground That Opened Its Mouth: The Ground's Response to Human Violence in Genesis 4." *Journal of Biblical Literature* 135, no. 4 (2016): 705–15.

Kraemer, David. *The Mind of the Talmud*. New York: Oxford University Press, 1990.

Lachower, Yeruḥam Fishel, and Isaiah Tishby, eds. *The Wisdom of the Zohar: An Anthology of Texts*. Translated by David Goldstein. 3 vols. Oxford, UK: Oxford University Press, 1989.

Laytner, Anson. *Arguing with God*. Northvale, NJ: Aronson, 1990.

Lévinas, Emmanuel. *Difficult Freedom: Essays on Judaism*. Translated by Seán Hand.

Baltimore: Johns Hopkins University Press, 1990.

———. *In the Time of the Nations*. Translated by M. B. Smith. Bloomington: Indiana University Press, 1994.

Levy, Steven, and Sarah Levy. *The JPS Rashi Discussion Torah Commentary*. Philadelphia: Jewish Publication Society, 2017.

Maher, Michael, trans. *Targum Pseudo-Jonathan: Genesis*. Collegeville, MN: Liturgical Press, 1992.

McNamara, Martin, Kevin J. Cathcart, and Michael Maher, trans. *The Aramaic Bible: The Targums*. Wilmington, DE: M. Glazier, 1987.

McNamara, Martin, Robert Hayward, and Michael Maher, trans. *Targum Neofiti 1 and Pseudo-Jonathan: Exodus*. Collegeville, MN: Liturgical Press, 1994.

Meyer, Michel. *What Is Rhetoric?* Oxford, UK: Oxford University Press, 2017.

Miles, Jack. *God: A Biography*. New York: Alfred A. Knopf, 1995.

Neusner, Jacob. *The Talmud: What It Is and What It Says*. Lanham, MD: Rowman & Littlefield, 2006.

Pearl, Chaïm, trans. *Rashi: Commentaries on the Pentateuch*. New York: Viking Press, 1973.

Perelman, Chaïm, and Lucie Olbrechts-Tyteca. *The New Rhetoric: A Treatise on Argumentation*. Translated by John Wilkinson and Purcell Weaver. Notre Dame, IN: University of Notre Dame Press, 1969.

Rosen-Zvi, Ishay. *Demonic Desires: Yetzer Hara and the Problem of Evil in Late Antiquity*. Philadelphia: University of Pennsylvania Press, 2011.

Ryan, Yvonne. *Roy Wilkins: The Quiet Revolutionary and the NAACP*. Lexington: University Press of Kentucky, 2014.

Scholem, Gershom, trans. *Zohar: The Book of Splendor*. New York: Knopf Doubleday, 2011.

Scult, Allen, Michael Calvin McGee, and J. Kenneth Kuntz. "Genesis and Power: An Analysis of the Biblical Story of Creation." *Quarterly Journal of Speech* 72, no. 2 (1986): 113–31.

Shulman, Dennis. *The Genius of Genesis: A Psychoanalyst and Rabbi Examines the First Book of the Bible*. New York: iUniverse, 2003.

Stern, David. "Introduction to the 2003 Edition" In Louis Ginzberg, *The Legends of the Jews*, translated by Henrietta Szold and Paul Radin, 1:xv–xxiii. Baltimore: Johns Hopkins University Press, 2003.

Stone, Suzanne. "Justice, Mercy, and Gender in Rabbinic Thought." *Cardozo Studies in Law and Literature* 8, no. 1 (1996): 139–77.

Waisanen, Don, Hershey H. Friedman, and Linda Weiser Friedman. "What's So Funny About Arguing with God? A Case for Playful Argumentation from Jewish Literature." *Argumentation* 29, no. 1 (2015): 57–80.

Weiss, Dov. *Pious Irreverence: Confronting God in Rabbinic Judaism*. Philadelphia: University of Pennsylvania Press, 2017.

Zornberg, Avivah. "Seduced into Eden: The Beginning of Desire." In *Longing: Psychoanalytic Musings on Desire*, edited by Jean Petrucelli, 193–225. London: Karnac, 2006.

CHAPTER 3

Political Theologies
of Sacred Rhetoric

STEVEN MAILLOUX

In February 2016, flying back to Rome after a visit to Mexico, Pope Francis was asked by a reporter if he would comment on a statement made during the presidential campaign in the United States. The reporter said, "Today, you spoke very eloquently about the problems of immigration. . . . One of the candidates for the White House, Republican Donald Trump, in an interview . . . said that you are a political man and he even said that you are a pawn, an instrument of the Mexican government for migration politics. . . . What do you think of these accusations against you?" ("Full Text"). With a wry smile, Pope Francis responded, "Well, thank God he said I was political because Aristotle defined the human person as *animal politicus*. At least I am [considered] a human person." Then more seriously, the pope added, "As to whether I am a pawn, well, maybe, I don't know. I'll leave that up to your judgment and that of the people. [But] a person who thinks only about building walls, wherever they may be, and not building bridges, is not Christian."

In this response, the first Jesuit pope gives us a practical example of political theology in action. Political theology deals with the connection between political praxis and religious belief. It is any implicit or explicit theory relating worldly action within power relations to speculative thinking about a world beyond (see Mailloux, *Rhetoric's Pragmatism*, 198). In this case, Pope Francis interprets and judges the international political situation through his religious beliefs, the Roman Catholic teachings on promoting social justice (see, for example, "Our Mission Today"). His particular employment of this terministic screen derives significantly from his formation as a member of the Society of Jesus, especially his practice of the Ignatian *Spiritual Exercises.*

In this essay, I describe political theologies of the sacred found within Jesuit intellectual and educational traditions, traditions whose rhetoric of *eloquentia perfecta* develops from the *Spiritual Exercises.* Through some concrete historical examples, I attempt to show how the Jesuits' political-theological rhetoric functions in revealing the sacred within a post-secular world. This rhetoric is a *theo*rhetoric—a speaking to, for, and about God—grounded in an Ignatian spirituality that turns the believer's inward attention outward toward actions aimed at contributing to the common good.[1]

We can think of the *sacred* as an appearance, extension, irruption of the supernatural in the natural, of the divine within the human. Such phenomena certainly resist rhetorical articulation, since human rhetoric—the use of signs in a context to have effects—is always limited by the natural, the conditioned, the finite, the contingent. Nonetheless, if we define *spiritual* as "concentrated attention to the sacred," there are spiritual rhetorics that relate us to the supernatural, spiritual rhetorics that have both individual personal and collective political effects. These rhetorics include community religious rituals as well as private prayers and meditations.[2] An influential example of such rhetorics can be found in the central document of the Jesuits, the *Spiritual Exercises* of Ignatius Loyola, the founder of the Roman Catholic order officially known as the Society of Jesus.

Ignatius composed the *Spiritual Exercises* and used them with his first companions even before the Society was formally established in 1540.[3] The principal instrument of Jesuit formation to this day, the text consists of a series of meditations, prayers, examinations of conscience, and other practices such as rule-guided moral discernment. Ignatius spread the performance of the *Exercises* beyond his order, using them with both lay men and women in the Roman Catholic Church. Today versions of the exercises are used not only by Catholics and other Christians but also by believers of non-Christian faiths and by those who are part of no organized religion. In doing the *Exercises*, the retreatant works with a spiritual adviser to improve his or her life with a stated goal of making an election, a vocational choice. Michel Foucault in his late lectures at the Collège de France called such exercises "technologies of the self" (see Foucault, *Hermeneutics*; and Hadot, *Philosophy*, esp. 126–27). The Ignatian *Spiritual Exercises* are a Jesuit self-technology that shapes character: there is an ordering of the retreatant's inner life, an ordering that might be called an aesthetics of experience, an ordering that is best understood as a self-directed ethics tied to an other-directed politics.[4]

The performance of the *Spiritual Exercises* makes time and space for the appearance of the sacred in the retreatant's life. One aspect of this performance is what might be called the rhetorical-hermeneutic circle. The classic twentieth-century description of this circularity is Martin Heidegger's: "Any interpretation which is to contribute understanding, must already have understood what is to be interpreted." However, this is not a "vicious" circularity but an enabling and unavoidable one: "What is decisive is not to get out of the circle but to come into it in the right way" (Heidegger, *Being and Time*, 194–95). The rhetorical performance of the *Spiritual Exercises* provides one approach to coming into the hermeneutic circle in what is claimed to be the right way. Motivated by an act of faith that derives from other readings of texts and life, the retreatant performs the exercises as a technology of the self that shapes one as a specific kind of believing subject. That is, as subjects already believing at least something about the *Spiritual Exercises*, Jesuit traditions, and other theological and political matters, retreatants are formed and form themselves as believing subjects in terms of Ignatian spirituality. Belief precedes and follows the performance of the exercises.[5]

To understand better how this works, we can turn to a book presenting a retreat based on the *Exercises* given by Cardinal Jorge Mario Bergoglio, the future Pope Francis. He first quotes the introductory "Principle and Foundation," which begins, "Human beings are created to praise, reverence, and serve God our Lord, and by means of this to save their souls" (Ignatius, *Spiritual Exercises*, 130). Bergoglio comments that "when the Lord gives us our mission, he founds our being," and later asserts that "our theology ought to be *pious* if it wants to be foundational, if it wants to live up to the claim that it was founded by the Lord. . . . The piety I am talking about is, so to speak, *the fundamental hermeneutic of our theology*" (Bergoglio, *In Him Alone*, 20, 27). This piety is the direct response to the experience of God in our lives: "It is only later that the human intellect tries to deepen our understanding and explain what it means that God is here. Thus we have the famous formula of Saint Anselm, 'faith seeking understanding' (*fides quaerens intellectum*)." The Jesuit cardinal summarizes in conclusion, "Let us never forget that we are called to found and to let ourselves be founded by the Lord" (28).

Anselm's definition of theology as "faith seeking understanding" is often associated with his declaration *Credo ut intelligam*, "I believe so that I can understand." Before him Augustine had given the imperative form: *Crede ut intelligas*, "Believe that you may understand." But Augustine also coupled the slogan with its inverse: "Understand so that you can believe" (see Przywara, *Augustine Synthesis*, 41–67; and Matthews, "Anselm," 65–66). Twentieth-century rhetorical theory and hermeneutic philosophy developed these Anselmian-Augustinian insights into various formulations of the hermeneutic circle.

One rhetorical-hermeneutic example was given by Kenneth Burke in a paper delivered before the 1965 meeting of the American Catholic Philosophical Association. In "Terministic Screens" Burke argues that our vocabularies reflect, select, and deflect reality for us. Our observations are filtered through these terministic screens. Indeed, many of our "observations" are really just "implications of the particular terminology in terms of which the observations are made" (46). Burke explains: "I have in mind the injunction, at once pious and methodological, 'Believe, that you may understand (*crede, ut intelligas*).' . . . The 'logological,' or 'terministic' counterpart of 'Believe' in the formula would be: *Pick some particular nomenclature, some one terministic screen*. And for 'That you may understand,' the counterpart would be: '*That you may proceed to track down the kinds of observation implicit in the terminology you have chosen, whether your choice of terms was deliberate or spontaneous*" (47). Thus, for Burke, the theological "injunction, 'Believe, that you may understand,' has a fundamental application to the purely secular problem of 'terministic screens'" (47). This is an illustration of how Burke reads theology, words about God, to get insights for his logology, words about words, which he reapplies in reading theology, including political theology, in a kind of hermeneutic circle (see also Burke, *Rhetoric of Religion*).

Even more explicitly, the philosopher Paul Ricœur applied and adapted the term *hermeneutic circle* throughout his long career. For example, in *Freud and Philosophy* writing on "the interpretation of religious symbolism," Ricœur focuses on a "new dimension" of the "problematic of faith," which he describes as "a call, a kerygma, a word addressed to me" from the "object of faith," the "Wholly Other" (*Freud and Philosophy*, 524–25).[6] Then Ricœur writes, "I speak of the Wholly Other only insofar as it addresses itself to me; and the kerygma, the glad tidings, is precisely that it addresses itself to me and ceases to be the Wholly Other. . . . The Wholly Other as logos . . . becomes an event of human speech and can be recognized only in the movement of interpretation of this human speech" (525). Ricœur concludes, "The 'hermeneutic circle' is born: to believe is to listen to the call, but to hear the call we must interpret the message. Thus we must believe in order to understand and understand in order to believe" (525).

Ricœur directly connects this hermeneutic circularity with access to the sacred in the modern age. He writes in *The Symbolism of Evil*, "Hermeneutics proceeds from a prior understanding of the very thing that it tries to understand by interpreting it. But thanks to that circle in hermeneutics, I can still today communicate with the sacred by making explicit the prior understanding that gives life to the interpretation" (352). Ricœur argues that in modern hermeneutics "'modernity' transcends itself, insofar as it is forgetfulness of the sacred" (352) This transcendence allows an openness to the sacred, "no longer, of course, under the precritical form of immediate belief, but as the second immediacy aimed at by hermeneutics" (352).

The practices of the Ignatian *Spiritual Exercises* embody the hermeneutic circle in action but with the aim of producing a more "immediate belief": believe in the foundation of the *Exercises* so that you can understand yourself and God's call for your vocation, and these understandings lead, in turn, to a deeper belief in how to act, including doing the *Exercises* and acting in accordance with their shaping effects. In certain contemplations, those Ignatius calls "compositions of place," the retreatant is asked to recall biblical stories and imaginatively participate in the narrative as a character (see Ignatius, *Spiritual Exercises*, 150; and Mailloux, *Rhetoric's Pragmatism*, 134, 156–57). In this way, the *Exercises* rhetorically rely on imagination to encourage emotions and inspire understandings, aiming to move the will motivated by a faith grounded and resulting in love (see Ignatius, *Spiritual Exercises*, 136, 176–77).

The Jesuit practice of spiritual discernment guides retreatants at each stage of their experiences in doing the *Exercises*: in examinations of conscience, responses to a vocational call, judging internal and external motivations, and determining God's will for future action. Especially distinctive is what has come to be called the Ignatian "rules for the discernment of spirits." These rules are intended to "aid us toward perceiving and then understanding, at least to some extent, the various motions which are caused in the soul: the good motions that they may be received, and the bad that they may be rejected" (Ignatius, *Spiritual Exercises*, 201). Ignatius provides a detailed guide for a kind of discernment that is simultaneously intellectual, affective, and sensory. Combining acts of imagination, intellect, feelings, and will, Ignatian discernment is a "complex art" of interpreting "interior experiences," including, for example, reflection on whether one is experiencing spiritual consolation or desolation in making certain decisions about courses of future action (424n130; see also Bergoglio, *In Him Alone*, 72–76). Interior movements of consolation characterize motions that increase one's faith, hope, and love, often resulting in feelings of satisfaction, happiness, and even joy. In contrast, spiritual desolation involves motions of "disquiet from various agitations and temptations," moving "one toward lack of faith and leav[ing] one without hope and without love." Discerning the nature of these internal motions aids retreatants in finding their way to the "right decision" about significant vocational choices (Ignatius, *Spiritual Exercises*, 202).

Ideally, these movements within become movements without. For retreatants, turning inward results in turning outward to become what Jesuits call "contemplatives in action": pious subjects becoming men and women for and with others (see Kolvenbach, "Jerome Nadal"; and Arrupe, "Promotion of Justice"). Here we turn from the inner world of the believing subject formed by the exercises toward that subject's agency in the sociopolitical world after their performance: from the interiority of discernment to the exteriority of political advocacy, an important dimension of being a contemplative in action.[7]

We can see this movement in Pope Francis's political-theological rhetoric of the sacred. In *Evangelii gaudium*, his 2013 apostolic exhortation on the proclamation of the Gospel, Francis speaks of the "ambiguous" nature of "the return to the sacred and the quest for spirituality" in contemporary culture—ambiguous because such motivated attempts can have positive or negative results—but he also refers unambiguously to "a fraternal love capable of seeing the sacred grandeur of our neighbour, of finding God in every human being" (para. 89, 92). In his 2015 environmental encyclical *Laudato si': On Care for Our Common Home*, Francis locates the sacred in a larger world not limited to human creatures, declaring that "God has written a precious book" and that "no creature is excluded from this manifestation of God. . . . Paying attention to this manifestation, we learn to see ourselves in relation to all other creatures" (para. 85). To conclude these thoughts, Francis quotes Paul Ricœur's declaration: "I express myself in expressing the world; in my effort to decipher the sacredness of the world, I explore my own" (see *Symbolism of Evil*, 13).

Those words signify differently in the pope's encyclical than they do in Ricœur's original text, yet the differences turn out to be complementary rather than contradictory. Put most simply, Francis's rhetoric is environmentally spatial while Ricœur's is cosmically and psychically temporal. In Francis's text, the self expresses and interprets the world outside to signify and understand the world inside; the ecological boundaries of self are simultaneously traversed and transformed, gone beyond and pushed out. While in its original context Ricœur's statement also has an outward/inward movement across space, its primary motion involves temporality: moving across universal cosmic time and across individual psychic time. Francis is making a specific point about a person's relation to the environment: in the terms of Jesuit spirituality, humans find God in all things—ourselves, other creatures, and everything else (see Traub, *Ignatian Spirituality Reader*, 47–85). Ricœur is making a general point about "the symbolisms of humanity," especially the symbolism of evil, which remain at the center of personal identity, interpreted from perspectives of both regression and progression, from its infantile origins to its mature possibilities. Ricœur declares that "to manifest the 'sacred' *on* the 'cosmos' and to manifest it *in* the 'psyche' are the same thing" (*Symbolism of Evil*, 12; see also *Figuring the Sacred*).

Ricœur presented his theory of symbolism in the second volume of *Finitude et culpabilité*, and it was taken up by the Jesuit philosopher Gaston Fessard in a conference paper soon after. Fessard's work has been receiving increased attention of late, including notice as a major early influence on Pope Francis during the latter's Jesuit formation (see Borghesi, *Mind of Pope Francis*, 6). It is to Father Fessard I now turn for my most detailed rhetorical examples of a political theology of the sacred. These examples will take us into the complex development of Fessard's philosophy, where the sacred emerges, disappears, and returns along the rhetorical path of his thinking about language and dialogue within private and public human experience.

––––––––

Gaston Fessard was a French philosopher whose Christian political theology derived from his dialectical thinking and his experience of the Ignatian *Spiritual Exercises*. Fessard's Hegelian commentary *La dialectique des "Exercices spirituels" de Saint Ignace de Loyola* was considered by his fellow Jesuit and noted rhetorician Walter Ong to be the best philosophical treatment of Ignatius's text yet written (Ong, "Interiority"). Fessard's commentary had a profound effect on a range of Catholic thinkers, including Pope Francis, who recently said, "The—in quotes—'Hegelian' writer—but he is not Hegelian, though it may seem like he is—who had a big influence on me was Gaston Fessard. I've read *La dialectique des "Exercices spirituels" de Saint Ignace de Loyola*, and other things by him, several times. That work gave me so many elements that later became mixed in [to my thinking]" (Borghesi, *Mind of Pope Francis*, 6).[8] Many non-Catholic academic and public intellectuals have also spoken highly of Fessard's reputation as an expert on and critic of Hegelian and Marxist traditions (see Rosen, "Kojève's Paris," 269).

As a Jesuit novice in 1931, Fessard wrote the core of his commentary, in which he developed dialectical thinking that became the basis for his political theology (Fessard, "Letter," xx).[9] In his writings of the 1930s and later, Fessard provides an exemplary illustration of how the rhetoric of the *Exercises*, focused inwardly on spiritual formation, could be turned outward in analyses of international politics. From 1935 to 1939, Fessard attended Alexandre Kojève's famous Sorbonne lectures on Hegel with their emphasis on the master-slave dialectic (Sales, "Gaston Fessard," 18).[10] During this time Fessard worked out a unique mixture of Jesuit-Catholic and Hegelian thinking and applied this political theology in analyses of the deteriorating international scene (see, for example, Fessard, *Pax Nostra*).

After addressing the possibility of Catholic-Communist dialogue in the 1930s (see *La main tendue*), Fessard turned his political theology in another direction, to criticize the justifying rhetoric of the Nazi-supported Vichy government in France during World War II. Fessard specifically condemned Vichy's claims to sovereignty and authority from a perspective influenced by his studies with Kojève and his interested reading of Carl Schmitt, the prominent German legal scholar and "self-appointed ideologue of the Nazis" (Schwab, "Introduction," 3). Fessard's 1941 pamphlet

"France, prends garde de perdre ton âme!" (France, take care not to lose your soul!) is often seen as a founding text of the French Catholic resistance movement. In political-theological terms, Fessard condemns National Socialism as a "conception of the world" that is "as totalitarian and intolerant as a religion, because founded on a mystique," and a mystique that is anti-Christian at that. It leads to a "spiritual terrorism," designating a "common enemy," such as Marxism and the Jews, to achieve the ultimate triumph of its thoroughly reprehensible politics (Fessard, "France, prends garde," 70–71, 86–87; see also Geroulanos, "Heterogeneities," 545–46).[11]

Fessard uses concepts of the National Socialist ideologue to condemn National Socialism. Though Fessard's pamphlet does not specifically cite Schmitt's texts, his unpublished notes highlight Schmitt's assertion in *The Concept of the Political* that the "requirement for internal peace compels [the state] in critical situations to decide also upon the domestic enemy" (46; see also Geroulanos, "Heterogeneities," 546).[12] Ultimately in his political-theological writings about Vichy, "Fessard turned Schmitt on his head," as Stephanos Geroulanos astutely puts it ("Heterogeneities," 548). Fessard negates Schmitt's understanding of the sovereign as "he who decides on the exception" (Schmitt, *Political Theology*, 5), arguing forcefully contra Schmitt that in emergency situations such as occupation during wartime, sovereignty "was fundamentally imperiled when it lacked the ability to demonstrate and practice its aim toward the 'common good'" (Geroulanos, "Heterogeneities," 548; see also Fessard, *Autorité et bien commun*).[13]

After the war, Fessard continued developing his political theology to interpret, evaluate, and comment on the transformed global scene. In November 1946 at the International Congress of Philosophy in Milan, Fessard compared the ideologies of Communism and Nazism, reading the texts of both Marx and Hitler through a Hegelian lens. His paper "Historical Materialism and the Master-Slave Dialectic" begins, "No matter how little existentially inclined he may be, the philosopher of today cannot completely ignore his own historical situation. He immediately sees there, dominating all political, economic, and social conjunctures, various conceptions of the world which, like the gods of Homer, direct the bloody struggles of humans" ("Le matérialisme historique," 57).[14] Fessard portrays ideologies such as Liberalism, Communism, and National Socialism as "the immortal divinities who in our day compete to lead humanity towards its destinies. Above our heads, or rather deep in our hearts, their dialogue continues even as our conflicts seem pacified" (57). Fessard employs the tropes of Hegelian dialectic to make his critical comparisons: "Marxism and Nazism both use the master-slave dialectic to explain the future of human reality, but the first places itself *exclusively in the point of view of the slave,* the second *exclusively in the point of view of the master*" (63). Marxism privileges the economic over the political in aiming for a classless society, while Nazism asserts the absolute primacy of the political in a racist nationalism. According to Fessard, neither of them provides a way to maintain an "*equal and reciprocal recognition* among all members of the polity" (67). After using Hegel to critique Marx and Hitler, Fessard uses Marx and Hitler to critique Hegel, in particular the separation and perpetual inversions of the political and economic in the master-slave dialectic.

In the end, Fessard calls not for another inversion but for a *conversion* of the political-economic opposition (68). He argues that the master-slave dialectic needs to be supplemented by the man-woman dialectic: "All of the constitutive elements of politics and economics—presented in the first dialectic as disjointed and opposed—appear in contrast in the second as reconciled and unified" (72). Fessard draws his analysis to a conclusion by putting all of his political-theological cards on the table: in the current international situation, "it is not difficult to recognize the true object of debate between National Socialism and Marxism, and the means of resolving it" (76). Appearing as a conflict over the supremacy of either the political or the economic, "it is in reality a question of the [human] attitude . . . towards God and the All of being." Thus Fessard proposes another dialectic, one that is "analogous to that between man and woman: the *dialectic of God and humanity.* Present in us and interior to all those dialectics which unfold in temporal events, this dialectic also directs them and becomes the principle of a genesis of humanity—a genesis which is still historical, though no longer only natural, but rather properly *supernatural* and truly spiritual" (76).

Fessard turns to a final dialectic to provide the transition to a specifically *Christian* political theology: this is the pagan-Jew dialectic (77). In brief: the pagan-Jew dialectic begins in the Old Testament as the chosen Jews are opposed to the idolatrous pagans, an opposition that is reversed in the New Testament as the converted pagans (Christians) are distinguished from the unbelieving Jews, until all are joined together in unity at the end of history (see Fessard, *Pax Nostra*; and Fessard, *De l'actualité historique*, 1:45–52, deriving the pagan-Jew dialectic from St. Paul's letters). Fessard concludes in summary fashion that the relations of master-slave, man-woman, and pagan-Jew are "the essential dialectics which a truly concrete existentialism must pursue to arrive at a *full analysis . . . of the structure of historical human being*" ("Le matérialisme historique," 77–78). Such an existentialism "would not of course provide the definitive solution to all of our problems" (77–78), Fessard admits. But "at least, by correctly analyzing our own historical situation," we could approach a solution. "Far from despairing before the finitude of our being and the absurdity of the world," we could become "capable of establishing that the unity of humanity—object of our wishes and supreme goal of our efforts—has as its essential condition" Paul's universalist declaration in Galatians 3:28, renouncing divisions between Jew and Greek, slave and free, man and woman, and proclaiming the unity of all in Jesus Christ (78).

In 1947, encouraged by his fellow Jesuits to publish his manuscript commentary on the *Spiritual Exercises*, Fessard wrote a preface that testifies to the Ignatian origin of the political-theological rhetoric we have seen at work during the 1930s and 1940s. Fessard describes the dialectical figures that form the basis, in form and content, for his intervention in contemporary politics. He suggests that anyone who has attentively read his past publications will have no trouble seeing how much the *Exercises* have "inspired" him every time he "encountered the problem of freedom and truth in history, as today, after Hegel, Marx, and Kierkegaard, it arises in our time" (*La dialectique*, 17). As for those who have read him more superficially, Fessard hopes the following connection may suffice: "The dialectics of Pagan and Jew, Master and Slave, Man and Woman—fundamental themes constantly used in our analysis of historical situations—are, in our view, not only the same type as the dialectic of the Before and After of the Election with which we explain the *Exercises*' structure, but also closely related through their content" (17). The before/after structure designates the times preceding and following the retreatant's vocational choice, their free election, prepared for and then reinforced in the performance of the *Exercises*.

The content of that before/after structure relates in various ways to the dialectics applied in Fessard's political theology. For example, as we have seen, the *Exercises* recommend rules of discernment to aid the retreatants in judging the internal and external forces motivating their free decisions, in particular their vocational elections. Fessard notes how Ignatius uses conjugal and military comparisons to describe these motivating forces, and Fessard observes that the basis of the comparisons—the man-woman relation, on the one hand, and war or the death struggle, on the other—are actually "two fundamental situations that refer directly to the genesis of freedom and permit us to analyze its diverse moments" (*La dialectique*, 247, interpreting rules 12–14 of "Rules for the Discernment of Spirits" in the *Spiritual Exercises*). He argues that "the Hegelian dialectic of the death struggle, from which emerges the master-slave relation, has as its indispensable complement a dialectic of man and woman, both dialectics together constituting a double aspect of the genesis of human reality" (247). That is, the discernment rules of the *Exercises* presuppose the man-woman and master-slave dialectics: "Man and woman are the two terms of a basic human relationship, that of love, which is at the source of every agreement. The military leader is the dominative agent of another basic human relationship, that of power or struggle, and his correlative is the 'slave'" (Pousset, *Life in Faith*, 217). Thus Fessard's commentary, finally published in 1956, represents spiritual practices as embodying and motivating the dialectical relations that he uses in his politico-theological analyses in public spheres seemingly far removed from the private performance of the *Exercises*. Again, if we think of the spiritual as concentrated attention to the sacred, then the "interior motion[s]" inspired by spiritual exercises provide, for Fessard, a sacred or supernatural basis for external actions (Ignatius, *Spiritual Exercises*, 202).

In the 1960s Fessard returned to the problem of Christian-Communist dialogue by explicitly focusing on the issue of language in contemporary partisan debates over religion, philosophy, and politics. He developed a rhetorical framework for discussing the possibility conditions of dialogue in general and for actualizing such dialogue in Europe and the United States between progressive Christians and anti-Stalinist Communists. Central to Fessard's framework was a complex rhetorical interpretation of the role played by "sacred mystery" and "supernatural symbolic structures" in Communist as well as Christian discourses. To explain this role, Fessard adapted terms and concepts from the structuralist anthropology of Claude Lévi-Strauss and combined them with the dialectical figurations he had developed earlier in his writings.

Fessard argues that the rhetorical conditions of possibility for dialogue begin with the requirement that all interlocutors must share beliefs in the existence of Truth and the value of Freedom. He goes on at great length to describe exactly what he means by those terms and subsequently addresses whether those possibility conditions can be actualized in the current political situation in which believing Christians and atheist Communists were attempting to engage one another in meaningful dialogue. It is to support these points that Fessard strategically turns to Lévi-Strauss's structural anthropology for rhetorical help. But Fessard is playing something of a double game as he develops his rather unorthodox application of Lévi-Strauss's cultural arguments. Fessard's rhetorical gambit is double in that he proposes a nonpartisan interpretive framework for understanding and enabling partisan dialogue even as the rhetoric of that same framework is derived from views of the sacred and the supernatural ultimately unacceptable to his ideological opponents.

In his 1969 essay "The Future of a Dialogue Now Possible," Fessard claims that according to the atheist Lévi-Strauss, "an ethnologist with Marxist orientations," language use requires the assumption of the sacred and the supernatural (100). Fessard notes how Lévi-Strauss's *Les structures élémentaires de la parenté* compares "the exchange of women in society with that of words in dialogue" (100). Lévi-Strauss describes the marital "interaction of truth (represented here by the universal law of the prohibition of incest), and of liberty (the condition of the alliance between the spouses and their families)," and brings out "precisely the major role played by language in such circumstances" (100). Fessard quotes the ethnologist: "'In the instant of marriage, . . . Nature and Culture or parental love and conjugal love meet and are absorbed in one another. Without doubt they meet only to substitute for one another and to crisscross one another. But what, for any social thought, constitutes marriage as a sacred mystery is the fact that, in order to cross one another, they must come together at least for an instant'" (100–101; see Lévi-Strauss, *Elementary Structures*, 489). Fessard remarks on Lévi-Strauss's use of the terms *sacred mystery*, finding it "rather surprising coming from the pen of an atheist" (101).[15]

If the sacred is a manifestation of the supernatural in the natural world of the human, then the sacred plays additional roles in the theory of Lévi-Strauss beyond that involved in the marriage ritual. Fessard focuses on the role of *Mana*, "the supernatural for the Melanesians," and points out that for Lévi-Strauss human dialogue is made possible, its inherent contradictions overcome, only through the assumption of "something analogous to *Mana*" (101). Fessard explains that this "notion of *supernatural*, whatever its name may be in different cultures, refers precisely to the relationship which, in connecting 'the servitude of any finite thought' with a divine understanding, serves as the principle of language and of all the mythical and aesthetic inventions such as even the possibility of dialogue." Fessard sees this Lévi-Straussian claim as simply universalizing the analysis of the "sacred mystery of marriage," extending it to all symbolic action, including dialogues (101).

Fessard's own rhetorical-hermeneutic strategy is to interpret and argue analogically: positing the conjugal union as the foundation of language and society, Lévi-Strauss, according to Fessard, sees the supernatural as the key to the unity of nature and culture, and Fessard analogizes this unity to the way Marx aims to unify man and nature and Christians relate human and divine. Fessard claims that Lévi-Strauss's nature-culture dialectic is founded on the symbolic nature of language and society as "one and the same autonomous reality," an identification that Fessard sees supported by the ethnologist's analysis of social structure. Lévi-Strauss "explains how every society rests on two kinds of *symbolic structures*, some of *communication* (rules of marriage, of kinship, economic relationships, etc.), and the others of *subordination* (associations, social classes, State, etc.)" (101). Fessard analogizes these two symbolic structures as dialectical relations: the man-woman dialectic is to communication as the master-slave is to subordination. Most important for Fessard's argument, Lévi-Strauss asserts that "the interplay of these two kinds of [symbolic] structures cannot be brought to order and regulated except by other analogous structures, but now 'thought-of' rather than 'lived-in': this is what *'we call the supernatural* . . . orders of myth and religion'" (101, quoting Levi-Strauss, *Structural Anthropology*, 312–13, emphasis added by Fessard; cf. Burke, *Rhetoric of Religion*, 7–42).

In a series of conference exchanges with Paul Ricœur also during the 1960s, Fessard explains in another way the semantic role of the supernatural in enabling symbolic action. At a 1962 Rome conference on "Demythisation and Image," Fessard delivered a paper titled "Image, symbole et historicité," which takes off from Ricœur's claim that the "greatness of myth" consists in its having "more meaning than a true history" (Fessard, "Image, symbole et historicité," 44; see also Ricœur, *Symbolism of Evil*, 236). The paper attempts to answer Ricœur's question: what is this "more meaning" of myth—for example, in the Adamic myth of the Fall? (Ricœur, *Symbolism of Evil*, 236). Fessard begins his answer summarizing and accepting the three dimensions of the symbol posited by Ricœur—cosmic, oneiric, and poetic—and adds another characteristic: the double aspect of the theoretical and the practical. Fessard connects this Ricœur-inspired description of symbolism to his own reflections on historicity: "Because of its three dimensions—cosmic, psychic, and poetic—and its two aspects—theoretical or speculative as well as practical or willing—the symbol necessarily has a relation to history and the historical" ("Image, symbole et historicité," 46; see also Ricoeur, *Symbolism of Evil*, 10–14).

Fessard finds this same relationship between symbol and history implied in an earlier Ricœur paper, "The Hermeneutics of Symbols and Philosophical Reflection," which asks, "Does not the movement from the Fall to the Redemption, a movement so full of meaning, exclude a 'logic,' whether it be nondialectical or dialectical? Is it then possible to conceive of a meaningful history, wherein the contingency of evil and the initiative of conversion would be retained and encompassed? Is it possible to conceive of a *becoming of being* in which the tragic of evil—of this evil always already there—would be both recognized and surmounted?" (313–14). Though Fessard rejects Ricœur's opposition of meaningful history to a dialectical "logic of being," he accepts the term *meaningful history* and asks, in his turn, "what history can accommodate the meaning of symbols such as the Fall," and what historicity would such a narrative have (Fessard, "Image, symbole et historicité," 47).

To answer these questions Fessard distinguishes three types of history—natural, human, and sacred or supernatural—and goes on to examine in detail the three "levels of historicity corresponding to this triple distinction" (47). Fessard notes that "in all cultures the first history to appear is sacred or supernatural history, which, along with 'myths,' includes a portion of human history and a portion of natural history" (48). Later these three histories separate, but they also sometimes re-converge. In the published version of his paper, Fessard adds a footnote that indicates the kind of analysis of political theology we have seen him practice in the public sphere beyond specialized scholarly conferences. Fessard writes that the historical "process of separation" between historicities "is constantly counterbalanced by an inverse process of confusion in a return to the primitive non-distinction," as illustrated in contemporary "ideological myths or conceptions of the world such as Communism and Nazism, which still offer an attitude as religious, despite appearances, as that of our distant ancestors" (49n4).

In his detailed analysis of the three historicities or ways of historical being, Fessard emphasizes the linear timeline of before and after for natural and human histories and underlines the importance of the "indissoluble link" between language and freedom within all human history (50). The most significant details for his paper's thesis in responding to Ricœur—and for my own argument about Fessard's sacred rhetoric of political theology— are the claims he makes about supernatural historicity: that the content of supernatural history is the interaction between humans and the gods or God, and its function is to give significance and value to the other historicities. Here, according to Fessard, we return precisely to Ricœur's "meaningful history": "as a unity totalizing human and natural histories, supernatural history is that which *gives them meaning*" (52).

To illustrate his theoretical point, Fessard returns to the Adamic myth with which he began his paper, the story of the Fall now viewed from the perspective of the supernatural historicity of Christianity: "As Son and Word of God made flesh, Christ, 'image of the invisible God,' appears in the messianic 'fullness of time' (Galatians 4:4), and He is the center of times, the 'Alpha and Omega, the Beginning and the End' (Revelation 21:6)." As the "founder of Christian theology," Saint Paul, "conceived supernatural history as giving meaning to universal [human] history" (55–56). Fessard develops this claim using the figures of Pauline and Hegelian dialectics and applying them in an interpretation of the Fall. He concludes in summary, "So then how does Paul, and Christian theology after him, attempt to think the 'Adamic myth'? . . . Exactly as Ricœur asks. That is to say, by capturing within 'the fullness of language' the symbols that make up this story in such a way as to recognize in them the maximum of cosmic, psychic, and poetic . . . expressivity. But to realize this maximum in its literal expressivity—that is to say, the most real and most true—it is important to use the existential and historical categories of man-woman, master-slave, and pagan-Jew" (58–59). These dialectical categories, of course, are the rhetorical figurations that Fessard himself had long been using to interpret historical actuality and spiritual development in his political theology of the sacred.

Later in the conference Ricœur and Fessard have a final exchange worth noting, this time over the definition of myth. Ricœur comments in rhetorical-hermeneutic fashion that "myth is not what I demythologize, it is what I interpret. In this sense, it should be said that there are myths at the very moment we begin to interpret. . . . It is within a hermeneutic that the myth is myth." In contrast but not in contradiction, Fessard declares that "what we call 'myth' is the final or supernatural historicity in which others live, and in which we do not believe. The Marxist lives in a myth in which I myself do not believe; and the Christianity in which I live, he calls mythical. Myth is the supernatural historicity of the other" ("Discussione," 313–14).

Fessard's political theology of the sacred derives from his dialectical interpretations of Pauline, Hegelian, and Ignatian texts, interpretations that get redeployed in his multiple interventions in the political controversies of his historical moment. A similar combination of spiritual and political commitments can be seen today in the words and actions of the first Jesuit pope, whose formation was strongly affected by the earlier Jesuit philosopher. Many others working in Jesuit traditions have found related ways to develop implications of this political-theological thinking. One striking example can be seen in current attempts to revive the rhetorical legacy of *eloquentia perfecta* in Jesuit colleges across the United States (see Gannett and Brereton, *Traditions of Eloquence*).

These pedagogical and curricular initiatives include the proposal of new rhetorical arts courses. One such course is described this way: "Based on the Jesuit rhetorical tradition, this course fosters articulate expression, critical thinking, and moral reflection, enabling students to engage in written and oral debate with persuasive force and stylistic excellence. . . . Emerging out of Renaissance humanism, Jesuit rhetoric (or *Eloquentia Perfecta*) developed the classical ideal of the good person writing and speaking well for the public good and promotes the teaching of eloquence combined with erudition and moral discernment" ("Rhetorical Arts"). This course attempts to reinvent *eloquentia perfecta* for the twenty-first century. First, it recombines the teaching of oral and written rhetoric, speech/listening with writing/reading. Second, Jesuit rhetoric today includes new forms of literacy. Just as the Jesuits of the sixteenth century came to terms with the media revolution of that era (the fifteenth-century invention and dissemination of the printing press), so, too, a Jesuit rhetoric now engages the digital revolution, including new media technologies that are visual, aural, and kinesthetic as well as verbal. Third, Jesuit rhetoric is taught within the Ignatian paradigm of experience, reflection, action, and evaluation, a pedagogy aimed at educating the whole person and producing men and women for and with others, serving faith that promotes justice. Jesuit rhetoric incorporates these pedagogical goals by integrating eloquence and critical thinking with moral discernment and a commitment to social justice, thus continuing the humanist tradition of conceiving the ideal rhetor as the good person writing and speaking well for the common good (see Duminuco, *Jesuit "Ratio Studiorum"*; Mailloux, *Rhetoric's Pragmatism*, 118–23; and Rhetorical Arts Working Group, "Jesuit Rhetorical Arts").

In all the rhetorical activities I have described throughout this essay—the performance of spiritual exercises, political-theological interventions in the public sphere, revivals of *eloquentia perfecta* within Jesuit college curricula—attention to the sacred plays a crucial role, sometimes explicitly, sometimes implicitly. In showing how such spiritual rhetorics function in different domains, I have tried to demonstrate how rhetoric, in theory and practice, is both enabled and constrained by the sacred as a manifestation of the supernatural and a target of the spiritual.

Notes

1. See *"Eloquentia Perfecta"*; on Jesuit theorhetoric, see Mailloux, *Rhetoric's Pragmatism*, 78–89.

2. On rhetoric and prayer, see Fitzgerald, *Spiritual Modalities*; and Mailloux, "Notes on Prayerful Rhetoric with Divinities." I am grateful to Molly Mailloux for our conversation leading to my working definition of *spiritual*.

3. For historical background, see commentary and documents included in Ignatius of Loyola, *Ignatius of Loyola: The "Spiritual Exercises"* (hereafter Ignatius, *Spiritual Exercises*); see also O'Malley, *First Jesuits*.

4. The aim of the *Spiritual Exercises* is "to overcome oneself, and to order one's life, without reaching a decision through some disordered affection" (Ignatius, *Spiritual Exercises*, 129). For discussion of the tropology of this ordering in relation to Kenneth Burke's logological analysis of terministic cycles in *The*

Rhetoric of Religion, see Mailloux, *Rhetoric's Pragmatism*, 120–22. On ordering in and of experience as aesthetic, see Dewey, *Art as Experience*. Cf. "aesthetics of existence" in Foucault, *Hermeneutics*, 434–35n14.

5. Cf. Foucault's description of the Christian model for care of the self, which begins with a circular hermeneutic relation between the textual truth of revelation and the purification of the interpreter's heart. That is, you must believe before you can understand the Word, but you must receive the Word before you can believe: "This circularity is . . . one of the fundamental points of the relations between care of the self and knowledge of the self in Christianity" (*Hermeneutics*, 255).

6. On Ricœur, compared to Heidegger and Emmanuel Lévinas on "the call," see Dierckxsens, *Paul Ricœur's Moral Anthropology*.

7. Cf. Richardson, "Contemplative in Action": "This constant effort to discern and realize, i.e., co-activate, the divine will in the world and collaborate with it is precisely what Ignatius meant by 'finding God in all things'" (118–19). J. Michelle Molina puts this movement in the more problematic sociopolitical context of its historical origin in her book *To Overcome Oneself*: "The Ignatian Exercises compelled the practitioner to develop a view of herself as active in a world whose contours were rapidly transforming, at a moment when the concept of 'the world' adopted the shape of a globe. 'Self' and 'other' were vitally linked in this series of meditative techniques that fostered a dynamic, active spirituality that linked its practitioner to the spiritual and material conquest of non-Christians. Spiritual self-reform had bearing upon the mobility of early modern subjects on scales large and small, as Ignatian methods prompted exercitants to be concerned with neighbors both proximate and distant" (50).

8. In notes for a preface to a never-published English translation of Fessard's book, Ong agrees with Francis's observation: "Père Fessard's thought is not dominated by Hegel; rather Hegel is dominated by Fessard, who raids Hegel for insights which will do service to Catholic truth" (MSS 64.2.2.1.195).

9. Fessard's draft circulated as an eighty-page manuscript among Jesuits until its 1956 publication in slightly revised and expanded form.

10. Fessard attended along with such later luminaries as Georges Bataille, Emmanuel Lévinas, Maurice Merleau-Ponty, Jacques Lacan, and Raymond Aron. See Kojève, *Introduction to the Reading of Hegel*; and "Kojève-Fessard Documents."

11. Cf. Kenneth Burke's 1939 essay on the English translation of *Mein Kampf*, where he demonstrates how Hitler's rhetoric relied "upon a bastardization of fundamentally religious patterns of thought" in scapegoating the Jews ("Rhetoric of Hitler's 'Battle,'" 219). A decade later, Burke wrote a long section called "The War of Words," originally intended for but ultimately not included in his *Rhetoric of Motives*. In the now published commentary, Burke analyzes the many rhetorical devices of politicians and media coverage during the early Cold War. One such device he calls "Spiritualization," a rhetorical strategy in which politicians and churchmen deflect attention by covering up profane-materialistic politics with sacred-idealistic religion.

12. Fessard owned copies of *The Concept of the Political* and other Schmitt books, which are now held in the French Jesuit Province Archives in Vanves, along with Fessard's handwritten notes.

13. For more recent appeals to the common good within Jesuit political-theological rhetoric, see Pope Francis's 2015 address to the United States Congress ("Address of the Holy Father").

14. I would like to thank Matthew Dowd, Vivian Folkenflik, and Daniela Ginsburg for their substantial assistance in translating Fessard's French texts quoted in my essay.

15. Elsewhere Fessard elaborates on his interpretation of Lévi-Strauss's expression: "Marriage would thus be a 'sacred mystery,' not only because 'nature and culture intersect for a moment,' but also and in a more profound sense because marriage symbolically represents a conjugal alliance between human nature and divine Nature, or more precisely— since all of this analysis takes place at the level of language—between speaking Humanity and the divine Word, origin of all nature as of all culture" (Fessard, "Symbole, surnaturel, dialogue," 124).

Bibliography

Arrupe, Pedro, SJ. "Promotion of Justice and Education for Justice." Society of Jesus. Accessed June 26, 2020. http://www.sjweb.info/documents/education/arr_men_en.pdf.

Bergoglio, Jorge Mario. *In Him Alone Is Our Hope*. Edited by Romain Lizé. Translated by Vincent Capuano, SJ, and Andrew Matt. New York: Magnificat, 2013.

Borghesi, Massimo. *The Mind of Pope Francis: Jorge Mario Bergoglio's Intellectual Journey*. Translated by Barry Hudock. Collegeville, MN: Liturgical Press Academic, 2018.

Burke, Kenneth. "The Rhetoric of Hitler's 'Battle.'" In *The Philosophy of Literary Form: Studies in Symbolic Action*, 3rd ed., 191–220. Berkeley: University of California Press, 1973.

———. *The Rhetoric of Religion: Studies in Logology*. Berkeley: University of California Press, 1970.

———. "Terministic Screens." *Proceedings of the American Catholic Philosophical Association* 39 (1965): 87–102. Reprinted in Kenneth Burke, *Language as Symbolic Action: Essays on Life, Literature, and Method*, 44–62. Berkeley: University of California Press, 1966.

———. "The War of Words." In *The War of Words*, by Kenneth Burke, edited by Anthony Burke, Kyle Jensen, and Jack Selzer, 41–257. Berkeley: University of California Press, 2018.

Dewey, John. *Art as Experience*. Edited by Jo Ann Boydston and Harriet Furst Simon. Carbondale: Southern Illinois University Press, 1989.

Dierckxsens, Geoffrey. *Paul Ricœur's Moral Anthropology: Singularity, Responsibility, and Justice*. New York: Lexington Books, 2018.

"Discussione." *Demitizzazione e Immagine*, edited by Enrico Castelli, 311–14. Padua: CEDAM, 1962.

Duminuco, Vincent J., SJ, ed. *The Jesuit "Ratio Studiorum": 400th Anniversary Perspectives*. New York: Fordham University Press, 2000.

"*Eloquentia Perfecta*: Writing and Speaking Well." Special issue, *Conversations on Jesuit Higher Education* 43 (Spring 2013).

Fessard, Gaston. *Autorité et bien commun*. Paris: Aubier, 1944.

———. *De l'actualité historique*. 2 vols. Paris: Desclée de Brouwer, 1960.

———. *La dialectique des "Exercices spirituels" de Saint Ignace de Loyola*. Paris: Aubier, 1956.

———. "France, prends garde de perdre ton âme!" *Cahiers du Témoignage chrétien*, no. 1 (November 1941). Reprinted in *Au temps du prince-esclave: Écrits clandestins, 1940–1945*, edited by Jacques Prévotat, 61–95. Paris: Critérion, 1989.

———. "The Future of a Dialogue Now Possible: To Become Actual or to Remain Impossible?" Translated by Oliva Blanchette, SJ. In *Demythologizing Marxism*, edited by Frederick J. Adelmann, SJ, 96–165. Chestnut Hill, MA: Boston College, 1969.

———. "Image, symbole et historicité." In *Demitizzazione e immagine*, edited by Enrico Castelli, 43–68. Padua: CEDAM, 1962.

———. "A Letter from Gaston Fessard, SJ." In *Life in Faith and Freedom: An Essay Presenting Gaston Fessard's Analysis of the Dialectic of "The Spiritual Exercises" of St. Ignatius*, by Édouard Pousset, SJ, edited and translated by Eugene L. Donahue, SJ, xx–xxviii. St. Louis: Institute of Jesuit Sources, 1980.

———. *La main tendue: Le dialogue catholique-communiste est-il possible?* Paris: Grasset, 1937.

———. "Le matérialisme historique et la dialectique du maître et de l'esclave." In *Atti del Congresso internazionale di Filosofia*, edited by Enrico Castelli, 57–78. Milan: Castellani, 1947.

———. *Pax Nostra: Examen de conscience international*. Paris: Grasset, 1936.

———. "Symbole, surnaturel, dialogue." In *Demitizzazione e morale*, edited by Enrico Castelli, 105–41. Padua: CEDAM, 1965.

Fitzgerald, William. *Spiritual Modalities: Prayer as Rhetoric and Performance*. University Park: Pennsylvania State University Press, 2012.

Foucault, Michel. *The Hermeneutics of the Subject: Lectures at the Collège de France, 1981–1982*. Edited by Frédéric Gros. Translated by Graham Burchell. New York: Palgrave Macmillan, 2005.

"Full Text of Pope Francis' In-Flight Interview from Mexico to Rome." *Catholic News*

Agency, February 18, 2016. http://www
.catholicnewsagency.com/news/full
textofpopefrancisinflightinterview-
frommexicotorome85821.

Gannett, Cinthia, and John C. Brereton, eds.
*Traditions of Eloquence: The Jesuits and
Modern Rhetorical Studies*. New York:
Fordham University Press, 2016.

Geroulanos, Stefanos. "Heterogeneities,
Slave-Princes, and Marshall Plans:
Schmitt's Reception in Hegel's
France." *Modern Intellectual History* 8,
no. 3 (2011): 531–60.

Hadot, Pierre. *Philosophy as a Way of Life:
Spiritual Exercises from Socrates to
Foucault*. Edited by Arnold I.
Davidson. Translated by Michael
Chase. Oxford, UK: Blackwell, 1995.

Heidegger, Martin. *Being and Time*. Translated
by John Macquarrie and Edward
Robinson. New York: Harper & Row,
1962.

Ignatius of Loyola. *Ignatius of Loyola: The
"Spiritual Exercises" and Selected Works*.
Edited by George E. Ganss, SJ. New
York: Paulist Press, 1991.

Kojève, Alexandre. *Introduction to the Reading
of Hegel: Lectures on the "Phenomenol-
ogy of Spirit."* Edited by Allan Bloom.
Translated by James H. Nichols Jr.
Ithaca: Cornell University Press, 1980.

"Kojève-Fessard Documents." Translated by
Hugh Gillis. *Interpretation* 19, no. 2
(Winter 1991–92): 185–200.

Kolvenbach, Peter-Hans, SJ. "Jerome Nadal:
Fifth Century of His Birth." *Review of
Ignatian Spirituality* 116 (2007):9–15.

Lévi-Strauss, Claude. *The Elementary
Structures of Kinship*. Translated by
James Harle Bell, John Richard von
Sturmer, and Rodney Needham.
Boston: Beacon Press, 1969.

———. *Structural Anthropology*. Translated
by Claire Jacobson and Brooke
Grundfest Schoepf. New York: Basic
Books, 1963.

Mailloux, Steven. "Notes on Prayerful
Rhetoric with Divinities." *Philosophy
and Rhetoric* 47, no. 4 (2014): 419–33.

———. *Rhetoric's Pragmatism: Essays in
Rhetorical Hermeneutics*. University

Park: Pennsylvania State University
Press, 2017.

Matthews, Gareth. "Anselm, Augustine, and
Platonism." In *The Cambridge
Companion to Anselm*, edited by Brian
Davies and Brian Leftow, 61–83.
Cambridge, UK: Cambridge
University Press, 2004.

Molina, J. Michelle. *To Overcome Oneself: The
Jesuit Ethic and Spirit of Global
Expansion, 1520–1767*. Berkeley:
University of California Press, 2013.

O'Malley, John W. *The First Jesuits*. Cambridge, MA: Harvard University
Press, 1993.

Ong, Walter J., SJ. "Interiority and Modernity
in the Spiritual Exercises." Paper
delivered at Saint Louis University,
St. Louis, MO, April 13, 1969.
Accessed March 13, 2016. http://cdm
.slu.edu/cdm/compoundobject
/collection/ong/id/1331/rec/14.

———. MSS 64.2.2.1.195. Walter J. Ong
Manuscript Collection, Saint Louis
University Archives and Digital
Services, Saint Louis, MO.

"Our Mission Today: The Service of Faith
and the Promotion of Justice." Decree
4 of the 32nd General Congregation
of the Society of Jesus, December 2,
1974–March 7, 1975.

Pope Francis. "Address of the Holy Father."
Holy See, 2015. http://w2.vatican.va
/content/francesco/en/speeches/2015
/september/documents/papafran
cesco_20150924_usauscongress.html.

———. *Evangelii gaudium: On the Proclamation of the Gospel in Today's World*.
Holy See, 2013. http://www.vatican
.va/content/francesco/en/apost
_exhortations/documents/papa
francesco_esortazioneap_20131124
_evangeliigaudium.html.

———. *Laudato si': On Care for Our Common
Home*. Holy See, 2013. http://w2
.vatican.va/content/francesco/en
/encyclicals/documents/papafran
cesco_20150524_enciclicalaudatosi
.html.

Pousset, Édouard, SJ. *Life in Faith and
Freedom: An Essay Presenting Gaston*

Fessard's Analysis of the Dialectic of "The Spiritual Exercises" of St. Ignatius. Edited and translated by Eugene L. Donahue, SJ. St. Louis: Institute of Jesuit Sources, 1980.

Przywara, Erich. *An Augustine Synthesis.* London: Sheed and Ward, 1936.

"Rhetorical Arts." Loyola Marymount University, 2020. https://academics .lmu.edu/cte/pedagogicalresources /corecurriculum/rhetoricalarts.

Rhetorical Arts Working Group. "Jesuit Rhetorical Arts: *Eloquentia Perfecta.*" Loyola Marymount University, February 27, 2013. https://academics .lmu.edu/media/lmuacademics/cen terforteachingexcellence/documents /Jesuit%20Rhetorical%20Arts.pdf.

Richardson, William J., SJ. "Contemplative in Action." In *Amor Mundi: Explorations in the Faith and Thought of Hannah Arendt,* edited by James W. Bernauer, SJ, 115–34. Boston: Martin Nijhoff, 1987.

Ricœur, Paul. *Figuring the Sacred: Religion, Narrative, and Imagination.* Edited by Mark I. Wallace. Translated by David Pellauer. Minneapolis: Fortress Press, 1995.

———. *Freud and Philosophy: An Essay on Interpretation.* Translated by Denis Savage. New Haven, CT: Yale University Press, 1970.

———. "The Hermeneutics of Symbols and Philosophical Reflection: I." Translated by Denis Savage. In *The Conflict of Interpretations,* edited by Don Ihde, 287–314. Evanston, IL: Northwestern University Press, 1974.

———. *The Symbolism of Evil.* Translated by Emerson Buchanan. Boston: Beacon Press, 1969.

Rosen, Stanley. "Kojève's Paris: A Memoir." In *Metaphysics in Ordinary Language,* 258–78. New Haven, CT: Yale University Press, 1999.

Sales, Michel. "Gaston Fessard (1897–1978): Un philosophe chrétien engagé dans l'histoire de son temps." In *Hegel, le Christianisme, et l'Histoire,* by Gaston Fessard, edited by Michel Sales, 17–21. Paris: Presses Universitaires de France, 1990.

Schmitt, Carl. *The Concept of the Political.* Translated by George Schwab. Chicago: University of Chicago Press, 1996.

———. *Political Theology: Four Chapters on the Concept of Sovereignty.* Translated by George Schwab. Chicago: University of Chicago Press, 2005.

Schwab, George. "Introduction." In *The Concept of the Political,* by Carl Schmitt, translated by Geoge Schwab, 3–16. Chicago: University of Chicago Press, 1996.

Traub, George W., SJ, ed. *An Ignatian Spirituality Reader.* Chicago: Loyola Press, 2008.

CHAPTER 4

How to Undo Truths with Words

Reading Texts Both Sacred and Profane in Hobbes and Benjamin

JAMES R. MARTEL

When it comes to thinking about reading sacred texts, Thomas Hobbes and Walter Benjamin may at first appearance seem singularly ill suited to being compared together. Hobbes is famously conservative and orthodox, a stern defender of royal prerogative against any incursions from other modes of politics as well as a defender of the Church of England against any pretenders with alternative readings of theology. Benjamin, on the other hand, is the epitome of the anti-orthodox; he is deeply radical and a foe of both the state and the church in any form. Despite all of this, in this chapter I will indeed be making a connection between these thinkers, arguing that they have remarkably similar takes not only on how to read a sacred text but also on what makes a text (or anything else for that matter) sacred in the first place. Although on the surface of things Hobbes appears to be against everything that Benjamin is for (and vice versa), we see that through their common notion of how to read and how to respond to the sacred more generally, there is an unexpected political upshot to which both thinkers subscribe.

It might also seem peculiar to be reading these authors in a volume about sacred texts. Although both authors devote a great deal of their time to theological questions, neither of them seems particularly interested in sacredness. Their emphasis in both cases is on the political rather than the sacred as such. Yet it is for this very reason that I find it useful to read both Hobbes and Benjamin in tandem (or in constellation, to use a Benjaminian phrase), as well as to read them in regard to the question of reading sacred texts. The key point I will be making in this argument is that in effect, for both writers, all texts are potentially sacred and furthermore that those texts that we ordinarily understand as sacred are not necessarily so. For both Benjamin and Hobbes, sacredness lies not so much in the text as such, but in our reading of it. Sacredness is an attribute that we, the readers, can—or also cannot—attribute to texts. Sacredness is a state of radical possibility, a way of taking a text out of its context and acknowledging our own failure to truly know what it is and what it means. Sacredness is thus, for these thinkers, a way of acknowledging, not so much the clear presence of a theological force or possibility, but rather a site in which that force is marked as unknowable. It is more a matter of wonderment at what we cannot know, see, or touch, and in this way is an effect that can be extended to any text, object, person, or experience.

In this way, I will finally be arguing that the question of a sacred text and how to approach it is deeply political for both of these thinkers in that they make access to sacredness maximally open, contingent, and local in ways that cannot be determined or directed in advance by any law or norm. Because of their focus on politics, reading these two authors in tandem in terms of their approaches to sacred texts shows us the sacredness of everyday life as well as the political value and power of that insight.

This insight may be especially helpful in our own time when questions of truth and interpretation have become perhaps especially fraught (although neither for the first nor the last time). With the rise of so-called populism, which is actually a form of political authoritarianism, and when notions of "fake news" and deepfake technology makes the very question of proof and meaning seem impossible and quixotic, it is good to revisit the notion of reading texts—any text—as sacred. As I will argue in what follows, for both Hobbes and Benjamin to think of a text as sacred means to think of it as being infinitely capable of being interpreted and reinterpreted, with decisions about truth and meaning left to the hands of the collective of readers rather than any one authority who claims to speak for the rest of us (yes, even Hobbes). By democratizing—or really anarchizing—reading and interpretation, Hobbes and Benjamin offer a response to the dilemma of truth and meaning wherein the very elusiveness of textual meaning—and perhaps sacred textual meaning in particular—becomes a way to guard against a text becoming merely a tool of orthodoxy and authoritarian control.

HOBBES'S NEGATIVE THEOLOGY

Let me begin to make this argument by looking first at Hobbes. Hobbes is, in a way, the more difficult case to make because he presents a scientific approach to epistemology that seems to accept, on the surface of things, the tangible and accessible reality of the material world and, by extension, a human politics based on the observation of and engagement with that world. He also argues that the sovereign is supreme in all things, very much including the question of what is sacred, further suggesting that, in liturgical matters at least, the sovereign should be seen as having the last word (not so much in terms of interpretation but at least in terms of liturgical practices derived from those texts). In this way, it would appear that Hobbes offers no ground (indeed his intention seems to eliminate) any notion of the sacred that is not state sanctioned or based on any kind of mystery.

This surface appearance can be misleading, however. For one thing, Hobbes's apparent empiricism is not what it seems. Hobbes's work is marked by a radical nominalism that subverts and renders problematic such an easy understanding of the material world. Hobbes is famous for saying that "there [is] nothing in the world universall but Names" (*Leviathan*, 26), meaning that we only know things by their name and, as such are committed to a purely representational approach to the world around us.

This nominalism also extends to matters theological for Hobbes (indeed, I would argue that it comes from his theology). Hobbes tells us in one of his most important statements about our relationship to God that "the nature of God is incomprehensible; that is to say, we understand nothing of *what he is*, but only *that he is*; and therefore the Attributes we give him, are not to tell one another, *what he is*, nor to signifie our opinion of his Nature, but our desire to honor him with such names as we conceive most honorable amongst our selves" (*Leviathan*, 271). In this way, human decisions about what is to be venerated (including in terms of what is sacred) are just that, decisions and projections onto the screen of a deity who is ever present and ever silent. This exercise is important then, not because it tells us what God actually wants (that is something that we can never know) but rather it is a way for human beings to determine what *they* think is "most honorable"—a way, in other words, to make a collective decision about what they most cherish and honor what they hold to be sacred.

It is true, as already noted, that Hobbes argued, much to the consternation of the Church of England, that the sovereign should be able to determine liturgy and not the clergy, suggesting that this public form of determination of the sacred is overridden by a centralized authority. But the roots of that claim do not stem from the fact that Hobbes thinks that the sovereign has access to some kind of higher truth the clergy lacks. Rather, Hobbes seeks to concentrate such decisions in one set of hands, even hands that are admittedly "arbitrary" (*Leviathan*, 471)—as he freely concedes the sovereign to be—simply to keep the peace.[1] Furthermore, this sovereign decision does not come out of a vacuum. For Hobbes language itself is a collective process of determining meaning, and so the sovereign can be said to only be authorizing decisions that have, for the most part, already been determined by a collective and public process. This, I would argue, very much includes decisions about the sacred insofar as these, too, reflect a radical nominalism that for Hobbes is determined not by law but by language, something that the sovereign does not and cannot control.

THE SACRED DURING THE TIME OF THE KINGDOM OF GOD

The practice of human beings determining their own desires by ascribing them to God is particularly relevant during what Hobbes and other thinkers of his time considered to be the present age when God ceased to speak to human beings. With God absent from direct communication with human beings, the burden of faith falls on a human hermeneutics. But even when God does speak to human beings, as was the case during the time of miracles and the Hebrew prophets—a period that Hobbes refers to as the "*Kingdome of God*" (*Leviathan*, 280)—Hobbes remains highly skeptical about the ability of human beings to ever directly perceive an act or will of God, much less God's presence—this, even in a time when God is actually king of ancient Israel (and hence the sovereign of all sovereigns).

In terms of the question of prophecy, of direct communication with and by God during that period, Hobbes writes, "Seeing then all Prophecy supposeth Vision, or Dream, (which two, when they be naturall, are the same,)

or some especiall gift of God, so rarely observed in mankind . . . there is
need of Reason and Judgment to discern between naturall, and supernaturall Gifts, and between naturall, and supernaturall Visions, or Dreams"
(*Leviathan*, 297). Even when God speaks "directly" to Moses, Hobbes says
that to interpret Exodus 33:2—"The Lord spake to Moses face to face, as a
man speaketh to his friend"—literally would be to presume that God actually has a face. Hobbes tells us even this speech "was by mediation of an
Angel, or Angels . . . and was therefore a Vision, though a more cleer Vision
than was given to other Prophets" (*Leviathan*, 297).

Speaking of a "more cleer Vision," Hobbes is still attesting to an invented
or phantasmic element of this vision. "More clear" merely means that the
vision seemed more real to Moses and therefore had a stronger effect on
his mind, but its effect remains within Moses's own imaginative and interpretive abilities. And clearly, if this is the case for Moses, who of all human
beings perhaps came closest to some kind of direct connection with God,
for the rest of us (human sovereigns very much included), any sense that
we can see or hear something directly from God is not only mistaken but
is, for Hobbes, idolatrous. Such beliefs were, in his view, the basis of much
of what he thought was wrong with his own time of the English Civil War
when England was wrenched by religious wars based on people's assumptions that they knew what the word of God said and meant.

There is therefore no recourse beyond representation when it comes to
matters both divine and secular for Hobbes. For this reason, decisions
about what is sacred and what is not cannot be determined by divine signs
but must themselves be rendered by human judgments. But critically, those
judgments must be recognized as *failures* to evoke what God actually is or
does. When we think that such judgments accurately represent God's own
desires and plans, we superimpose human judgment over God's own and,
in this way, separate ourselves from God, overwriting God's blankness with
a substance of our own devising. This is another reason why Hobbes pre-
ferred to put the ultimate power of determination of the sacred in the hands
of the king instead of the clergy; because the king, as a political figure, was
not to be mistaken for someone who actually knew what God meant. The
arbitrariness of the king is in fact a positive for Hobbes in this sense because it
keeps the failure to represent God—at least potentially—alive (and once
again this failure exists not in law but in language itself that the sovereign
speaks but does not determine).

In general, Hobbes is a very stern guardian of the dividing line between the human and the divine. Even when it comes to miracles, which seem like a way for God to directly communicate with human beings through signs and supernatural events, Hobbes argues that a miracle is more in the eye of the beholder than a tangible and expressible fact of God's power. Thus he writes, "The first Rainbow that was seen in the world, was a Miracle, because the first; and consequently strange; and served for a sign from God. . . . But at this day, because they are frequent, they are not Miracles, neither to them that know their naturall causes, nor them to them who know them not" (*Leviathan*, 301). There is thus nothing in the phenomenon of a rainbow that is inherently miraculous. The miracle in this case effectively lies in the *reading* of the phenomenon as being miraculous and therefore is itself an artifact of language and representation and, once again, of a human decision as to what is and what is not sacred.

Hobbes reinforces this idea when he considers the supernatural tricks that the Egyptian priests were able to perform that came without God's sanction during the time of Moses:

> For it is evident enough, that Words have no effect, but on those that understand them; and then they have no other, but to signifie the intentions, or passions of them that speak. . . . Therefore when a Rod seemeth a Serpent, or the Waters Bloud, or any other Miracle seemeth done by Enchantment; if it not be to the edification of Gods people, not the Rod, nor the Water, nor any other thing is enchanted; this is to say, wrought upon the Words, but by the Spectator. So that all the Miracle consisteth in this, that the Enchanter has deceived a man; which is no Miracle, but a very easie thing to doe. (*Leviathan*, 304)

Here, we see even more evidence that doing something beyond the ordinary powers of human activity and imagination does not constitute either a miracle or something sacred. Supernatural powers themselves are not what creates sacredness. They do not give their wielder the right to expect worship and reverence in return. Once again, the decision to regard something as sacred comes from within the community of the humans who receive these signs and events (or who judge that they have been given such signs) to decide for themselves if and what such signs portend.

Despite Hobbes's penchant for seeking a centralizing authority for questions of what is sacred, there are once again myriad ways that Hobbes seeks not the concentration but the dissemination of such forms of interpretation. Or perhaps more accurately, he recognizes that these kinds of decisions about what is sacred and what is not, what counts as a miracle and what does not, are inherently social decisions and that no one authority—not even the sovereign—can or even should have the power to unilaterally determine such things.

Thus, for example, in *De Cive*, Hobbes tells us that during the period of the Kingdom of God a prophet occasionally challenged the interpretive power of the Levite priests. Thus "the supreme civil power was therefore *rightly* due by God's own institution to the high-priest; but *actually* that power was in the prophets to whom (being raised by God in an extraordinary manner) the Israelites, a people greedy of prophets, submitted themselves to be protected and judged, by reason of the great esteem they had of prophecies" (323). Critically, for Hobbes the role of prophet is itself screened by the people as a whole: "Others did judge of the prophets, whether they were to be held for true or not. For to what end did God give signs and tokens to all the people, whereby the true prophets might be discerned from the false; namely, the event of predictions, and the conformity with the religion established by Moses; if they might not use those marks?" (325).

In *Leviathan* as well, Hobbes offers some ways for the people to be able to discern between a true and a false prophet. He writes, for example, "That which taketh away the reputation of Wisedome, in him that formeth a Religion or addeth to it when it is already formed, is the enjoyning of a beliefe of contradictories: For both parts of a contradiction cannot possibly be true: and therefore to enjoyne the beliefe of them, is an argument of ignorance; which detects the Author in that; and discredits him in all things else he shall propound as from revelation supernaturall" (84). Hobbes goes on to discuss the way that a lack of both sincerity and also (unexpectedly) love can similarly identify a false prophet. For the latter, Hobbes says that if the prophecy seems to accord too much to the speaker's own private ends "but not for love of others" (84) it can be rejected.

In this way, a public and collective judgment about what constituted sanctified prophecy and what was false was determinant. Declaring oneself a prophet, even convincing a king that this was the case, did not grant one the status of someone who spoke on behalf of God. Instead, such decisions remained in collective hands, in the way that the people as a whole responded to and decided on the sacredness of what such a prophet had to say.

Such signs and ways to judge were available to one and all during the time of Hebrew prophets. Yet even for some time after the kingdom of God fell (the period when God's rule over ancient Israel was revoked and the Israelites elected Saul, a human king, issuing in a model of human-based rule ever after), prophecies continued to erupt from time to time directly challenging the interpretive power of kings that Hobbes ordinarily supports. In *De Cive*, he tells us that "the civil power therefore, and the power of discerning God's word from the words of men, and of interpreting God's word even in the days of the kings, was wholly belonging to [prophets, among others]" (326) And, in this way, it continued to fall to the people to judge whether the prophet spoke for God or not (perhaps with some help from the prophet him- or herself).

In Hobbes's view, in his (and our) own time, God no longer speaks even to prophets, but Hobbes continues to insist on public interpretation and decision even in the face of his contention that the sovereign should have the last word in all matters. Thus he writes in *Behemoth* that despite the problems that widespread access to scripture may have posed for the English monarchy and church, Hobbes defends it nonetheless because, in his view, "there are so many places of Scripture easy to be understood, that teach both true faith and good morality . . . of which no seducer is able to dispossess the mind (of any ordinary readers), that the reading of them is so profitable as not to be forbidden without great damage to them and the commonwealth" (53).

In other words, even given the risk of misinterpretation of Scripture, Hobbes saw that widespread access to sacred texts was vital for a polity that was to have a basic sense of ethics and decency. If the sacredness from these texts comes not from the texts as such, but rather from the decision of the people to read and interpret them accordingly, we also see here a way for a community to discipline and order itself via the way it chooses to interpret (or not interpret) a text. This is an exercise that cannot be simply left to sovereign decision because the production of moral and ethical beliefs—something that for Hobbes was required for the public as a whole—lies in and is produced through the reading and interpreting of such texts. In this way the act of reading sacred texts is in some sense a practice of social self-production, a function, once again, of language rather than of law. It could even be said that the ability to determine that a text is sacred (or not) or valid (or not) is the basis of a political power, an anarchic power that is forever shifting as linguistic usages change and that always resides among the entire community of speakers and readers; reading texts as sacred or true, a community is, in effect, reading itself and its own interpretive authority into being.

READING SACRED TEXTS

Given the critical nature of textual interpretation, and especially of sacred texts described here, the question becomes: how are these texts actually to be read? In fact, in several of his works, Hobbes offers a great quantity of examples of how to read a sacred text properly. Here, too, his views on reading sacred texts are no different than his views on reading texts in general, returning us to his general and radical nominalism. In all cases, Hobbes calls for a reading that reduces and undermines attempts to interpret texts as conveying magical elements that represent not the blank screen of God, but rather some already predetermined pseudo truth promulgated (dangerously) in God's name. For this latter kind of reading, Hobbes has a name: daemonology, which he defines as that "fabulous Doctrine concerning Daemons, which are but Idols, or Phantasms of the braine, without any reall nature of their own, distinct from humane fancy" (*Leviathan*, 418).

Daemonology consists of seeing (or reading) things that are not there and mistaking them for things that are. It is in effect the opposite of the way Hobbes tells us that we should speak about God because, instead of being about what we do not know about God, it becomes a pretense that we *do* know something after all.

For Hobbes, the practice of daemonology leads to a "kingdome of darkness" (the name of the fourth and final part of *Leviathan*). He saw his own time as constituting such a kingdom whereby falsities were promoted as truths and attributed to sacred texts whose authority was not to be questioned.

Because of such dangers, Hobbes sharply polices the way we ascribe supernatural powers to God even—or especially—in reading Scripture. Hobbes is especially concerned that we do not read in ways that are overly metaphorical wherein the metaphor becomes a vehicle for falsities. Instead, he seeks in every case to reduce the metaphor to its most basic (and nominal) meaning, rendering it unavailable for false and bloated claims.

Hobbes writes, for example, that the biblical term "Spirit," was much overinterpreted in his day to mean a plethora of things that it had nothing to do with. He tells us therefore that "for metaphoricall significations [of 'Spirit'] there be many" (*Leviathan*, 270) and also that "[of the] signification of *Spirit* I find no where any; and where none of these can satisfie the sense of that word in Scripture, the place falleth not under humane Understandings; and our Faith therein consisteth not in our Opinion, but in our Submission; as in all places where God is said to be a *Spirit*; or where by the *Spirit of God*, is meant God himself" (271).

As ever, Hobbes is careful to distinguish between God's own actions and powers, which are completely separate from human existence, and those actions that we attribute to God that are within our own purview and power to determine. Here again Hobbes is not saying here that we cannot or should not talk about God and God's actions, but only that we have to understand that when we do so we are speaking from our own limited perspectives. Hobbes recognizes that we cannot really do otherwise since human language is the only way to talk about God at all, but we must speak and write with caution, avoiding what he calls a "metaphorical" reading insofar as metaphors can readily be misread as literal terms. More accurately, for Hobbes we must remain aware precisely of the inherently metaphorical nature of all language but limit the way that metaphor is an invitation to fill the blankness of language with some imagined truth. The danger for Hobbes is that people forget the limits—and human-derived nature—of language and use these metaphors as projections of their own anxieties and wished-for powers.

In order to combat this danger, Hobbes seeks to have people read Scripture in as literal a manner as possible. Thus he tells us that when in the Bible the term "the Spirit of God' is used, he writes that "*as long as the Spirit of God is in my nostrils*, [Job 27:3] is no more then to say, *as long as I live*" (*Leviathan*, 272). And he interprets "*the Spirit entred into me, and set me on my feet* [Ezek. 2:30]," as meaning "*I recovered my vitall strength*" (272–73). In this way, Hobbes seeks to reduce the ability to read things into Scripture that are not there.

Hobbes's focus on the word "Spirit" is not accidental; one of the most pernicious forms of misreading for Hobbes has to do with the Holy Spirit, a figure that was much revered by the Puritans of his day. For the Puritans, the Holy Spirit was a force that connected separate human beings from one another. For Hobbes this was a dangerous form of thinking that threatened to enchant the world with fake and projected forms of magic and, in that way, seriously reduce the actual sacredness of the world (since it will be hijacked by projection and fetishism) as well as—and thereby—reducing the salubrious effect that the collective honoring of God can have on a political community when they exercise the determination of what is sacred and what is not according to their own decisions and judgments.

Hobbes makes a similar case for the term "Word of God," writing:

> If we say the *Word of God*, or of *Man*, it may bee understood some-times of the Speaker . . . as the words that God hath spoken, or that a Man hath spoken: In which sense, when we say, the Gospel of St. Matthew, we understand St. Matthew to be the Writer of it: and sometimes of the Subject. . . . That which is here called the Word of God, was the Doctrine of Christian Religion: as it appears evidently by that which goes before. And (Acts 5:20) where it is said to the Apostles by an Angel, *Go stand and speak in the Temple, all the Words of this life*; by the Words of this life, is meant, the Doctrine of the Gospel; as is evident by what they did in the Temple. (287)

In this way, Hobbes radically reduces the chances that we will read too much into the sacred text. The term "Spirit" of God can only mean the kind of inspiration that we draw from the idea of God or a power that we attribute to God of which we know nothing further. The "Word of God" can only mean the words that we humans attribute to God, the "Doctrine of Christian Religion." Both readings return us the world of human devising, to the human yielders of language and their own judgments and decisions.

When Hobbes insists on reading Scriptural phrases literally he is not, as it might at first seem, merely seeking to strip the world of sacredness altogether (although plenty of people said that he was doing just that both in his own lifetime and subsequently). I would argue that instead—and this is where the connection to Benjamin becomes most apparent, as I will soon show—he is seeking to disallow interferences with the notion of God and Spirit by human agents in order to allow that sacredness itself be available to us in a purely negative way. By encountering the absence of the sacred, its failure to appear in the world, it remains a source of inspiration and wonder, something that is destroyed as soon as we begin to ascribe false and knowable truths to it.[2]

In this way, as with reading a rainbow as a miracle, the ability to see something afresh, free from the constraints of idolatry and projection, allows us to see what could be called the sacredness of the everyday, the way that God's non-presence is available in texts deemed sacred and profane alike.

In this way, too, Hobbes's literalism does the opposite of what it initially appears to do; rather than serve as a secularizing force that strips the world of any divine presence, it runs interference in that world, allowing the public a chance to consider what the sacred is and what it is not in ways that avoid all certainties and biases. In doing so, these communities are able to experience, once again, their own political—and I would once again say anarchic—power.

BENJAMIN'S COSMOLOGY

Moving on to Benjamin's own way of reading the world in general and sacred texts in particular, the first thing to note is that, just like Hobbes, Benjamin partakes in a radically negative theology. Benjamin tells us in "On Language as Such and On the Language of Man" that whereas in paradise, Adam had a direct relationship to God and to the material world around him—his function was to give a spoken name to those objects and the animals in the Garden that corresponded to the mute name God had already given them—since the Fall, "knowledge of good and evil abandons name; it is a knowledge from outside, the uncreated imitation of the creative word" (72). Human beings since that time substitute knowledge for truth; representation, projection, and myth become our only recourse.

Accordingly, Benjamin also tells us that subsequently human beings "fell into the abyss of the mediateness of all communication, of the word as mean, of the empty word, into the abyss of prattle" (72). As such, we are cut off both from God and from the material objects that surround us. As with Hobbes, we are reduced to a radical nominalism, but for Benjamin this is a nominalism that has been "abandoned." To name no longer acknowledges what is present; now it grasps and strains to reproduce something that is forever lost to us, leaving us with nothing but "prattle."

In this context, what appears divine or sacred is merely projection. For Benjamin the world is full of false messiahs, partaking in what he calls "mythic violence" ("Critique of Violence," 248). This is the violence of projection itself, of assertion without basis.[3] For Benjamin two of the clearest instances of mythic violence are law and capitalism. Benjamin tells us that law, at least in the way it is ordinarily practiced, has no real basis for its authority. Accordingly, it turns to capital punishment as a way to demonstrate (or even produce) its right to exist: "If violence, violence crowned by fate, is the origin of law, then it may be readily supposed that where the highest violence, that over life and death, occurs in the legal system, the origins of law jut manifestly and fearsomely into existence. [The purpose of capital punishment] is not to punish the infringement of law but to establish new law" (242).

As for capitalism, in "Capitalism as Religion" Benjamin writes, "[It] is a purely cultic religion, perhaps the most extreme form that ever existed. In capitalism, things have a meaning only in their relationship to the cult; capitalism has no specific body of dogma, no theology" (288). In such a context, the sacred becomes readily confused with the profane and, as we see, the very notion of what constitutes a "religion" becomes muddied by attempts to reproduce paradise in a human, secular (and idolatrous) guise.

If Hobbes's response to this situation is to seek to narrow our reading of words and signs and other forms of representation to their pith, reducing or eliminating the possibility for misreading, Benjamin's solution is quite the opposite. Rather than "clarifying" the meaning of words, Benjamin seeks to render representation itself obscure—that is, to demonstrate the failure that representation always performs but that is not usually apparent to us. In this way he takes his nominalism further than Hobbes does himself.

Benjamin's key tool for this kind of reading is his turn to allegory. In his *Origin of German Tragic Drama*, contrasting allegory to the symbol (the attempt to make an object actually stand in for the truth), Benjamin tells us, "Whereas in the symbolic destruction is idealized and the transfigured face of nature is fleetingly revealed in the light of redemption, in allegory the observer is confronted with the *facies hypocritica* [the face that reveals impending death] of history as petrified, primordial landscape" (166). In this way, the allegorical focuses on the material body of objects (including people's own material bodies) as a way to counter the false symbolism that we otherwise would read into these things. Allegory as a trope is, for Benjamin, always focused on failure, the failure to represent, the failure to be true. Such failures serve to undermine the certainties that otherwise directly interfere with our attempts to recognize the absence of truth from the world and, in particular, the truth that comes from God.

As already noted, for Benjamin, the appearance of what is deemed to be sacred is, far from something to cherish and seek out, rather something to shun because its expression in the world is always false (as symbol). In this way, what is "sacred" about a text is not its provenance but rather its ability to remain opaque via the very medium of transmission that normally gives it over to our interpretations. Accordingly, Benjamin writes, "For sacred script always takes the form of certain complexes of words which ultimately constitute, or aspire to become, one single and inalterable complex. So it is that alphabetical script as a combination of atoms of writing, is the farthest removed from the script of sacred complexes. . . . The desire to guarantee the sacred character of any script—there will always be a conflict between sacred standing and profane comprehensibility—leads to complexes, to hieroglyphics" (175). Here we see once again that for Benjamin the way to fight false readings of the sacred is not to insist on "literal readings," as with Hobbes, but rather to break the word down into its component parts so that the figures of representation (in this case letters) serve as a barrier to comprehension, so that all you see are the trees instead of the forest.

An example of this kind of reading comes in a passage in *The Arcades Project* that Benjamin cites from G. K. Chesterton in his book *Dickens*, which in turn cites directly from Dickens himself: "On the allegorical element. 'Dickens . . . mentions among the coffee shops into which he crept in those wretched days, one in St. Martin's Lane, [had] "a glass plate with COFFEE ROOM painted on it, addressed towards the street. If I ever find myself in a very different kind of coffee room now, but where there is such an inscription on glass, and read it backwards on the wrong side, MOOR EEFFOC . . . a shock goes through my blood." That wild word, 'Moor Eeffoc,' is the motto of all effective realism" (233). This "wild word" is a case of the symbolic being reduced to the allegorical. Rather than tell us something true, the letters have become a weapon against the very meaning that they would otherwise convey. Not unlike the general strike, which Benjamin offers as a key form of nonviolent confrontation with the law and with capitalism, this allegorical or hieroglyphic form of reading refuses to participate in an economy of meaning whose outcomes are always presupposed and that serve only to foster more phantasm, more idolatry, and more violence. Granted, in this instance, the words "MOOR EEFFOC" are spelled backwards, giving the words a strange shape or form, but in fact backwards or forwards, clear or obscure, letters, images, signs, and all other forms of representation are always failing. It is the mark of that failure (Benjamin also speaks of the allegory as a form of ruin) that allows us to resist the temptation to read things into the world that are not there.

Benjamin's confrontation with the symbol and with the false manifestations of the sacred go so deep as to even interfere with the way we read the most clear and evident statements in Scripture. A prime and well-known example of this is when he reads the biblical commandment "Thou shalt not kill." Thus, in the "Critique of Violence," Benjamin writes, "Neither divine judgment nor the grounds for this judgment can be known in advance. Those who base a condemnation of all violent killing of one person by another on the commandment are therefore mistaken. It exists not as a criterion of judgment, but as a guideline for the actions of persons or communities who have to wrestle with it in solitude and, in exceptional cases, to take on themselves the responsibility of ignoring it" (250). In other words, even a commandment as central and seemingly clear in its meaning as the condemnation of killing is not straightforward at all. Struggling with the meaning of this, as with all other texts, Benjamin offers that at best this commandment is a mystery to be puzzled with, a statement that ultimately leads to our own responsibility and our own interpretation, just as with Hobbes. Once again, mystical obfuscation gives way to political and collective decision, not to find truth after all but to decide what, in the clear absence of truth, human beings are going to do, how they will act, and what they will decide together in the face of a God that tells them nothing at all.

In cases such as this—and again in a way that I would argue is quite similar to Hobbes—it is not that Benjamin seeks to deny the sacred altogether. Rather, by exposing the failure of the sacred to be present even in the most sacred of objects or texts, Benjamin is allowing the sacred to be what it always must be for us—mysterious, separate, unknowable. This is the closest thing to a "truth" that we are permitted for Benjamin (and Hobbes, too, for that matter). To refuse to fill the spaces of our world with false manifestations of the sacred is to remind us that the sacred is everywhere and nowhere at once and that it cannot be summoned or used to serve our purposes by the power of our reading, by representation.

Drawing on Kafka, who has always been one of Benjamin's greatest muses, he tells us that access to Scripture is in a sense the undoing of the sacred as we thought we understood it and constitutes instead the path to contemplate the sacred and the messianic in everyday life (as with the commandment "Thou shalt not kill" to ignore or turn one's back on whatever we think God must mean by this phrase). Thus he writes that "the gate to justice is study. And yet Kafka does not dare attach to this study the promises which tradition has attached to the study of the Torah. His assistants are sextons who have lost their house of prayer; his students are pupils who have lost the Holy Writ" ("Franz Kafka," 815). For Benjamin those students who have "lost the Holy Writ" have gained something far more precious: a space within which they are free from mythical projections and violence.

To be broken off from what passes for sacred in the world does not condemn us to meaninglessness and evil. Rather, to experience the failure of the pseudo sacred has a strong effect on us, not so much in the sense of giving us even a glimmer of the sacred itself but simply in encountering the space where it is not.

For Benjamin, when meanings and symbols are broken and obscured, they do not cease to have an influence or power over us, but that power becomes something else. Thus he writes, for example in *The Origin of German Tragic Drama*, about a play by Pedro Calderón de la Barca in which Mariamne, the wife of Herod, sees the fragments of a ripped-up letter in which Herod states that in the event of his own death, Mariamne should be killed to preserve his honor. Mariamne reads not a coherent text, but fragments that nonetheless convey to her something critical: "She picks up these fragments form the ground and gives an account of their content in extremely evocative lines. 'What do they contain? / Death is the very first word / which I encounter; here is the word honour / And there I see

Mariamne. / What does this mean? Heaven help me! For much is said in the three words / Mariamne, death, and honour / . . . But what doubts can there be? I am already informed'" (207–8).

Benjamin goes on to say that "even in their isolation the words reveal themselves as fateful. Indeed, one is tempted to say that the very fact that they still have a meaning in their isolation lends a threatening quality to this remnant of meaning they have kept" (208). In other words, as broken up, as allegorical, words and signs can and still do convey impulses, thoughts, powers, and the like. They can be in fact "more threatening" (but also more anything else) in their broken state than they are when apparently whole. In this way, we can tell that the sacred remains among us, even as we turn our backs (or ignore) its "clear and obvious" manifestations. For, as Benjamin tells us in "On the Concept of History, "for the Jews every second was the small gateway in time through which the messiah might enter" (397). In other words—and by extension—every moment and every object is already infused with sacredness for Benjamin. It is not up to us to discover the sacred but rather to fight our tendency to overwrite the sacred with our own wishes and desires. We must, for Benjamin, aspire to be like Kafka's students, having "lost the Holy Writ" but continuing to pursue the sacred, not so much for its own sake but for theirs.

CONCLUSION

In looking at the connection between Hobbes and Benjamin—however unexpected it might be—we see a commonality that helps us to think further about the place of the sacred and furthermore how to "read" sacredness in texts and in the world more generally. Both thinkers offer that the sacred is not something that inheres in a certain place or a certain text. The sacred is mysterious to us and it has no specific location. Indeed, to deem something as sacred and off-limits in some sense reproduces a larger archism in society, a way of creating hierarchies and rules that are unimpeachable. For this reason, as already noted, for both authors, sacredness lies in our reading of it, in our decision to deem something sacred rather than seeing it as residing in any particular object, place, or text as such.

This is not to say that we control our own access to the sacred; as I have tried to show, quite the opposite is true. The only thing we can control, or at least resist, is our tendency to project and seek to represent the sacred, thereby guaranteeing (or so we believe) some access to, and thereby power over, the sacred.

There are, of course, critical differences between Hobbes and Benjamin. Of the two of them, I would say that Benjamin is even more careful to guard against the sense that meanings are available via correct forms of reading. When Hobbes reduces the meaning of words and metaphors down to their representational pith, he could be read (and usually is) as meaning that this is the correct and true meaning of a sentence. I think that is not quite the case with him, that his nominalism is a bit more radical than that, but he leaves us with an ambivalent impression (one that is reinforced by his many claims to science and a geometry of human knowledge). Benjamin, on the other hand, is a wholehearted opponent of textual clarity and meaning. He seeks in all cases to override even his own authority in a text (something that I think Hobbes does, too, but in a much more complicated way).

Even so, Hobbes reminds us, perhaps more certainly than Benjamin, that the question of what is sacred is an entirely political one. It involves the way people chose to respond to and interpret various phenomenon. For Hobbes, decisions about how to interpret and respond to the challenge of the sacred serves as a key form of political cohesion, a way for a community to consider what they hold in, what they have decided will pass for truth. We see this in Benjamin, too, when he writes that in the face of a commandment like "Thou shalt not kill," we must struggle both as individuals and as a collective with the meaning and with the responsibility of such terms. What both thinkers offer us is a model for how this kind of struggle can resist being superimposed over by some arbitrary and singular authority. Although Hobbes sullies this somewhat with his insistence that the sovereign ought to be the one that ultimately makes decisions about the sacred (among other things), as I have argued he does so in a context in which the bulk of such decisions have in effect already been made via myriad and collective acts of reading and interpretation that precede any sovereign decision. For Hobbes, even the sovereign must give way to popular decisions about the meaning of words and, as we saw in the example of the time of human kings after the "kingdom of God," when opinions about the sacred and about whether a prophet spoke on God's behalf or not were left to the people as a whole.

By removing any sense of the sacred as cohering in one thing, one time, one place, or one person, both thinkers have rendered legible and accessible the anarchist possibility of the sacred as being everywhere and every time ("for the Jews every second was the small gateway in time through which the messiah might enter"). This serves as a way to defy and subvert any kind of centralized or overarching dogma. The sacred becomes a fount of resistance to such forms of authority and, as such, offers a counterpart to sovereign and liturgical forms of authority. By showing us that any text or any object can be as sacred as any other, the very distinctions that generally undergird the hierarchies and powers of the state, the law, and the church are unmade and redistributed across a newly anarchized notion of time, space, and authority that is where the sacred always actually resides.

To return, once again, to our own time, one of deep anxiety about truth and the sources of that truth, Hobbes and Benjamin offer us, I think, a way to resist the blandishments of populism and other false messiahs. Rather than straining after truth or dutifully recognizing that some things are sacred and some things are not (and the difference is always given by some higher, archist, authority), they show us that we can *never* have access to truth and hence, the very decision to consider a text, or any other object, sacred only reinforces, rather than undermining, the anarchist and collective power of interpretation that both Hobbes and Benjamin will protect at all costs.

Notes

1. Hobbes writes, "And that which offendeth the People, is no other thing, but that they are governed, not as every one of them would himselfe, but as the Publique Representant, be it one Man, or an Assembly of men thinks fit; that is, by an Arbitrary government: for which they give evill names to their Superiors; never knowing (till perhaps a little after a Civill warre) that without such Arbitrary government, such Warre must be perpetuall; and that it is Men, and Arms, not Words, and Promises, that make the Force and Power of the Laws" (*Leviathan*, 471).

2. This is yet another reason why the sovereign's determination is not ultimately that important for Hobbes; the sovereign cannot remove the aporia of language. They can argue that sacredness means this or that but such positive determinations are ultimately erroneous (indeed arbitrary).

3. Although the word Benjamin uses in German—"Gewalt"—is not necessarily the same as "violence" in English (which tends to connote physical acts of violence whereas the German term means something broader like force), actual physical violence is often the result of such projection.

Bibliography

Benjamin, Walter. *The Arcades Project.* Translated by Howard Eiland.

Cambridge, MA: Harvard University Press, 2003.

———. "Capitalism as Religion." In *Walter Benjamin: Selected Writings*, vol. 1, *1913–1926*, edited by Marcus Bullock and Michael W. Jennings, 288–91. Cambridge, MA: Harvard University Press, 2004.

———. "Critique of Violence." In *Walter Benjamin: Selected Writing*, vol. 1, *1913–1926*, edited by Marcus Bullock and Michel W. Jennings, 236–52. Cambridge, MA: Harvard University Press, 2004.

———. "Franz Kafka: On the Tenth Anniversary of His Death." In *Walter Benjamin: Selected Writings*, vol. 2, *1927–1934*, edited by Michael W. Jennings, 794–818. Cambridge, MA: Harvard University Press, 1999.

———. "On Language as Such and on the Language of Man." In *Walter Benjamin: Selected Writing*, vol. 1, *1913–1926*, edited by Marcus Bullock and Michael W. Jennings, 62–74.

Cambridge, MA: Harvard University Press, 2004.

———. "On the Concept of History." In *Walter Benjamin: Selected Writing*, vol. 4, *1938–1940*, edited by Howard Eiland and Michael W. Jennings, 389–400. Cambridge, MA: Harvard University Press, 2006.

———. *The Origin of German Tragic Drama.* Translated by John Osborne. New York: Verso Press, 2003.

Hobbes, Thomas. *Behemoth; or, The Long Parliament.* Edited by Stephen Holmes. Chicago: University of Chicago Press, 1990.

———. *De Cive.* In *Man and Citizen: ("De Homine" and "De Cive"),* by Thomas Hobbes, edited by Bernard Gert, 87–386. Indianapolis: Hackett, 1991.

———. *Leviathan: Revised Student Edition.* Edited by Richard Tuck. New York: Cambridge University Press, 2006.

CHAPTER 5

Chanting the Supreme
Word of Information

"Sacred?! Redundant?!"

RICHARD DOYLE AND TREY CONNER

The word for word is word.

 —WILLIAM S. BURROUGHS, *MY EDUCATION: A BOOK OF DREAMS*

I am not myself.

   —PHILIP K. DICK, *VALIS*

From within me, as part of me, it looked out and saw itself.

   —PHILIP K. DICK, *THE EXEGESIS*

In his nearly nine-thousand-page, mostly handwritten manuscript *The Exegesis*, the writer Philip K. Dick (PKD) developed a theory and description of the human encounter with information ecologies resonant with the technological and scientific shifts developing across the planet in the early 1970s. The resulting model for understanding the influence of information technology on human culture has enormous implications for the evolution of rhetoric as an attribute of human behavior by which we alter and transform ecosystems. We are now unmistakably aware of the effect our consciousness has on the biosphere. We cannot avoid the conclusion that we are recursively self-aware beings whose activities are linked to a larger-scale ecosystem, and that this larger-scale ecosystem, dubbed by Lynn Margulis and James Lovelock "Gaia," is heating up under the influence of conscious attention's penchant for extracting and dissipating energy (see Schneider and Sagan, *Into the Cool*). But can we *experience* this feedback loop between consciousness and the planet? Does this feeling feel something like the sacred?

It is no doubt true that PKD's habitat, California, was a particularly potent biome for this nascent evolution in ecosystemic signaling systems learning to signal to themselves recursively as awareness, but this evolutionary shift was, as is true of most things Phil Dickian, a transformation not easily pinned down to a particular location. It was, in short, ubiquitous. Where, *exactly*, was it happening? Nowhere in particular, distributed and devoid even of a reliable label, it has occurred, apropos the equally visionary prophecies of Teilhard de Chardin, on the scale of the earth itself.[1]

To wit: While PKD was living across the bay from Douglas Engelbart's 1968 "Mother of All Demos," the debut of the first computer mouse as a pointing device extended a digital index finger into a cybernetic dimension. France pioneered online dating in 1977. Under the influence of the second-order cybernetics of Austrian polymath Heinz von Foerster, Chile *almost* had an internet in the 1970s, while Columbus Ohio, in alliance with Atari, enjoyed a two-way cable linkup that was an experiment in electronic democracy and the commodification of participatory attention: Qube. In 1986 Helsinki, Finland, a young computer science student posted to an electronic bulletin board as he sought a work-around for an expensive operating system required by his curriculum, Minix, yielding the distributed labor of Linux, a family of open-source software that now runs most of the Internet. The Soviets practically specialized in cybernetics.[2]

In the Phil Dickian universe of *The Exegesis*, it is precisely this impression of no longer experiencing a proprioceptive sense of location that can be said to be symptomatic of the attentional shift that was already underway as what Alvin Toffler titled "The Third Wave" unfolded. What were the effects on consciousness of these massive standing waves in human attention, a finite resource, as it shifted from domain to domain?[3] What were the effects of human consciousness on these waves? Were there patterns in the shift?

Just as the emissions, high sulfur or not, that emerge from a coal-fired plant's smokestack are part of the externality effect of industrial production, shifts in the human ecosystem of information processing were having unintended and nonconscious effects on the lived conscious experience of humans. The widespread "attention deficit" is perhaps the oblique sign of an extraordinary surplus of informatic events, transmissions that sometimes result in ego death: the total exhaustion of the "I" as a sufficient reporter on experience. Have we broken the narrative barrier now that techno-cultural change and the information to report on it can no longer be made coherent?

It was the Nobel Prize–winning economist and architect of the information society Herbert Simon who rendered the dynamic of this shift in the ecosystem of information into the local language of attention: "What information consumes is rather obvious: it consumes the attention of the recipient" ("Designing Organizations," 40–41). Simon can be seen, in this 1971 quote on information overload, to be the social scientific doppelgänger for the more mystical PKD, who transcribed the direct experience of this attention *consumption* through a galaxy of tropes that included the cosmic-scale "VALIS," a Vast Active Living Intelligent System that "nailed" him with information (*VALIS*, 16). In the face of this *nailing*, PKD transduces the very physicality and lived subjective experience of this distributed consciousness into a domain apparently capable of larger-scale and, to the participant, coherent experiences of massive spikes of information. It would appear that PKD's sense of being a "recipient" dissolved when he was "nailed" with information: "From within me, as part of me, it looked out and saw itself" (*Exegesis*, 6). Was his "I" consumed in an action of attention consumption scaled to the cosmic magnitudes of VALIS?

It may well be, as observed by researchers such as Walter Pahnke in the 1960s, that the psychological response to such a shifted scale whereby the "I" itself is consumed or swallowed up into a cybernetic white whale of an attention sink, is ego death: the arrival of a sense of being embedded in a system or process much larger in scale than the self. "I am not myself" (*VALIS*, 16). In such a context, whatever one is, one is not a "recipient," as such a being implies being distinct from a "sender." Sometimes the sacred rhetoric of "God" is used in subjective reports for this phenomenon where scaling and dissolution of the sense of a separate "I" occurs, even in the relatively profane domains of science fiction; however, as physician and researcher Andrew Newberg has demonstrated in *How Enlightenment Changes Your Brain*, these episodes of a likely massive dwindling of the

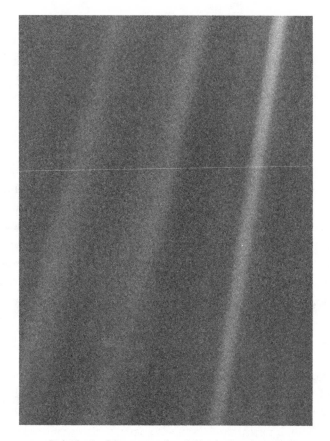

FIG. 5.1 "Pale Blue Dot." Can you spot the pale blue dot from that spot whence you spot it? Courtesy NASA / JPL-Caltech.

parietal lobe, among other things, can be experienced by atheists, theists, and the indifferent through some larger-scale structure—such as the cosmos itself—as a figure into which one can dissolve as in a figure/ground gestalt shift of attention. "I am not myself" (*VALIS*, 16). As attention consumption spikes toward infinity, ego death can occur. The ego itself can become astronomer Carl Sagan's pale blue dot (see fig. 5.1)[4]—almost unimaginably insignificant against the background of cosmic magnitudes.

Ego death, and the reports of ineffability that often accompany it, offers insight into why and how rhetorical acts can prove conducive to the sacred even as they rather famously cannot represent it. Researchers at Johns Hopkins University titled one of their breakthrough studies "Psilocybin Can Occasion Mystical-Type Experiences Having Substantial and Sustained Personal Meaning and Spiritual Significance" precisely because that is what they found (see Griffiths et al., "Psilocybin"). While other recent texts have treated the psychonautical techniques for activating apparently inner landscapes, Dick's writings offer techniques for arriving at these insights—what he would dub the scale of "ultra-meta-cognition"—without, or alongside, ethnobotanical means.[5] How might these rhetorical scripts or "softwares" work?

In this chapter we suggest that these sacred rhetorics—linguistic recipes or algorithms—can under appropriate conditions yield experiences beyond the domains of space or time (see Eliade, *Cosmos and History*). And, as with a shaman's rattle or the cow bell of a heavy metal song, these sacred rhetorics sometimes achieve their effects through a *redundancy* rather than a *content* of information. "More cowbell!" Through repetition, Simon's recipient is overloaded and can discover a larger-scale ecosystem by which the information was being processed all along. While the conscious mind, for example, has been measured to process information at a rate of sixty bits per second, the nonconscious mind processes at a rate of twenty-five million per second. This suggests that the "I" can process reality at a rate approximately four hundred thousand times slower than the human organism itself. Egoity minor indeed!

ATTEND TO THE SENSE "I AM" AND GIVE ATTENTION TO
NOTHING ELSE, OR ELSE

Is it this aforementioned nonconscious mind that can be encountered by an experience of the larger-scale distributed consciousness of "I am not myself" (*VALIS*, 6). An example from the practice of Nisargadatta, an Advaita teacher of twentieth-century India with whom PKD was likely familiar, elucidates and actualizes this recipe for redundancy and ego death. Nisargadatta's teacher instructed him to simply "attend to the sense 'I am' and give attention to nothing else" (Maharaj, *I Am That*, 376). We can translate this attentional discipline of inward focused attention—dubbed *atma vichara* or "self-inquiry" by the Advaita tradition in which Nisargadatta practiced—into a chant as follows:

I am
I am
I am

Who is this who chants?

I am
I am
I am

The repeated enunciation of the chant is not linear but critical: like a sand dune, it is a repetition (grains of sand) that can undergo sudden shifts (the dune collapses) (see Sagar, Murthy, and Radhakrishnan, "Avalanches"; and Rotman, "Counting"). In these shifts, the pattern of a larger-scale (fractal?) structure to address the query may manifest, as perhaps it did for Moses:

I am that I am (chanting)
I am that I am (chanting)
I am that I am (chanting)

Here, along with shifts of scale, the sense of an interior and the exterior can dissolve. The twentieth-century mathematician and philosopher sage Franklin Merrell-Wolff (FMW) dubbed these types of events "introceptive," as an apparently direct experience of self-awareness becomes accessible from the inside out (*Transformations*, 103). Instead of feeling, seeing, sensing, smelling, touching a world that somehow feels "external" to us, we discover that an entire "invisible landscape" of "I am" is available for our exploration—the domain of an apparently inner and self-aware consciousness dubbed the Self or "I am" consciousness by Nisargadatta and the Vedanta traditions he transmits. For FMW, when we encounter this inner domain through the practice of introception, we have an "imperience" as distinct from an "experience." William S. Burroughs argues, "The way out is the way in" (*Naked Lunch*, 191).

And imperience, of course, is the next domain of hyper-capitalist attention capitalism. Whoever uncorks the galaxy of value available for the infinite exploration of nonconscious human attention will become indistinguishable from Palmer Eldritch, PKD's intergalactic antihero and demonic drug dealer. If the current economic shift is about the increasingly compressed conversion of attention into money, the domains of dreams, visions, and even mindfulness become the logical next attention sink. As conscious attention is rapidly swallowed up by social media, the nonconscious attention economy becomes the next, enormous layer of the market. Perhaps not surprisingly, PKD's 1966 short story "We Can Remember It for You Wholesale" names this incipient economic tactic in a title.

Yet the shift in the technological means by which human society produces economic value and narratives about itself is as much discussed as it is little understood. The mutation occurring within human culture under the pull of a distributed consciousness is both completely familiar and absolutely out of context. Placelessness is as close as the nearest Starbucks. On the spatial register—what PKD will experience as VALIS—the emergence of the network and the shift from an ontology implicitly based on matter to an ontology explicitly based on attention could be registered as placelessness, and in this placeless place, ego can disappear as well: the capacity to share fragments of reality from across the planet at 186,000 miles per second or so meant humans suddenly felt an extraordinary proximity to one another. Social distancing is only the latest mutation in this panic at proximity. With unprecedented levels of external perceptual and cognitive stimuli, introception can get crowded out, and the recipient is no longer consumer but consumed. Are you imperienced? "What information consumes is rather obvious: it consumes the attention of the recipient" (Simon, "Designing Organizations," 40–41).

In many diverse global cultures from across space/time, the awareness of the extraordinary proximity of all things becomes articulated as "interbeing." Interbeing is the Vietnamese monk Thich Nhat Hanh's offered translation of the Buddhist concept of dependent origination or "interdependent Co-Arising." The Sanskrit term *pratiya samutpada* suggests impermanence and effervescence as much as it does interconnection: "*Pratitya samutpada* is sometimes called the teaching of cause and effect, but that can be misleading, because we usually think of cause and effect as separate entities, with cause always preceding effect, and one cause leading to one effect. According to the teaching of Interdependent Co-Arising, cause and effect co-arise (*samutpada*) and everything is a result of multiple causes and conditions" (Nhat Hanh, *Heart*, 221–22). PKD's informatic metaphysics, what writer Erik Davis calls a "techgnosis," offers a latticework of concepts for inhabiting this strange shift toward an experience of *pratitya samutpada* that can manifest as the sense of separation falls away under the influence of extraordinary proximity and redundancy: "Attend to the sense 'I am' and give attention to nothing else" (Maharaj, *I Am That*, 376). Through the practice of exploring apparently inner states such as "I am," we can discover the continuity between the inner and the outer. In involution, we discover our nondual dependent origination. When we introcept and discover that there is no "I" to be separate from any other being, we get an inkling of dependent origination.

As used here, "involution" names rhetorical practices that take the grammatical and rhetorical form of the I as their object (see Doyle, *Darwin's Pharmacy*, 236–50): "Attend to the sense 'I am' and give attention to nothing else" (Maharaj, *I Am That*, 376). Once taken as an object or a sense—rather than an assumed major premise to being human—the I can transform. While verbs usually take things as their object (e.g., "The pink light hit me in the noggin"), involutionary speech acts directly address the observed space, time, and causal characteristics of the implicit ego structure of any given discourse. If, for example, the slightly different self-inquiry script of fellow twentieth-century Indian teacher's Ramana Maharshi's "Who am I?" is to be anything but an abstraction, a sequence of signs, we must turn, trope, our consciousness toward . . . itself, and observe, "Who am I?"[6] Am I, for example, the idea I have myself, or something else, nowhere else but now here?

And if we will experiment with turning our consciousness back onto itself through chanting, meditation, self-inquiry, dancing, entheogens, fasting, percussion, or quite simply breathing, we will find there no "response" at all to the sacred by rhetoric: "Attend to the sense 'I am' and give attention to nothing else" (Maharaj, *I Am That*, 376). Such practices tend not toward response—which is always perhaps gleefully haunted by the specter of an identity that never existed in the first place, some sort of being-responsible—but instead resound, and they tend to resound with redundancy: all are essentially and not accidentally iterative practices resounding with redundancy. Maharshi offers an interrogative version of the same *atma vichara* practice and instruction that Nisargadatta received from his guru: "Attend to the sense 'I am' and give attention to nothing else" (376). These repetitions can function alone or as part of any suite of techniques for encountering and inhabiting these apparently "inner" states—states that might shift any concept or practice we might have for responding to or resounding with the words "sacred" or "rhetoric."

And despite appearances, these states offer no identity but only ipseity. Along with ubiquity and placelessness, the fascination with and dissolution of identity is perhaps the most obvious and obscure symptom on this informatic turn of the evolutionary screw in human culture. The early and persistent fascination with anonymity often found in nascent online culture can be seen as an index of this shift. Eric Hughes's 1993 "Cypherpunk's Manifesto" resonates with the 2,600-cycles-per-second signals of Captain Crunch and other early phone phreaks, who sought to bridge space and time through free telephonic communication of what Aurobindo would describe in *The Future Poetry* as "mantra" or the charged word, a resonance of the redundancy of What Is: "That possibility is the discovery of a closer approximation to what we might call the mantra in poetry, that rhythmic speech which, as the Veda puts it, rises at once from the heart of the seer and from the distant home of the Truth—the discovery of the word, the divine movement, the form of thought proper to the reality" (10). Information technology increased in interconnection as well as bandwidth, and the more that ubiquity and proximity were registered on human experience, the more the question of any particular agency became vexed, and language was pushed beyond the semantic register into a redundancy of information and the ipseity threshold was broached: who am I? Redundancy refers to the lack of surprise value of any given piece of information, while the information value of any string, *pace* Claude Shannon and his mathematical theory of communication, is its difference from any expected value (Shannon, "Mathematical Theory").

This perspective on redundancy suggests that Kenneth Burke's inquiries into identification offer a suturing of identity rather than its dissolution through iterative self-inspection. "To begin with 'identification,'" Burke writes in *A Rhetoric of Motives*, "is . . . to confront the implications of *division*" (22). Diane Davis diverges from this division, noting that "published reports on the activity of mirror neurons and resonance mechanisms can be read as eloquent deconstructions of Burke's ultimate order of things, shattering the presumption of an originary biological disconnect between self and other" ("Identification," 131–32) While Davis treats this operation conceptually—using the evidence of contemporary neuroscience to warrant a "shattering" of a "presumption" of division—it is the presumption of any self whatsoever that is dissolved through the practice of involution suggested by Nisargadatta. We concur with Davis when she observes that there can be no disconnect between any alleged "self" and/or "other" and their biological characteristics, as through the practice of involution the self/other "division" can dissolve. In other words, in involution the self can dissolve in the gnostic light of self-inspection, and so too can the alleged "body." Our discussion below of Adi Shankara's "Nirvana Shatakam" may enable readers to inquire into this presumption directly, but for now let us note that the strategies for this dissolution are themselves massively repetitious and, yes, redundant. The *Ribhu Gita*, an Advaitan text (the sixth part and the heart of the twelfth-part *Shivarahasya Purana*) touted by Ramana Maharshi as a direct route to awareness, points to a release of any concept of the body through the experience of repetitious chanting:

> *Deho hamiti ya buddhir tusta shaiva hi chocyate*
> *Kalatrayapi tannasti sarvam brahmeti kevalam*
> The perception of myself as the body is the great distortion
> In all of the times there ain't nothing but fracking brahman[7]

On these terms, categories such as "self," "other," and "body" become aspects of an unbridled monism reminiscent of the bolder and more ecstatic visions of Deleuze and Guattari. Here identity itself, where and when and to whom the information occurs, approaches pure redundancy in a "Body Without Organs" (see Deleuze and Guattari, *Thousand Plateaus*, 149–66). If identity, for example, is the result of a series of attributes or data points available to perception, then we look in vain for its location and approach total redundancy in our search. Identity never arrives as information, but is instead critically redundant repetition. Even multimodal biometrics, combining DNA, facial recognition, gait recognition, finger prints, and so on, pinpoints no identity at all, only a swarm of traces that can be updated as quickly as a credit report in response to anomalous routine spending: organs without bodies. Each fragment repeats an assertion of identity without arriving at one: "*Attend to the sense 'I am' and give attention to nothing else*" (Maharaj, *I Am That*, 376).

Is the contemporary political fascination with and obligation toward identity and identification a subjective correlative to the distributed nature of informatic networks? Both the political left and right are riveted by these identitarian responses to redundancy. Absent, identity must be asserted. Elsewhere, one of us has suggested that it is this experience of "distributed consciousness" of "I am not myself" that allows one to read Dick's works as an allegory about this global human encounter with a massive spike in the quantity of informatic events in the human ecosystem (see Doyle, "Afterword"). And the experience of "being distributed" under the influence of information is the veritable decoder ring for *The Exegesis* itself, where PKD discovers over and over again what it feels like to be ecstatically distributed "living information": "Attend to the sense 'I am' and give attention to nothing else" (Maharaj, *I Am That*, 376).

Yet what was PKD's quirk becomes our practice. If we will practice exegesis of *The Exegesis*, we might have the experiences described therein. For PKD, exegesis is a synonym for involution: ultra-metacognition. When we do exegesis on *The Exegesis*, we do exegesis: redundancy in thousands of pages!

And the experience is invariably involved in a unique dissolution of the very boundary of the inside and the outside. When information supplants matter as the fundament of creation, as it does for PKD and, eventually, his willing exegetical reader, then "inside" and "outside" become experimental labels for any particular imperience rather than any attribute of an object or process "out there." If the universe is mapped as information, there is no "out there" or "in here"—only information events with experimental labels. We might call this position, exemplified by PKD's mobiusing of himself in our epigraph, "informatic monism" as it posits a universe of information signaling to itself: "From within me, as part of me, it looked out and saw itself" (*Exegesis*, 6).

But this informatic monism was already encountered by psychonauts such as scientist and professor Timothy Leary in his meditations, sampling from the *Tao Te Ching*,[8] of the "serpent coil" or ouroboros of DNA: the serpent coil of DNA. We meet it everywhere. But we do not see its front. We follow it everywhere. But we do not see its back (see Leary, *Psychedelic Prayers*, 67). Without a spatial boundary, this ouroboros is also temporally loopy, "curling" back into the Now or present moment: "When we embrace this ancient serpent coil, we are masters of the moment. And we feel no break in the Curling back to primeval beginnings. This may be called Unraveling the clue of the life process" (67). No back, no front, the action of embracing the ancient serpent coil becomes a recipe for encountering the neither inward nor outward nature of reality, in the unique ipseity of Now. Recovered literary critic Eknath Easwaran's translation of the Mandukya Upanishad sums this up as the fourth state of consciousness, neither waking, dreaming, nor dreamless sleep, but Turiya, that which the other states emerge from, or "I am that I am": "The fourth is the superconscious state called Turiya, neither inward nor outward, beyond the senses and the intellect" (Easwaran, *Mandukya Upanishad*, 7). Dick has recourse to this continuity between inside and outside in one of his more direct descriptions of VALIS or the Logos:

> I saw the active agent, a gold and red illuminated-letter like plasmatic entity *from the future*, arranging bits and pieces here: arranging what time drove forward. Later I concluded that I had seen the Logos. What is important is that this was perceptual to me, not an intellectual inference or thought about what might exist. It came here from the future. It was/is alive. It had a certain small power or energy, and great wisdom. It was/is holy. It not only was visible around me but evidently this is the same energy which entered me. It was both inside and out. (*Exegesis*, 5)

At another moment, PKD is more concise in his description of this informatic monism with two aspects of redundancy, "inside" and "outside": "I think it's all the same thing, one found inner, one found outer" (6).

Is it this experience of distributed consciousness with no inside or outside that emerges in 1960s counterculture that offers a way "out" of the ego and the suffering that attends to it? If our claim about redundancy and the dissolution of identity as a path to distributed consciousness has merit, and in practice it seems to, to understand the books, you need to have the *experience* of the books (e.g., "It's all the same thing, one found inner, one found outer"). It is not enough, or anything at all, to "shatter the presumption" of a separation of biology from identity; this dissolution must *occur*. To whom does it occur? An involute, Now. The books must be experimented with as what brain-science pioneer John Lilly dubbed the "as-if-true." It is rather easier to inhabit the perspective that it is "as-if-true" that you are a star-child if you can imagine yourself on a cosmic scale. Oh involutes, perhaps listening to Parliament and reading Carl Sagan can help you understand Philip K. Dick, and vice versa?!

But even as a bardic, psychedelic, or "ecodelic" experience of consciousness as a distributed field rather than a point can enable one to understand Philip K. Dick's books on the metanoia of involution, perhaps you can also have this imperience of distributed consciousness if you read and even chant books! But if you wish to understand the books, you will very likely need some other practice to potentiate an awareness of distributed consciousness. In the remainder of this essay we hope to help catalyze an imperience of distributed consciousness—just mayhaps worth labeling as "the sacred" by directing attention at moments of "dehiscence" where the inward experience of consciousness becomes strangely actual: subjectivity can be felt to feel like a field rather than a point. Stranger still, we have found that this experience of being a field can be experienced together, hence our dual authorship: "Since each of us were several, we were already quite a crowd" (Deleuze and Guattari, *Thousand Plateaus*, 3). Distributed consciousness is perhaps the very hallmark of the sacred: "Where two or more are gathered in my name, there I am": "Attend to the sense 'I am' and give attention to nothing else" (Maharaj, *I Am That*, 376). Is our contemporary fascination with and even weaponization of identity a reaction formation to this arrival of a technologically induced distributed consciousness as the very touchstone of an authentic life?

VALIS VEDANTA

> To reach, not the point where one no longer says I, but the point where it is no longer of any importance whether one says I.
> —GILLES DELEUZE AND FELIX GUATTARI, *A THOUSAND PLATEAUS*

PKD himself has recourse to the eighth-century yogi, philosopher, and rhetorician Shankara to articulate the way he has experienced these states of distributed consciousness, so it may be useful to look to one of Shankara's techniques for imperiencing involution if we are to test the claim that distributed consciousness is actual and that it might just capture the feeling of Dick's diversely labeled menagerie of deities for us together. One way to activate this "distributed" aspect of consciousness without conceptualizing it is to systematically and playfully negate any ideas or sensations that might constitute an identity. Shankara's "Nirvana Shatakam," for example, begins with the negation of the familiar experience that I am my mind: *Mano buddhya ahankara cittani naham* (I am not my mind, intellect, memory, or ego). While the experience that we are our thoughts, particularly our internal monologue, may seem as natural, familiar, and true as absolutely any claim whatsoever, Shankara directs our attention to our nonidentity with our mind or ego. The very declaration of the strange performative "I am not my mind" (Shankara, "Nirvana"), uttered aloud and, as science fiction author Robert Heinlein might put it, grokked fully, can fracture the experience of identity, as it begs us to consider the *who* who could possibly not be the contents of my mind. If I am not my mind, I may rightfully ask, who am i?!

Recoiling from involution, we look outward for a clue.

Perhaps, *pace* Diane Davis, I am, at least in part, my biological body. The *Ribhu Gita*—that Advaitan text taught by Ramana Maharshi as a recipe for liberation—calls this identification with the body the "great distortion." Shankara asks us to repeat the observations that we are not our breath or our blood or our skin either: *Na ca prana sangyo na vai pancha vayu* (I am not my life, my blood, my breath neither). If we are asked to even provisionally inspect what we are if we are not our mind or our body, we probably simply recoil from the insight or reject it without any contemplation. But if we will contemplate "I am not my mind," we look to the work that the language and concepts can plausibly do for and with consciousness. "I am not my mind" can open up into a vertigo of freedom, as even the consideration of the possibility that there is no better reason to identify with a stream of thoughts than there is to identify say, with my breath or even my toenails, can alter our relation to our usual sense of self (Shankara, "Nirvana").

And how can I identify with my body when it keeps changing? How can a body identify with an I that cannot be located? Is not the transcendental condition of possibility for even uttering "I am not my mind" or "I am not my tongue" a dehiscence in thought, a momentary wrinkle in cognition wherein we get a glimpse of our ordinary way of thinking that presumes a self? (Shankara, "Nirvana").

Mano buddha ahankara cittani naham can induce, in readers willing to chant it, extraordinary states of consciousness where we experiment by observing our nonidentity to ourselves: "I am not myself" (Dick, *VALIS*, 128).

Even an inkling of this nonidentity with ourselves, can, though, send us running for certainty, and it is likely to that specter "the body" that we take flight. Of course, I am not my mind, I might say, as my mind is not even always aware in sleep (or at work), so clearly, I am something other than just my mind. And where does the mind come from? The body. Or so it would seem.

But what happens when we chant the following?

> *Mano buddha ahankara cittani naham*
> *Mano buddha ahankara cittani naham*
> *Mano buddha ahankara cittani naham* (Shankara, "Nirvana")

If we will practice a rhetorical analysis of this chanting, we might observe and imperience the following ways: (a) there is a chanting that consists both of a sequence of sounds and the experience of those sequences of sounds; (b) in chanting, the origin of this sequence of sounds can be searched for but not found; and (c) whatever the chanting is, it is not a body, and nor is it the chanter. These attributes of chanting can be practiced by any reader willing to slow down and engage in this refrain:

> *Mano buddha ahankara cittani naham*
> *Mano buddha ahankara cittani naham*
> *Mano buddha ahankara cittani naham* (Shankara, "Nirvana")

If we will let this repetition work on us until we experience its redundancy, we might notice that other thoughts, perhaps all of them, become crowded out by the redundancy of the chanting:

> *Mano buddha ahankara cittani naham*
> *Mano buddha ahankara cittani naham*
> *Mano buddha ahankara cittani naham* (Shankara, "Nirvana")

Is the field of awareness that is experienced through this chant a body? Or is that which observes a body, and, with which it usually identifies? Turiya?

The more we work with these rhetorical effects without drawing any conclusions about their ontological value, the more we can become comfortable with mapping ourselves as "fields of awareness" rather than "isolated bags of flesh" divided at the "level of the organism" (Davis, "Identification," 132), which is itself conceptual and not actual. While the discourses of ineffability point to representation's incapacity to, well, *represent* the sacred, the involutionary practices of Shankara, Nisargadatta, Maharshi, PKD, and others offer a series of refrains that systematically erode any idea that one may have of oneself, allowing the sacred to occur (see Deleuze and Guattari, *Thousand Plateaus*, 310). Instead of attempting to portray or signify the sacred, then, Shankara's practice works to eliminate obstacles to an already immanent and luminous reality (a plane of immanence?!) through the iteration of a massive redundancy. We chant, *Chidananda rupah shivo'ham shivo'ham* (I am pure awareness, I am errythang) (Shankara, "Nirvana"). And the involutionary obstacles that can be hacked through these practices of redundancy are both difficult and simple to overcome—ideas and thought: "Attend to the sense 'I am' and give attention to nothing else (Maharaj, *I Am That*, 376). In contemporary Neo-Vedanta—a global discourse that traces much of its lineage to Shankara and Vedanta even as it mutates in profound ways—material scientist and long-term meditator Gary Weber has placed perhaps the most emphasis on the practice of chanting as a technique conducive to awakening. Chanting, for Weber, can lead to a "happiness beyond thought." "Beyond thought," like "I am not my mind," asks us to focus the mind on the release of ideas that can be distilled into the paradoxical "Shut up and chant!" While "enlightenment" is the usual English word that is used to describe the meta-abstraction and understanding associated with the insights of self-knowledge, the Sanskrit "moksha" is perhaps more appropriately translated as "liberation." It is also worth experimenting here with the language of healing, where etymologically the "healing" comes from "to make whole."

And a plausible candidate for the mechanism of this healing could well be the decrease in the activity of the default mode network (DMN) of the human brain. One reason the "sacred rhetorics" associated with mindfulness have circulated is their capacity to diminish stress-related diseases. Stress—long a black box for a nonspecific cause of almost everything—becomes legible as at least partially an effect of activity of the DMN. The self-referential self-talk disappears "beyond thought," and with it, the stress that is its correlative. Beyond thought, what do we find?

> *Mano buddha ahankara cittani naham*
> *Mano buddha ahankara cittani naham*
> *Mano buddha ahankara cittani naham* (Shankar, "Nirvana")

RESONATING WITH AUROBINDO

> All creation is expression by the Word.
>
> —AUROBINDO, *KENA*

Out of the silence that occurs out of chanting, we might immediately glimpse that Aurobindo Ghose's treatment of human speech directs our attention to something other than the body, the mind, or the allegedly external world. Aurobindo does not analyze language as persuasion, but as a manifestation of something larger in scale that we cannot comprehend but can only witness through an exercise in self inquiry: "*to attend to the sense 'I am' and give attention to nothing else*" (Maharaj, *I Am That*, 376; emphasis added). By linking "creation" to an "expression" of an uppercased "Word," Aurobindo already solicits readers into an inquiry: Whence or when comes this Word of which the empirical world itself, "creation," is a redundant "expression"? (Aurobindo, *Kena*, 29): "to attend to the sense 'I am' and give attention to nothing else" (Maharaj, *I Am That*, 376).

If, as Aurobindo and the Vedic traditions in general concur, the creation of the empirical world is not the starting point but rather the *outcome* of an eloquent deployment of language, then the implications for sacred rhetorics are diverse and vital: "In the beginning was the word, and the word was with God, and the word was God" (John 1:1). Rather than looking out at a situation to be analyzed and cut it into parts, with an action that might be rationally deliberated and enacted, as in "I will act upon an audience not familiar with the work of Aurobindo Ghose as if they were separate from me," sacred rhetorics hereby become oriented to self-inquiry—the investigation of the speaker or writer. "Whence comes this discourse? Where is the author? Who is the reader?": "Attend to the sense 'I am' and give attention to nothing else" (Maharaj, *I Am That*, 376).

This involutionary turn, though, is not a narcissistic one, but is, as Slavoj Žižek often tropes, "precisely the opposite" (*Puppet*, 13). By turning the usually outward gaze inward, one can discover that there is no object (or its merism doublet, the subject) there at all to be found, only a field or "great space" (FMW) of awareness—subjectivity without any subjects. The very pretense of the division between the author and the audience disappears as we inquire into the domain, in space or time, of the supreme Word as the subjective component of awareness, and find it to be anything but discrete.

When we investigate what we will label below as the "enthymeme of our suffering" the presumed existence of the "I," we find that the presumption of an "I" is always asserted but never warranted. This "presumption" of the "I" does not even need to be shattered. In the sacred, the claim for the suppressed major premise, the "I," dissolves: "Attend to the sense 'I am' and give attention to nothing else" (Maharaj, *I Am That*, 376).

ALREADY REDUNDANT IS THE ENTHYMEME
OF OUR SUFFERING

Already, the reader is being welcomed to look beyond the sensible for the Word. It cannot be found through the analysis of data, qualitative or quantitative. Indeed, in some sense the Word as mapped by Aurobindo cannot be found, nor can it be lost. Aurobindo asks us to contemplate a higher order of abstraction than either "lost" or "found," and it is here that we might have an inkling of the Word manifesting into and through creation.[9] By definition, this higher order of abstraction cannot be found in the apparently external world, nor can it be found simply through a turn inward (see Aurobindo, "Knowledge by Identity").

Beyond inner or outer, Aurobindo points to and speaks from a higher order of abstraction than Aristotle, for example, when the latter asks rhetors to see the available means of persuasion in each case. Aristotle—or the crowd of students who likely prepared *The Rhetoric*—asks us to look outward here in our observation, gathering data, hypotheses about the audience and the kinds of arguments they might love. Aurobindo, instead, asks us to turn our consciousness back on itself, observing empty awareness—there is only a knowing without a knower—for the source of that creation that we think we wish to alter. And the word for that source of creation, for Aurobindo, is not the "I," but Word.

Notes

1. This is appropriate given the planetary-scale mirror-stage event reflected through the "big blue marble" image that brought the planetary scale into the planetary imaginary.

2. See Axel Berg: "*I* do not know about other scientists, but for me cybernetics is a working tool for the builder of communism, and first and foremost an absolutely necessary means for the speediest construction of communist society" ("Cybernetics and Education," 14; emphasis added).

3. A standing wave one that "oscillates in time but whose peak amplitude profile does not move in space." See Wikipedia, s.v., "Faraday Wave," last modified May 15, 2020,

7:01, Wikipedia, http://en.wikipedia.org/wiki/Faraday_wave.

4. See "Solar System Portrait: Earth as 'Pale Blue Dot,'" Nasa Visible Earth, n.d., https://visibleearth.nasa.gov/images/52392/solar systemportraitearthaspalebluedot.

5. In Buddhist discourse, *upaya*, or "skillful means," provides a language for a suite of techniques that include everything from mushrooms to meditation.

6. This invocation of involution involves the extraordinary vision of the integral evolutionary yoga of Aurobindo Ghose as well as the biological meaning explored in *Darwin's Pharmacy*. See Chandra, Lata, and ElSohly, *Cannabis sativa L.—Botany and Biotechnology*.

7. Author's translation of *Ribhu Gita*. See Weber, *Evolving Beyond Thought*; and Sudha, *Nectar of Chanting*.

8. See James Legge's widely circulated translation: "We meet it and do not see its Front; we follow it, and do not see its Back" (*Sacred Books of China*, 57).

9. Easwaran's translation of the *Mandukya Upanishad* describes a domain that is "Neither inward nor outward" (204).

Bibliography

Aurobindo. *The Future Poetry*. Twin Lakes, WI: Lotus Press, 1994.

———. *Kena and Other Upanishads*. Pondicherry: Sri Aurobindo Ashram, 2001.

———. "Knowledge by Identity and Separative Knowledge." In *The Divine Life*, 523–52. Pondicherry: Sri Aurobindo Ashram Press, 2005.

Berg, Axel. "Cybernetics and Education." *Anglo-Soviet Journal* 25, no. 2 (Spring 1964): 13–20.

Burke, Kenneth. *A Rhetoric of Motives*. Berkeley: University of California Press, 1969.

Burroughs, William S. *My Education: A Book of Dreams*. New York: Penguin, 1995.

———. *Naked Lunch*. New York: Grove Press, 1956.

Chandra, Suman, Hemant Lata, and Mahmoud A. ElSohly, eds. *Cannabis sativa L.—Botany and Biotechnology*. New York: Springer, 2017.

Davis, Diane. "Identification: Burke and Freud on Who You Are." *Rhetoric Society Quarterly* 38, no. 2 (2008): 123–47.

Davis, Erik. *TechGnosis: Myth, Magic, and Mysticism in the Age of Information*. Berkeley, CA: North Atlantic Books, 2015.

Deleuze, Gilles, and Felix Guattari, *A Thousand Plateaus*. Translated by Brian Massumi. Minneapolis: University of Minnesota Press, 1987.

Dick, Philip K. *The Exegesis of Philip K. Dick*. Edited by Pamela Jackson and Jonathan Lethem. New York: Houghton Mifflin Harcourt, 2011.

———. *VALIS*. New York: Houghton Mifflin Harcourt, 1981.

———. "We Can Remember It for You Wholesale." In *We Can Remember It for You Wholesale*, 35–52. Toronto: Carol, 1987.

Doyle, Richard M. "Afterword: A Stairway to Eleusis: PKD, Perennial Philosopher." In *The Exegesis of Philip K. Dick*, edited by Pamela Jackson and Jonathan Lethem, 897–900. New York: Houghton Mifflin Harcourt, 2011.

———. *Darwin's Pharmacy: Sex, Plants, and the Evolution of the Noösphere*. Seattle: University of Washington Press, 2011.

———. *On Beyond Living: Rhetorical Transformations of the Life Sciences*. Stanford, CA: Stanford University Press, 1997.

Easwaran, Eknath, trans. *Mandukya Upanishad*. Tomales, CA: Blue Mountain Center of Meditation, 1987.

Eliade, Mircea. *Cosmos and History: The Myth of the Eternal Return*. Translated by Willard R. Trask. New York: Harper, 1954.

Griffiths, R. R., W. A Richards, U. McCann, and R. Jesse. "Psilocybin Can Occasion Mystical-Type Experiences Having Substantial and Sustained Personal Meaning and Spiritual

Significance." *Psychopharmacology* 187, no. 3 (2006): 268–83.

Leary, Timothy. *Psychedelic Prayers and Other Meditations.* Berkeley, CA: Ronin, 1997.

Legge, James, trans. *The Sacred Books of China: The Texts of Tâoism.* Oxford, UK: Clarendon Press, 1981.

Maharaj, Sri Nisargadatta. *I Am That: Talks with Sri Nisargadatta Maharaj.* Edited by Sudhakar S. Dikshit. Translated by Maurice Frydman. Durham, NC: Acorn Press, 1988.

Merrell-Wolff, Franklin. *Transformations in Consciousness: The Metaphysics of Epistemology.* Albany: SUNY Press, 1995.

Newberg, Andrew, and Mark Robert Waldman. *How Enlightenment Changes Your Brain: The New Science of Transformation.* New York: Avery, 2016.

Nhat Hanh, Thich. *The Heart of the Buddha's Teaching: Transforming Suffering into Peace, Joy, and Liberation.* New York: Harmony Books, 1999.

Rotman, Brian. "Counting on Non-Euclidean Fingers." In *Mathematics as Sign: Writing, Imagining, Counting,* 125–53. Stanford, CA: Stanford University Press, 2000.

Sagar, B. S. Daya, M. B. R. Murthy, and P. Radhakrishnan. "Avalanches in a Numerically Simulated Sand Dune Dynamics." *Fractals* 11, no. 2 (2003): 183–93.

Schneider, Eric D., and Dorion Sagan. *Into the Cool: Energy Flow, Thermodynamics, and Life.* Chicago: University of Chicago Press, 2006.

Shankara, Adi. "Nirvana Shatakam." Isha Foundation, December 21, 2012. https://isha.sadhguru.org/us/en/blog/article/mysticchantsnirvana shatakam.

Shannon, C. E. "A Mathematical Theory of Communication." Pts. 1 and 2. *Bell System Technical Journal* 27, no. 3 (July 1948): 379–423; 27, no. 4 (October 1948): 623–56.

Simon, Herbert. "Designing Organizations for an Information-Rich World." In *Computers, Communication, and the Public Interest,* edited by Martin Greenberger, 40–41. Baltimore: Johns Hopkins University Press.

Sudha, Muktananda Swadhyaya. *The Nectar of Chanting.* Ganeshpuri: Shree Gurudev Ashram, 1972.

Weber, Gary. *Evolving Beyond Thought: Updating Your Brain's Software.* North Charleston, SC: CreateSpace, 2018.

———. *Happiness Beyond Thought: A Practical Guide to Awakening.* Lincoln, NE: i Universe, 2007.

Žižek, Slavoj. *The Puppet and the Dwarf: The Perverse Core of Christianity.* Cambridge, MA: MIT Press, 2003.

PART 2

Sacred Practices

CHAPTER 6

Hacking the Sacred (or Not)

Rhetorical Attunements for Ecodelic Imbrication

JODIE NICOTRA

> I now see how the lives of all these creatures depend upon unseen organisms that they live with but are unaware of, that contribute to and sometimes entirely account for their abilities, and that have existed on the planet for far longer than they have. It is a dizzying change in perspective, but a glorious one.
>
> —ED YONG, *I CONTAIN MULTITUDES*

The summer before college, I experienced what I can best describe as a spontaneous, profound recognition of unity, a cellular realization of my inseparability from all things. As a blue-collar Catholic kid raised in the suburbs of Pittsburgh, I lacked the intense rhetorical training with which one typically prepares for such a world-shattering experience (which in the Zen tradition is known as *kenshō*, a *rōshi* told me a few years later), nor did I have a context to which I could comfortably assign it, though maybe I had been unconsciously prepped by multiple readings that summer of *Siddhartha*, Hermann Hesse's novel about the Buddha. In any case, after that night I found myself persistently drawn to schools of thought and traditions that offered techniques for direct interaction with the divine—typically those traditions that fall within the category of "mysticism." Such traditions, regardless of their time and place, tend to hold two presuppositions in common: first, that despite the commonsense appearance of a world of individual, separate beings, everything is actually one, and is an aspect of the divine; and second, that it is possible to access the divine through direct experience, aided by a system of texts and practices. Despite claims to ineffability of the mystic experience itself, the mystic tradition would seem to place us immediately in the realm of the rhetorical.

Though it took me a while to recognize it, this general attunement to mystical notions of interconnectedness probably explains why I found myself attracted in the late aughts to news stories about the human microbiome, which had recently gained the interest of the scientific community. The *microbiome* can be swiftly defined as the colonies of bacteria, fungi, and viruses that inhabit every multicellular living organism and shape many of its biological and social functions. Though not overtly addressing the divine, the positing of ecologies of invisible organisms that by some estimates make up at least half of all living creatures seems at the least to warrant a radical ecological perspective wherein all living creatures are part of one another—quite a mystic take for Western science, and one that leads, as the epigraph by science writer Ed Yong's suggests, to a "dizzying change in perspective," a "grander view of life" (Yong, *I Contain Multitudes*, 55). Indeed, my seventeen-year-old self would have recognized and taken some comfort in the promise of this view.

What, though, does mystical experience and the microbiome have to do with rhetoric? As the editors point out in the introduction to this collection, the notion that there are *limits* to rhetoric in responding to the sacred holds only if rhetorical practice is conceived in representational or epistemic terms. Such a rhetoric, focused on discursive representation or human ways of knowing the world, might imagine a "sacred" that exists somewhere outside of and separate from us, impossible to capture with our inadequate forms of human expression. A rhetoric grounded in such assumptions reduces worldly (and other-than-worldly) things to a distinctly human scale; as Casey Boyle and Scot Barnett write in their introduction to *Rhetoric, Through Everyday Things*, "If we continue to think of things exclusively in terms of language, appearance, or representation . . . we will likely go on believing that human beings alone determine the scope and possibilities of rhetoric and that humans, as a consequence, are the only true legislators of nature" (4).

In their collection, Boyle and Barnett argue for an *ontological* conception of rhetoric rather than the human-centric epistemological one adopted by the rhetorical tradition at large. An epistemological rhetoric, implicitly positing a human knower apart from the world, makes rhetoric a human-sized enterprise. An ontological rhetoric, on the other hand, conceives of the rhetor less as an objective observer of the world and autonomous rhetorical agent than as an entity inextricably bound up with and habituated by a confluence of material and discursive forces. Here, the human self is not actually separate (as it is with an epistemological understanding of rhetoric), but it can be habituated into perceiving itself as separate, a view pithily captured by Gilles Deleuze in *Empiricism and Subjectivity*: "We are habits, nothing but habits; the habit of saying 'I'" (x). In an ontological conception, rhetoric functions less as communication between separate entities than as a force of attunement: in this case, a force that potentially enables the recognition of self as densely entangled with, even inseparable from, the world. Along with post-humanist rhetoric and philosophy, such a conception of the inseparability of self and universe can be seen most readily in ancient sacred texts like the Upanishads:

> On this ever-revolving wheel of being
> The individual self goes round and round
> Through life after life, believing itself
> To be a separate creature, until
> It sees its identity with the Lord of Love
> And attains immortality in the indivisible
> whole. (Easwaran, *Upanishads*, 218)

In keeping with the insights of rhetoric conceived as ontological, in this essay I define rhetoric's role in responding to the sacred not as an attempt to represent human experience, but as the building of a capacity to enable the recognition of the self's dense interconnectedness with all things. This moment of recognition has names in many traditions (like *kenshō*), but here I borrow rhetorical theorist Richard Doyle's term "ecodelic imbrication"— namely, "a sudden apprehension of immanence, a connectivity that exceeds the rhetorical capacities of an ego" (*Darwin's Pharmacy*, 20). As he outlines in *Darwin's Pharmacy*, the realization of this ecodelic imbrication can be abetted by discursive and nondiscursive rhetorical technologies that help facilitate the human recognition of its profound interconnection—what we might call "hacking the sacred." Doyle's book specifically highlights the rituals around the human use of psychedelics (a term that literally means "mind-manifesting") as examples of such rhetorical technologies; however, he acknowledges a plethora of other rhetorical technologies aimed at provoking human recognition of immanence—which, given the frequency of such experiences and the capacities of the human brain, seem to be a feature rather than a bug: "No doubt the practices of immanence are as diverse as the planet itself; fasting, inhaling carbon dioxide, and even working with latex have all provoked encounters with immanence, suggesting that in some fashion human perception is indeed 'wired' for a periodic recognition of the dense imbrication of organism and environment and is highly tunable by our practices" (9). While certainly the mystic tradition contains a plethora of material that attempts to describe experiences of ecodelic imbrication (from St. Teresa of Avila's accounts on Erowid.org of her raptures to "trip reports" describing ayahuasca visions) that may persuade others to similar pursuits, this passage by Doyle suggests that it is the call to immanence provoked by this human "wiring" itself around which discursive and nondiscursive rhetorical technologies and practices grow.

In this essay, I consider the rhetorical practices that foster ecodelic imbrication; first, in contexts that are recognizably "sacred": specifically, the Apsáalooke (i.e., Crow) Sundance ceremony, and *zazen*, the meditative discipline affiliated with the Zen Buddhist tradition. Next, I consider contexts that are secular: specifically, the cluster of disciplines and practices that can loosely be called microbiome science. It might seem incongruous to pair contemporary scientific practice with overtly religious rituals; however, like other sciences grounded in ecological thought, microbiome science is founded on the assumption that all things are deeply enmeshed with one another in relations of mutual interdependence. With its attendant concepts of the "holobiont" and disruption of the entrenched notion of the "biological individual," microbiome science seems especially poised to disrupt human-centric relations to the world and to provoke recognition of our ecodelic imbrication. What is interesting is that unlike mystic rhetorical practices designed to provoke a recognition of the self as ecodelically imbricated, microbiome science more often than not attunes us to familiar scientific frameworks of logical efficiency and economic imperative, forestalling such an "ecodelic recognition." Attending to the various ways that our attunement can be blocked, I argue, gives us insight into the limits of rhetoric in responding to the sacred.

SACRED ATTUNEMENTS

In the heat of midsummer each year, the Apsáalooke (Crow) people hold their traditional major ceremony, the Ashkísse, or Sundance.[1] A postcolonial melding of the traditions of several Native peoples, the contemporary Sundance typically involves several days of ritual dancing in a lodge built anew each time for the occasion. Before the ceremony, dancers offer a private vow to Akbaatatdía ("The One Who Has Made Everything") expressing their greatest need and their willingness to make personal sacrifice to attain deeper spiritual connection or to aid in the healing of a family or community member. This vow is an expression of the spiritual power known as *baaxpée* (sometimes translated in English as "medicine"), a connection with a power greater than the individual mortal self. The tangible or material expression of *baaxpée* is *xapáaliia—xapáaliia* can take the form of a "medicine bundle," objects revealed in a vision that are sacred to an individual and their family, though it also refers to the people and things that are touched by *baaxpée*. A typical way to receive medicine is by way of an individual vision quest, where the seeker gives up food and water with the hope of receiving the gift of *xapáaliia*, but fasts are also practiced during the Sundance.

Ashkísse literally means "big lodge" or "imitation lodge," referring to the ceremonially constructed structure in which the Sundance is held. The forked top of a large central pole (typically made from a cottonwood) supports twelve trees arranged in spokes like a medicine wheel. Unlike what the translation of Ashkísse might suggest, the lodge is not meant to be symbolic, a mere imitation or representation of the cosmos; rather, it would be better described as a *microcosm*, a conduit of communication between the dancers and Akbaatatdía that needs to be activated by the elements of the Sundance ceremony. The songs and drums set a rhythmic pace as tobacco smoke sends prayers heavenward; the dancers charge toward the central pole and fall back, charge and fall back, blowing in unison on eagle bone whistles and brushing the central pole with eagle plumes. Occasionally a dancer may receive a vision from Akbaatatdía, mediated through an Ililápxe like the Buffalo, the Eagle, the Otter, or the Sun—the revealed character of an Ililápxe often seen as part of the natural world and a tangible extension of Akbaatatdía.

While structurally similar to the individual vision quest, the Sundance is ultimately aimed at strengthening and deepening the clan. The Apsáalooke word for "clan," *ashammaléxia*, literally translates in English "as driftwood lodges." Just as the force of a river causes driftwood to pile up and stick together, so, in the clan, "each individual is like a piece of driftwood, orienting himself or herself around, and depending on, the others of the prescribed group" (Frey, *World of the Crow Indians*, 3). But such "driftwood" includes more than just human kin: the clan of the Apsáalooke also incorporates all other entities and phenomena, including the transcendent or spiritual, in an interconnected web: "animal with plant with land with animal with spirit" (4). When you dance for the clan, you are dancing to manifest your interconnection with all of life.

Like the Sundance (though quieter, maybe), the Zen practice of zazen relies on discursive and nondiscursive rhetorical technologies aimed at fostering a realization of the false perception of a Self that is individual and separate from the world: in this case, the algorithmic repetition of physical actions on the part of participants (e.g., sitting with the spine erect, repeatedly returning the attention to a point of concentration like breath or a koan, and concentrated walking), combined with the intention to achieve what has variously been called self-realization, the recognition of the unified nature of all things, and "full rapport with life" (Kapleau, *Three Pillars*, 11). More than just symbols or representations, these rhetorical practices aim to stitch the participant into the sacred. As Philip Kapleau writes, in a passage specific to zazen (but applicable to other practices that aim for the mystical sacred), "[Zazen] is more than just a means to enlightenment or a technique for sustaining and enlarging it, but is the *actualization* of our True-nature" (20). Like the Sundance, the practice of zazen is not conducted on a representative or symbolic level, nor is it conducted instrumentally, as a mere physical means by which one channels the divine to an already-existent subject. Rather, these practices serve as the direct means by which participants realize their imbrication with all things. In other words, both of these recognizably sacred practices partake of an ontological rhetoric that presupposes the Self as always-already ecodelically imbricated, and organizes discursive and nondiscursive practices around prompting the realization of this imbrication.

To understand the importance of rhetorical frameworks to attunement to the sacred, one need only consider the title of the 2014 *HuffPost* UK blog post "Is Meditation the Best Kept Anti Ageing Secret?" The article describes a study performed at a Zen retreat center where researchers found that people who had taken part in a meditation retreat had significantly higher levels of telomerase (the enzyme that enables the lengthening of telomeres, which control cellular aging) than a control group, and wonders, "In a world where we are bombarded by the latest anti aging beauty products at every corner, often at exorbitant prices, could the secret to eternal youth really be in something as simple as meditation?" (Photi, "Is Meditation"). While the cosmetic benefits of meditation are the most overtly shallow, it is true that meditation typically gets sold in America as a primarily individualistic enterprise, aimed at fulfilling certain instrumental purposes. Everyone from Blue Cross Blue Shield to millennial lifestyle websites like mindbodygreen tout the virtues of meditation as individualistic improvement: it will make you less stressed, happier, more focused, more productive, and more successful, they say.

Thus, even those rituals and practices that may appear superficially identical to the ones in the sacred contexts described above can fail at tuning the mind to ecodelic imbrication. Considering such cases draws our attention to the importance of what Thomas Rickert, drawing on Martin Heidegger, calls the *mood* of a world. "Mood" here is the entanglement of world and body that attunes people in certain ways and not others (Rickert, *Ambient Rhetoric*, 14); to use one of Rickert's examples, for a person who is depressed the world shows up differently—drained of luster—than for someone who isn't. While mood, by virtue of being a product of the entanglement of world and body, cannot be the result of a singular, controlling rhetorical agent, it is still possible to rhetorically tune mood so as to create the likelihood of certain effects. Rickert uses Brian Eno's start-up music for Microsoft Windows 95 as an example of an element that contributes to a positive mood (and potentially a feeling of an operating system as easy to use and better able to enable quality work). Just as music can work as an attunement device, the discursive and nondiscursive rhetorical elements of overtly sacred contexts like the Sundance and zazen can modulate moods that predispose attunement to ecodelic imbrication. Without such deliberate modulation, the practitioner attunes to something that more likely falls within typical Western frameworks of engagement with the world.

Understanding the attention to mood in these more overtly sacred practices can help us understand how microbiome science—which at least initially would appear to be equally invested in a mystic view of life as radically interconnected—can fail to provoke a recognition of the ecodelic imbrication of the Self.

MICROBIAL ATTUNEMENTS

For almost the entire twentieth century, the study of microbes was dominated by the rhetorical framework of germ theory, the focus on microbes as the agential causes of disease. The entangled rhetorics, bodies, and technologies (broth and agar cultures, glass plates, pipettes, a plethora of discursive acts including ads for antibiotics and anti-germ cleaning products, PSAs warning of infectious disease, etc.) of this warlike "world" of early microbial science served to illuminate certain relations with microbes and to cast others in shadow. Humans were attuned to relationships of antagonism against microbial agents, which in turn pulled into the world a network of other bodies and technologies; generating an attention, for instance, to the molds, soil, and sulfanilamide antibacterial agents that could be harnessed against microbial aggressors.

This framing of our relationships with microbes tapped into and reinforced the familiar humanist understanding of humans as distinct from other organisms. In biology, this notion reached its apotheosis in the notion of the "biological individual," which for centuries was the fundamental unit of Western science. The biological individual has been defined in its commonsense or intuitive characteristics as being spatially and temporally continuous, clearly bounded, made of heterogeneous, causally related parts, developed from a single cell to a multicellular body, subject to impaired function if some of these parts are removed or damaged, and genetically homogenous (Wilson, *Biological Individuality*, 9). Even scientific disciplines like ecology, ostensibly concerned with multivariate systems, have been premised on examining how whole organisms relate to one another (Bouchard and Huneman, *From Groups*, 2). Partly this is owing to a perception influenced by Western attention to categorization since Aristotle, wherein things like horses, oak trees, and other countable organisms are distinct to the naked human eye from their surroundings and other organisms like them (Wilson, *Biological Individuality*, 9). Considered from this perspective, it is easy to see how the individualist notion of biological species has kept such a firm hold, and how it showed up in the rhetorical framing of a hostile relationship between humans and microbes.

Of course, this rhetorical attunement to microbes as aggressors did work admirably for a while, at least in its impacts on human health. In the so-called golden age of antibiotics, between the 1950s and 1970s, antibiotic discovery and manufacture flourished, and these antibacterial agents were so effective that many Western scientists prematurely declared the end of infectious disease (Aminov, "Brief History"). But in fairly short order, biological forces like "horizontal" genetic transmission enabled bacteria to develop exponentially quicker resistance to specific antibiotic agents, even as pharmaceutical companies began to slow down and eventually end development of new antibiotic drugs, exhausted by the unprofitable attempts to keep pace with evolution.

With the failures of a germ-centric rhetorical attunement to microbes, other relationships became more legible—specifically, those insights developed by microbial ecology. Considered to be only a minor and fairly inconsequential subfield for much of the twentieth century, microbial ecology had laboriously studied what was considered the "dark matter" of microbiology—the in situ dynamics of microbial interactions with other species of microbes as well as with eukaryotic cells and within organisms. We now know that such interactions make up the bulk of microbial activity, since, as contemporary microbiologists have estimated, almost 99 percent of bacteria cannot be cultured in laboratory conditions. The renewed attention to the commensal ("friendly"), ecological dimensions of microbes was intensified by the completion of the Human Genome Project, which heralded an era of increasingly cheap, quick, "next-generation" DNA sequencing, along with an array of "omics" technologies (like proteomics, metabolomics, metagenomics, and epigenomics) and big data statistical and modeling techniques that allow them to process the "wide, dirty" data sets that come with massive amounts of genomic data. Consequently, microbiologists began to shift their focus from studying laboratory bacterial cultures and sequencing individual organisms to sampling and sequencing entire communities of microorganisms: among others, in the guts, skin, nose, and vaginas of humans and other organisms; near superheated vents on the ocean floor; and on New York subways. Thus emerged a collaborative, cross-disciplinary enterprise that could loosely be called "microbiome science,"² which brings together older fields like microbial ecology, molecular biology, microbiology, population ecology, and computer science with brand new ones like bioinformatics. Microbiome science focuses on the ecological dimensions of microbial interactions (including bacteria, archaea, fungi, and viruses, among others). As one paper outlining the benefits of next-generation sequencing and other technologies for studying the microbiome remarks, even though the new technology requires massive amounts of computer processing power, advanced assembly software, and data mining tools, ultimately it promises "a great leap forward in our ability to explore the great unknown territory of complex microbial ecosystems. . . . Insights into microbial ecology, evolution, and genomic diversity will follow from biological interpretation of the data obtained" (Snyder et al., "Next-Generation Sequencing," 2). Indeed, the effects and attributes of the microbiome on human health have been so vociferously touted both in the scientific literature and in the popular press that even microbiome scientists are somewhat bemused by the attention—at a recent microbiome science conference I attended, one quipped, "So, how has the microbiome saved the world today?"

It took this confluence of technological circumstances, scientific projects, and obvious shortcomings of germ theory to prompt a more widespread rhetorical attunement to the radical interdependence of organisms. In line with this more ecological attunement, microbiome science seems poised to revolutionize our understanding of the human place in the world. Along with deposing multicellular organisms as the top of the hierarchy, microbiome science has unseated the individual organism's genome as the locus of development and redistributed it among a host of organisms. The rhetorical frameworks undergirding microbiome science would thus seem to prompt an attunement to the ecodelic nature of Self; for instance, as one article examining the philosophical consequences of the microbiome suggests, "Immunologically speaking, self is not a human trait but the product of complex interactions between human cells and a multitude of microbial cells. Differently put, what has traditionally been called self is partly contingent on what has traditionally been called nonself" (Rees, Bosch, and Douglas, "How the Microbiome Challenges").

Yet—despite all the attention and money currently directed at microbiome science; despite the massive technological infrastructure associated with DNA sequencing and data modeling; despite the breathlessness with which connections between intractable human health problems and the human microbiome is described; it is doubtful that the insights of micro-biome science have provoked the same sort of intense ecodelic awareness described by those who have directly experienced it through practices like the Sundance, zazen, or interfacing with plant psychedelics. In the next section, I attempt to discover why not.

EYES UP?

> The time has come to replace the purely reductionist "eyes-down" molec-ular perspective with a new and genuinely holistic, eyes-up, view of the living world, one whose primary focus is on evolution, emergence, and biology's innate complexity.
>
> —CARL WOESE, "A NEW BIOLOGY FOR A NEW CENTURY"

As a recently published article explains, the "modern synthesis," which wedded Darwinian natural selection with Mendelian genetics, was concep-tualized at a time when germ theory dominated microbiology; thus both the dominant rhetorical attunements and the available technologies made it difficult to see an ecological role for microbes (Bordenstein and Theis, "Host Biology"). The article calls for a "postmodern synthesis" that would install a more ecological conception of life, "reboot" elements of Lamarck-ian evolution, and unify long-standing divisions between zoology, ecology, botany, and microbiology. This more ecological conception of life might be seen in the main conceptual figure associated with microbiome science, the "holobiont"—defined as the "macro" organism or host along with its colony of archaeal, bacterial, fungal, and viral symbionts. Even vocabulary like "host/guests" in relation to holobionts is not entirely correct for some sci-entists, who conceive of the holobiont as the collection of genetic material of the entire organism and its associated microbes—the organism as colony or assemblage. Associated with the language of holobionts is hologenomes, defined as "the complete genetic content of the host genome, its organelles' genomes, and its microbiome" (5). Some microbiologists now argue that holobionts and hologenomes, not individual organisms, should be consid-ered the basic units of biological organization, a shift in perspective that would also prompt a reconsideration of the specific evolutionary principles that govern them.

At first glance, the potential of this ecological framework would seem to lead us back to the notion of "responding to the sacred" as the use of rhetorical technologies to provoke the human recognition of our dense entanglement or inseparability from all things. One could potentially assign the holobiont as the mascot of the microbiome science era, and use it as a figurehead for the realization that we are all inextricably and immanently connected—a shift away from biological individualism that would lead to radical changes in the biological unit of study, its research questions, and its conception of problems (Hunter, "Revival"; Gilbert, Sapp, and Tauber, "Symbiotic View"; Gilbert and Tauber, "Rethinking Individuality"). Owing to its deep connections with Western thought and its association with the scientific traditions of positivism and instrumentalism, microbiome science would stand to have more widespread rhetorical effects in helping realize our sacred nature than relatively small-scale religious traditions like the Sundance and zazen. But just as not all meditation practices lead to ecodelic imbrication, by and large the seemingly radical insights of the holobiont and hologenome have been eclipsed in workaday science, pointing to something of a paradox at the heart of microbiome science. While microbiome science has produced profound ecological insights, these same rhetorical frameworks also serve to block these insights.

The confusion is evident in the scientific literature, which has been fraught with controversies about how to characterize the human microbiome: for instance, what the "ome" in "microbiome" actually means. One school of thought takes the "ome" as a reference to genomics and other "ome" technologies—here, the term "microbiome" refers to the total of genomic material in a given community, a mode of thinking that would reinstall totality on a larger level. The other school of thought places more emphasis on the "biome" as an ecological unit, thus understanding the microbiome as the "microbial biome." As John Huss explains, "One strategy is fundamentally molecular, and uses the techniques of systems biology to integrate information about molecular mechanisms and pathways. The other strategy is fundamentally ecological, and uses the techniques of genomics to identify the ecological actors in the microbial community" ("Methodology")—what Carl Woese (in reference to the epigraph to this section) might call an "eyes-down" versus an "eyes-up" approach ("New Biology," 175). Huss argues that, regardless of whether studies of the microbiome take a molecular or an ecological approach, its conceptualization has been largely driven by the "translational imperative," the pressure to create clinical applications or consumer products from basic research. Huss links this translational imperative to 2003, where leaders of the Human Genome Project argued that given the economic exigencies of postwar funding for basic scientific research, the scientific community using genomics needed to create a more reliable "pipeline from 'bench to bedside'" ("Methodology").

A similar contradiction and tension underlies all of microbiome science. This contradiction is illustrated clearly in the book *The New Science of Metagenomics: Revealing the Secrets of Our Microbial Planet*, a 2007 report written by the Committee on Metagenomics (among other organizations). Sponsored by the National Academy of Sciences, the report aims to explain and promote the science of metagenomics, which sequences the DNA of microbes at a community, rather than an individual level. The report reveals that even radical new technologies like metagenomics (described by the report as "akin to a reinvention of the microscope in the expanse of research questions it opens to investigation . . . a new way of examining the microbial world that not only will transform modern microbiology but has the potential to revolutionize understanding of the entire living world" (2) can fall back into the same old positivist frameworks. While the technology is currently in its early stages, the report asserts that when amplified, "The ultimate goal, perhaps in sight by 2027, would be a metacommunity model that seeks to explain and predict (and retrodict) the behavior of the biosphere as though it were a single superorganism. Such a 'genomics of Gaia' would be the ultimate implementation of systems biology" (139).

The reference to Gaia especially would appear to hark back to mysticism, or at least a radically interdependent view of life on earth. Yet for all its apparent potential for being an engine and technology for ecodelic imbrication, the insights the committee focuses on seem very much like business as usual, a tension or paradox illustrated on the first page of the book: "All plants and animals have closely associated microbial communities that make necessary nutrients, metals, and vitamins available to their hosts. The billions of benign microbes that live in the human gut help us to digest food, break down toxins, and fight off disease-causing microbes. We also depend on microbes to clean up pollutants in the environment, such as oil and chemical spills. All these activities are carried out by complex microbial communities—intricate, balanced, and integrated entities that adapt swiftly and flexibly to environmental change" (1). While the authors focus on some of the ecological dimensions of microbes in this passage, by far the overall focus is instrumentalist and human-centric—that is, how can we make these newly identified microbial communities work for capitalism? With this particular rhetorical attunement, microbiome science produces results and understandings that reproduce typical Western conclusions, even when the specifics of the science (here, one that could in other circumstances install a radically ecological conception of life) would seem to undercut it. A similar stumbling block can be seen in many microbiome studies, where the technological attempts to gain understanding of a complex, unknowable ecology is reduced by understanding it as not an end in itself, but as a means: many studies of the gut microbiome, for instance, have as their end goal the purpose of making a better probiotic, essentially a magic pill that would metonymically substitute a well-balanced food system for an industrialized one founded on the same logics of efficiency and economics that inform much of Western science, or a means of harnessing bacterial power to clean up the oil spills and toxic waste produced by the same system. Such technologies, though they would appear at least superficially to promise the ecodelic imbrication of more recognizably "sacred" technologies like those of the Sundance and zazen, tend more often than not to fall back into the very thinking that prevents these insights.

One of the questions this collection asks is "what is the relation between rhetoric (defined as a medium of communication) and the sacred (which is defined as beyond the communicative)?" In response to this question, the present essay has pointed to the importance of rhetorical attunements in realizing our relation to the sacred, here defined as a direct experience of the interconnectedness of all things. While the potentiality for such experience most obviously lies in realms already marked as sacred (as in my examples here of the Native religious ritual of the Sundance and the Zen Buddhist practice of zazen), it also potentially lies in the realm of everyday experience and in arenas of human endeavor that have traditionally been conceived as the antithesis of the sacred, like science. Rhetorical frameworks, comprising both discursive and nondiscursive factors, including material technologies and technologies of the self, can either help to manifest this relation or block it through enmeshment in frameworks of thought that recast the human as separate from, in control of, and dominant over the rest of the world. Owing both to its potential for prompting a recognition of our ecodelic imbrication and the ways it rhetorically pulls its punches via its investments in humanist and capitalist logics, microbiome science proves to be an interesting case study. We might ask what it would mean if microbiome science retooled its rhetorical attunements to be more like the more overtly sacred ones. What if it took the encouragement toward direct experience of ecodelic imbrication, or the interconnectedness of all things that is more overtly present in sacred practices? How would this change its research questions, its uses of technology, its experiments and studies? What new insights might emerge? My suspicion is that at the very least it might enable some radically ecological thinking, the "eyes-up" view called for by Woese.

More to the point of this collection's title, I hope I have shown here that there are not particular limits to rhetoric, at least as far as the sacred is concerned. There are only different attunements that it can cast, different moods it can create, and the different relations that result.

Notes

1. I am grateful to my colleague Rodney Frey, who as an ethnographer and participant in many Sundances, explained the ritual and the meaning to me. Everything in this section either comes from personal discussion or Frey's two books on the Apsáalooke people, *The World of the Crow Indians* and *Carry Forth the Stories*.

2. While the concept has been in use since the 1960s, the term "microbiome" gained notoriety in 2001, when microbiologist Joshua Lederberg (who won the Nobel Prize in 1958 for his work on the exchange of viral genetic material among bacteria) published a short but oft-cited article defining the microbiome as "the ecological community of commensal, symbiotic, and pathogenic microorganisms that literally share our body space and have been all but ignored as determinants of health and disease" ("Ome Sweet Omics," 8).

Bibliography

Aminov, Rustam I. "A Brief History of the Antibiotic Era: Lessons Learned and Challenges for the Future." *Frontiers in Microbiology* 1, no. 134 (2010). https://www.doi.org/10.3389/fmicb.2010.00134.

Barnett, Scot, and Casey Boyle. "Introduction." In *Rhetoric, Through Everyday Things*, edited by Scot Barnett and Casey Boyle, 1–14. Tuscaloosa: University of Alabama Press, 2016.

Bordenstein, Seth R., and Kevin Theis. "Host Biology in Light of the Microbiome: Ten Principles of Holobionts and Hologenomes." *PLoS Biology* 13, no. 8 (2015). https://www.doi.org/10.1371/journal.pbio.1002226.

Bouchard, Frédéric, and Philippe Huneman, eds. *From Groups to Individuals: Evolution and Emerging Individuality.* Cambridge, MA: MIT Press, 2015.

Committee on Metagenomics, National Research Council, Division on Earth and Life Studies, and Board on Life Sciences. *The New Science of Metagenomics Revealing the Secrets of Our Microbial Planet.* Washington, DC: National Academies Press, 2007.

Deleuze, Gilles. *Empiricism and Subjectivity.* Translated by Constantin V. Boundas. New York: Columbia University Press, 1991.

Doyle, Richard. *Darwin's Pharmacy: Sex, Plants, and the Evolution of the Noösphere.* Seattle: University of Washington Press, 2011.

Easwaran, Eknath, trans. *The Upanishads.* Oakland, CA: Nigiri Press, 1987.

Frey, Rodney. *Carry Forth the Stories: An Ethnographer's Journey into Native Oral Tradition.* Pullman: Washington State University Press, 2017.

———. *The World of the Crow Indians: As Driftwood Lodges.* Norman: University of Oklahoma Press, 1987.

Gilbert, Scott F., Jan Sapp, and Alfred I. Tauber. "A Symbiotic View of Life: We Have Never Been Individuals." *Quarterly Review of Biology* 87, no. 4 (2012): 325–41.

Gilbert, Scott F., and Alfred I. Tauber. "Rethinking Individuality: The Dialectics of the Holobiont." *Biology and Philosophy* 31, no. 6 (2016): 839–53.

Hunter, Philip. "The Revival of the Extended Phenotype." *EMBO Reports* 19, no. 7 (2018): 1–4.

Huss, John. "Methodology and Ontology in Microbiome Research." *Biological Theory* 9, no. 4 (2014): 392–400.

Kapleau, Philip. *The Three Pillars of Zen.* Boston: Beacon Press, 1965.

Lederberg, Joshua. "Ome Sweet Omics: A Genealogical Treasury of Words." *Scientist* 15, no. 7 (2001): 8.

Photi, Stella. "Is Meditation the Best Kept Anti Ageing Secret?" *HuffPost* UK, April 4, 2014. https://www.huffing tonpost.co.uk/stellaphoti/meditation antiageing_b_5206754.html.

Rees, Tobias, Thomas Bosch, and Angela E. Douglas. "How the Microbiome Challenges Our Concept of Self." *PLoS Biology* 16, no. 2 (2018). https://www.doi.org/10.1371/journal .pbio.2005358.

Rickert, Thomas. *Ambient Rhetoric: The Attunements of Rhetorical Being.* Pittsburgh: University of Pittsburgh Press, 2013.

Snyder, Lori A. S., Nick Loman, Mark J. Pallen, and Charles W. Penn. "Next-Generation Sequencing: The Promise and Perils of Charting the Great Microbial Unknown." *Microbial Ecology* 57, no. 1 (2009): 1–3.

Wilson, Jack. *Biological Individuality: The Identity and Persistence of Living Entities.* New York: Cambridge University Press, 1999.

Woese, Carl. "A New Biology for a New Century." *Microbiology and Molecular Biology Reviews* 68, no. 2 (2004): 173–86.

Yong, Ed. *I Contain Multitudes: The Microbes Within Us and a Grander View of Life.* New York: Ecco / HarperCollins, 2016.

CHAPTER 7

Divining Rhetoric's Future

MICHELLE BALLIF

Rhetoric, as a disciplinary art and practice, has been theorized as (among other things) a deliberative art. Famously, Aristotle claimed that deliberative rhetoric was one of the three species of rhetoric (the other two, of course, being judicial and epideictic). The species were so designated based on the types of intended audiences addressed: deliberative rhetoric hailed an audience of judges that were tasked to instantiate, perhaps even legislate, an "advantageous" *future* outcome (*On Rhetoric* 1358b; Kennedy ed., 49); the other two, as we know, were intended to address audiences of judges of past fact (judicial) or of spectators of the present (epideictic).

In the case of all the species, but for our purposes regarding deliberative rhetoric, the judgments must be made without the benefit of certain knowledge of which deliberative choice would play out in the *future* of having been the most beneficial outcome for the intended audience. So the rhetor must present arguments for consideration based on "the possible and the impossible and . . . whether it will or will not come to be" (1359a; Kennedy ed., 51). As the goal is to portend an unknowable future, Aristotle suggests that we look to the past for examples because "we judge of future events by *divination* from past events" (emphasis added). He argues that such a divination is not particularly complicated because "generally, future events will be like those of the past" (1394a; Kennedy ed., 181).

Advocating for this future, then, requires a *calculation* of the possible and the impossible, and divining this future requires an *accounting* of past events: all such accounting is done by *human* agents and portends a *future* that is predictable "in general." My desire, here, is to problematize these founding assumptions by offering an alternative: that of "divination."

To begin, I want to pose this challenge from an earlier moment in our long history—a challenge that cohabited rhetoric's beginning, evident in Plato's *Phaedrus*, for example. Historically—or at least coincidental with rhetoric's "birth"—"divination" or other methodologies of portending a future from para-human sources were *not* seen as extraneous to any form of rhetorical deliberation, but they have in more current times been dismissed as forms of, at best, "divine madness." These para-human sources are what I consider "sacred," in that they recognize that there is more to any rhetorical moment than can be humanly, rationally accounted for.

This essay is an attempt to point to how "divination" might be a productive methodological model to think about rhetoric's future: for a future (that is to come, admittedly) that challenges the binary of the "rational and the divine," and that more (pre)originarily establishes the divine responseability of every rhetorical encounter. That is, I am suggesting, deliberation is "para-rational" in that it cannot count on logistical calculations to make just decisions about the future, precisely because to do so renders a *replication* of the past. Aristotle said as much, in general. But deliberation is not "irrational" in that it does entail reasoned judgments. But these judgments are made without any sure knowledge; rather, they are guided only by probability, contingency, and exigency—and perhaps by the whisperings of a still, small daimon.

Such judgments are akin to the kinds of decisions a farmer may make, such as when would be the best time to plant seed. One might, say, then, that such judgments rely on a certain practice of divination. But as we might, as we will, we could say so much more.

As the reader may know, the practice of divination played a significant role in the practices of ancient Athenians. As we recount our originary narrative tale of the "birth of democracy," rhetoric is figured as the protagonist guiding processes of deliberation among the *living, human* members of the *demos* to decide facts of past, present, and future; the art of rhetoric conceived as human agents deliberating to advance the advantages of a democratic union.

History shows that the gods (and the dead) also participated in this deliberation, serving as key interlocutors in such debates, rendering opinions on whether something was just or good, or whether an army should go to battle or not. Scholars have demonstrated that "divination" played an important role in the civic deliberations of classical Athens (see Bowden, *Classical Athens*; Johnston, *Ancient Greek Divination*; Struck, *Divination*). That is, contrariwise to the contemporary incantation of the "birth of rhetoric" narrative, para-human, para-rational, and even para-normal agencies were recognized as important parts of the deliberative process.

Contemporaneously, our understanding of this construction of rhetorical agency is a presumption that "we" exist independently of "rhetoric," and that rhetoric is perhaps a tool that "we" use to do a variety of work—work of our choosing—and work that advantageously benefits us.

Thomas Cole has theorized rhetoric as a uniquely "human" art of "communication," as "a speaker's or writer's self-conscious manipulation of his medium with a view to ensuring his message as favorable a reception as possible on the part of the particular audience being addressed" (*Origins*, ix). So many presumptions, but to begin: that "we" exist prior to "rhetoric" and that "rhetoric" is a *techne* or tool to be picked up, after the fact, of our presumed, preexisting rhetorical agency, employed, as needed, to do our work, to serve our human, all-too-human purposes.

But contra to such human-centric articulations of rhetoric that make no place for divination, I suggest that rhetoric is always a function of the "divine," if you will, and of the dead, as you must. By "divine," I mean any "para-human"—indeed, "para-normal"—influence, agency, or condition of possibility (the prefix signifying at or to one side of).

But more, pre-originary, I use the "divine" to point to that which paranormally inheres in a rhetorical relation. As Diane Davis writes, rhetorical agents are "by definition something other than distinct individuals or self-determining agents, and whose relations necessarily precede and exceed symbolic intervention" (*Inessential Solidarity*, 3). I am not saddling her with the burden of my ultimate claims, but her point is that there *is a relation that* "*precedes and exceeds*" any communication. I want to repeat this, which I will, and this entire essay could be reduced to this insight: *a relation that* "*precedes and exceeds*" any communication. A yes, yes. (Jacques Derrida says there are a number of "yeses," incalculable.)

There is more than we can *account* for in any rhetorical exchange. This fundamental, "pre-originary" relation is what Derrida has called "a response to a call" from "the other" (qtd. in Royle, "Ouijamiflip," 236). Davis characterizes this as a response-ability to the wholly other. According to Derrida, there is a pre-originary "yes, yes"—a call and response—that brings "you" and "me" into being and most certainly a "we." Yet none of the pronouns are stable, never present; it is a rhetorical relation that simultaneously does and undoes us; it is simultaneously the possibility and impossibility of a "we."

This response-ability *is* the ethical necessity of answering the other, the wholly other, and this response-ability *is* what brings any rhetorical agency into being. I am suggesting—as a thought experiment—that reconceiving this call and response as a "divine" enterprise and using "divination" as a pretext to discuss potential methodologies, "we" can envision a future—a future to come that is not predicated on the past.

I feel obligated to offer several caveats/clarifications before we go any further. Lest I be misread, my focus on the para-rational is not an advocation for irrational or irresponsible rhetoric that disregards "facts," advances demagoguery, or promotes neoliberalist politics: all instances in which the needs of the (systematically protected) (self-same) one outweigh the needs of the many (indeed, which are guaranteed at the expense of the many).

On the contrary, what is being advanced here is altogether different: a rhetoric that attends to the other—to all of the other others—and that divines a future, distinct from what Aristotle envisioned: a future that replicated the past, in general. As Aristotle has told us, if you plant an acorn, you will grow an oak tree. The *future* is already contained in the seed, in its potentiality. This is not the kind of future we are invoking. We are heralding a new future, without any knowledge or ability to calculate its arrival, but with a commitment to responding to the wholly other.

DIVINATION: ARISTOTLE AND PLATO

According to Hugh Bowden's *Classical Athens and the Delphic Oracle*, the Oracle—particularly that of Delphi—played a significant role in the democracy of ancient Athens (87). That is, democracy did not begin when the gods were put to bed. Democracy did not mark its birth when only rational deliberation among living humans became the only communication game in town. The gods continued to be questioned; the gods continued to be consulted. The divine haunts democracy. Let me repeat: the divine haunts democracy.

Bowden further argues that for the Greeks living during the fifth and fourth centuries BCE, there was a great concern for conciliating the gods with lavish festivals in their honor but also for consulting with the gods for fear of punishment for not following their counsel. Bowden writes that hepatoscopy (the divination of the livers of sacrificed animals) was "literally an everyday occurrence in democratic Athens" that was used not only by farmers to reduce risks associated with the "variability of harvest" (10), but also by military strategists to divine choices in war to produce favorable outcomes.

Divination was also sought by those in the law courts and the Athenian Assembly when issues arose that "could not be resolved by debate," and in these circumstances, "ambassadors were sent to the sanctuaries of gods noted for their oracular powers" (6): chief among these is Apollo at Delphi. Although "scholars disagree about what happened in the actual consultation, and no ancient writer gives an explicit account," "it was quite probably very simple: the petitioner would ask his question, and the Pythia would reply directly to him, speaking clearly and straightforwardly. The petitioner would normally write down the response word-for-word, and then leave the consultation room. The god had spoken" (21).

The Pythia was the medium for the god's message; she was a local woman from Delphi, and although she would be "past childbearing age" when she performed the role, she "dressed in the clothes appropriate to an unmarried girl, thus appearing symbolically as a virgin" (21). Although Bowden does not think there is evidence in support, he notes that the Pythia "is sometimes portrayed as wild and incoherent, or as giving deliberately ambiguous responses" (21). He also acknowledges that there is "some dispute about the gaseous, hallucinatory environment" of the temple at Delphi, but he writes of recent geological investigations that indicate the site of the temple was built at the crossing of two fault lines and that various gasses were indicated, included ethylene—a gas used for anesthetic purposes in the mid-twentieth century—which in low dosages could produce a trance effect (19). I will leave this discussion to Thomas Rickert.

Plato is complicated in terms of his relations to the gods and divination. As this essay is not really purposed to survey this query, I point the reader to Peter T. Struck's *Divination and Human Nature*, who records extensive research on Plato, and more, as the title suggests (37–90), as well as to Sarah

Iles Johnston's *Ancient Greek Divination*, which includes incredible bibliographies at the end of each chapter. But to attempt a summation for the present purposes, I point to the dialogue of the *Phaedrus* as *symptomatic* of issues we are addressing. No doubt, the dialogue is familiar to most students of rhetoric, so I only briefly recount the salient points here: Phaedrus tells Socrates that he will set up a golden statue of him at Delphi if he can deliver a better speech than the one Lysias has composed. Socrates coyly takes the challenge; as he concludes his speech, he divines that he has offended the gods, and begins anew, with another speech, in which he glorifies madness, one species of which is the madness of love, but another of which is divination or prophesy. Of course, Socrates ends his "dialogue" by resisting the seduction, and asserts that he will not be led astray by rhetoric, but will remain a lover of dialectic. So be it. But in this same exchange, he has acknowledged that the gods have influenced his deliberative processes.

Of note, Aristotle wrote a brief, skeptical work, "On Prophesying by Dreams." He does not conclude with much enthusiasm, but he thought enough of it to write the treatise (for more on Aristotle and his relation to divination, see Struck, *Divination*, 91–170, and subsequent notes). I am glossing here the fact that, as Bowden argues, for Plato (an Athenian, but not involved in Athenian politics) and for Aristotle (not an Athenian, but very involved in political issues), Delphi was symptomatic of the times, representing that para-human forces needed to be consulted "on issues where human wisdom cannot be expected to know the correct answers, either because they concern the wishes of the gods or because they require knowledge about the character, or perhaps future fortunes of individuals—knowledge not available to mere mortals" (Bowden, *Classical Athens*, 85).

Johnston queries why "divination so fascinated ancient intellectuals" as opposed to other practices associated with the divine, such as sacrifice. She concludes that "part of the answer is that divination more clearly involves participants in a two-way conversation. . . . When you cast the dice or read the entrails or put a question to the Pythia, you get an answer almost immediately. *Interpreting* it may take you longer, but at least you know that someone" (*Ancient Greek Divination*, 4) . . . has answered your call.

THE DIVINE YES, YES

Hence figuring "divination" as a call-and-response *conversation* with the "divine" opens for us a space to address the "response-ability" of the pre-originary rhetorical relation that Davis argues, and that Derrida exposes as a "yes, yes," as the most foundational (put that under erasure) gesture of hospitality/equation of communicational relation.

Of this "yes, yes," Derrida writes, "It is never *present* as such," and it is irreducible to any linguistic theory ("but not from any theory of its linguistic effects") ("A Number of Yes," 239). Before we move on, because it is important: the yes, yes has *effects*. It can and will materialize. Derrida explains:

> Let us suppose a first *yes*, the archi-originary *yes* that engages, promises and acquiesces before all else. On the one hand, it is originarily, in its very structure, a response. It is *first second*, coming after a demand, a question, or another *yes*. On the other hand, as engagement or promise, it must *at least* and in advance be tied to a confirmation in another [*prochain*] *yes*. *Yes* to the other [*au prochain*], that is, to the other *yes* that is already there but nonetheless remains to come. The "I" does not preexist this movement, nor does the subject; they are instituted in it. I ("I") can say *yes* ("yes-I") only by promising to keep the memory of the *yes* and to confirm it immediately. . . . This "second" *yes* is a priori enveloped in the "first." . . . This last, the first, is doubled in advance: *yes, yes*. (239–40)

At first read, this "explanation" seems dizzying, to be sure, but the irreducible suggestion is that any rhetorical activity, agency, effect is always already, simultaneously, a response (yes) to a call (yes), both of which are "doubled" in their atemporal nonbeing, but that materialize effects. "A *yes* cannot be counted" (240), but its effects can be witnessed.

This essay from which I am drawing is contextualized by Derrida's "conversation" with Michel de Certeau about what he "writes about writing in the mystical text" and the relationship between various gods and the "boundless *yes*," and invites us, as well, to think of this "response to a call from the other," which is always mise en abyme, in terms of the divine and, here, divination. In contrast to the divination practices outlined above, especially as appropriated by modern-day thinkers, we are refiguring divination as not a communication from one stable addressor (the one who asks the question) to a stable addressee (Apollo of Delphi, for example), but as a con/fusion of the addressor and the addressee in that, as we have seen above, the so-called first yes of the one asking the God (yes, I answer to you, God) is always already a response to the God's *yes* (I am).

Furthermore, and of more import here, that *relation* is what I am considering "divine." There is a promise and a prayer in every yes, an infinite chain of response-ability. Every question is always already a response to a previous question. Question: will you recognize me? Answer: yes. The "original" question, however, is *already* a response to the question: will you recognize me as the one who recognizes you? Answer: yes. I realize this example is highly psychologized, but back up the scenario with God as a player: Same series of questions. Same answers. Even in this—what I hoped to be a useful example—I rendered the actors a priori ("you" or "God"). What I want to stress is that this relation of "yes, yes" is more pre-originary, in that this doubled call comes *before* "you" are even a "you"—or, it must be said, before "God" is even a "God." It calls *all* into being.

In any event, alongside Derrida, every other (the questioner, the Pythia, and the God—and all the other others) is wholly other ("tout autre est tout autre"). Even this equation does not work because I have pre-identified the beings, already categorically depriving them of their wholly otherness by rendering them, *as such*: "questioner" (addressor), "Pythia" (medium), and "God" (audience)—each, *as such*.

And if every other is wholly other—which means every other, and we are not just talking humans here—each being (and put that under erasure) is completely and singularly unique (and who decides the boundaries of where one being begins and/or where one ends?). Therefore, if every other is radically singular, then every other is unknowable, *as such*. This is because our systems of knowledge *categorize* "tout autre" into a category in order to make the "thing" recognizable, *as such*. The example I have used for decades to explain how this works is Friedrich Nietzsche's discussion of the leaf. To wit: every leaf in the universe is unique ("tout autre"); in order for it to be recognized as a "leaf," however, it must be categorically distinguished from tree trunks, mushrooms, dirt (each subject to the same categorical assignation). For the leaf to be an "oak leaf" it must undergo a further set of categorizations: not a pine tree, not a magnolia tree. Point: all these radically singular presentations of/to the world are reduced into categorical constructs in order to "know" them, as such.

So the ethical challenge is: how to avoid this epistemic exercise, which results in so much violence? Is it avoidable if one is "to know"? As a thought experiment, trade the "leaf" example, above, for the "undocumented immigrant" or for "the terrorist." How to know, but more to the point, how *not* to know. Derrida has advanced a "non-knowing," a "without knowing" (*sans savoir*), a "passion of non-knowing" (*Cinders*, 75), which has "more to do with bearing an ethico-political witness to justice than with the *docta ignorantia*" (Caputo, *Prayers*, xxiv).

No fear: I am not suggesting that we want those who are uninformed divining our future. But we want—and aspire to be—those who have a respect for the *unknown*, a profound humility toward the wholly otherness of the other. Demagogues and tyrants are those who *know* what the future should be—and who and who not should be included in it as deliberative participants.

SYMPTOMATOLOGY AS DIVINATION

And so to return to the "divination" of rhetoric's future. To assume that every other is wholly other (including to one's self), then we take up the question of how to divine the messages of the wholly other. Not for our purposes today, but moving forward, I might suggest necromancy as a methodology to study (the dead have so much to say)—but understand that divination is a *not* a simple act of "cryptology." For, oh my goodness, once you open that crypt! But any "divinatory" methodology employed must avoid the hermeneutical cycle, which merely (re)appropriates what is already known, refashioning an already known *future*.

Derrida suggests symptomatology as a methodology with which to proceed. But I need to stress that what he calls symptomatology is not a pathologized symptom to be rendered according to some diagnostic protocol. Here is Derrida:

> Beyond all forms of verification, beyond discourses of truth or knowledge, the symptom is a signification of the event over which nobody has control, that no consciousness, that no conscious subject can appropriate or control, neither in the form of a theoretical

or judicative statement, nor in the form of a performative production. There is symptom in what's happening here, for instance [at
his lecture]: each of us interpreting, foreseeing, anticipating, and
feeling overwhelmed and surprised by what can be called events.
Beyond the meaning that each of us can read into these events, if
not enunciate, there is the symptom. (*Cinders*, 457)

The symptom might be otherwise addressed as the "remainder effects"—
what he has theorized as the trace, *différance*—the surplus of meaning that
destabilizes any meaning, any signification.

Hence to refigure rhetorical divination as symptomatology is not to—
once again—play the hermeneutic game of de-termining the message, the
encrypted message of the symptom.

ARISTOTLE AS SYMPTOM AND OUIJA

So the (debatable) question being posed here: why is *Aristotle* our symptom, as a discipline? First of all, wrap your heads around the fact that there
existed some person named Aristotle who died a couple of thousand years
ago, and yet we dedicate so many textbooks and introductory speech and
writing courses in his name, invoking his spirit, daily. But despite that fact,
we do not believe in seances? In hearing voices beyond the grave? I have
more to say, but that awaits another occasion.

Here, I will begin with Christian Lundberg's and Joshua Gunn's "'Ouija
Board, Are There Any Communications?' Agency, Ontotheology, and the
Death of the Humanist Subject, or, Continuing the ARS Conversation."
This essay provides a model for the kind of symptomology work that the
discipline can undertake. They ask specifically, to our point, why does the
field have such an investment in the idea of a rhetorical agent who has no
para-influences?

As Lundberg and Gunn explain, new technologies in the nineteenth
century, such as the telephone and the telegraph, awakened dormant anxieties about human agency as the "Second Great Awakening" of religious
thought in the United States that emphasized "a conviction in the capacity
of humans to act morally and secure their own spiritual salvation," opposing
earlier notions of Calvinist fatalism. Coincidental with this Awakening was
the development and use of new technologies as the aforementioned

telegraph. Could be a chicken-and-egg quandary. But the point, regarding the Ouija board, was that once the spiritualist movement took force, all sorts of communications with the para-human, the dead, were undertaken. Nineteenth-century messages were sent with "rappings" on surfaces, which "a given 'medium' would count to discern if they denoted a 'yes,' a 'no,' or a letter of the alphabet" (Braude, *Radical Spirits*, 10–31, qtd. in Lundberg and Gunn, "Ouija Board," 83). "Excepting toddlers and accountants, counting is a somewhat tiresome exercise of agency, and so it was only a matter of time before a number of enterprising individuals would develop the 'talking board' to ease the labor of mediation" (Lundberg and Gunn, "Ouija Board," 83), as the effort of *calculation* of divination became too great! But more to their point: "As a technology ultimately inspired by the Second Great Awakening, the Ouija board illustrates the anxiety surrounding our many fantasies about human agency, particularly in respect to communication as a transcendent, or even transparent event" (84). They write, "However ironic, the belief that one or another could literally speak with the souls of the dearly departed reflects an evangelical subject enthusiastically wedded to a humanist gospel that has elevated agency to the status of the godly, lording over the material and spiritual universe. This transcendent sentiment, sometimes discussed as 'ontotheology,' was heavily critiqued by Heidegger, who lamented that 'it seems as though man everywhere and always encounters himself, even beyond death'" (84).

As Lundberg and Gunn argue, "The practice of a séance also directs our attention to a problem implied (but also somehow beyond) the transparency or transcendence of the moment of communication: the instabilities of the Cartesian self, or the self-transparent and self-possessed subject of thoroughly conscious intention" (84). "Using a Ouija board, for example, demonstrates that while the exercise of agency takes place in the movement of the planchette, the status and possibly even the existence of the agent who originates the action is undecidable" (84). Who is exercising agency in these moments? they ask. One of the players? Someone from beyond? A combination? And how could one decide? How could one calculate the "ratios" of agency operative in this communicational moment? How could one know? They use the example of the Ouija board to foreground an anxiety, expressed by Cheryl Geisler's report on the concept of rhetorical agency of the now-dead Alliance of Rhetorical Studies conference, that the human rhetorical agent should be, indeed is, "'given' and godly" (Geisler, "How Ought We"; Lundberg and Gunn, "Ouija Board," 86).

So my argument, alongside that of Lundberg and Gunn, is that rhetoric theorized as divorced from any para-human influence is symptomatic of an anxiety of a need to establish the human as more powerful, more influential, than any "divine" influence.

For my purposes and from my perspective, the "divine" is simply what Socrates himself would have called the daimon, but a daimon that had no transcendental currency. And the Ouija board, although patented, simply means "yes, yes" (*oui* in French and *ja* in German: you do the math—that is at least two yeses). Admittedly, the daimon was co-opted by "self-consciousness" and became merely a "background check" to advise for or against certain choices. But if we look back at that proverbial "birth of rhetoric" moment, we will see that divination was part of it. I am suggesting— alongside Lundberg and Gunn—that we, as a contemporary discipline, chose to embrace Aristotle in order to deny para-human influences and *that* is our discipline's symptom.

To be clear, if possible, I am acknowledging that rhetorical agency exists and is exercised every day; effects of the para-normal, para-human, para-language are experienced every day. These effects materialize as rhetorical agency. The question before us is how to divine a future for us—for *all of us*. A future to come.

FROM THE DEAD TO THE FUTURE TO COME

What the séance example of the aforementioned period foregrounds, and helps us to ponder, is the role of the *medium* in a rhetorical construction. The Pythia who renders the God's message; the telegraph or the telephone that allows for telepathy; the medium who counts the rappings; the Ouija board that spells out the communications from one source to another.

But there is an even more haunted and complicated medium—and that is language itself (as if we knew what we were talking about when we name it *as such*), which troubles all of the elements of the so-called rhetorical situation and which exposes (but does not reveal) the aporetic quality of all the heretofore distinguishable players and contexts of the so-called rhetorical situation.

Let us begin by acknowledging that language is, itself, a medium—taking continuous dictation from beyond. As Christine Berthin, author of *Gothic Hauntings*, asserts, "Language is always 'from the other,' inherited and heavy with history," but "language differs from other media because of its pretense at transparency and immateriality" (22). This supposed transparency is effected through the repression of all that remains: "There are residues in language of something that is not language" (23). Uncanny residues, they "are foreign to the message and live a life of their own within the words of the subject who unknowingly conveys them" (23). Language, structured as a medium, is thus dictating or channeling the para-human, the para-rational: the divine.

This returns us to our starting point: rethinking deliberation as divination—in a post-Aristotelian manner—affords us the opportunity to hail futures-to-come that are not predicated on a predicted past, but rather that invite futures as yet to be seen. Brooke Rollins, in her new book *The Ethics of Persuasion*, summons voices from the past who speak to such possibilities. Of Isocrates, she notes that his vision of rhetorical education fundamentally acknowledges "a future so boundlessly unfathomable" that "is beyond the human capacities of knowledge and expectation. Further, while he points to this necessary ignorance about what is to come, he also hints at a *beyond* of this epistemological limit, gesturing toward an event that is not simply unknown (as in, yet to be known), but that is in excess of knowledge itself" (123). The future-to-come pushes us against and beyond the *limit* of the known. Deliberation, as the Aristotelian legacy has proffered, avoids this limit by rhetorically engineering futures that are based on the divination of the knowable *past* in accordance with time-honored theorized presumptions: deliberation involves *human* agents who can "manipulate" language, as per the rhetor's "self-conscious" desire, eliminating any para-human influences. Further, this deliberative space is inhabited and voiced by the very "self-conscious" agents who are granted voice and who are conditioned to reproduce an "advantageous" future that will serve their interests. Reconceiving deliberation as divination tasks us with listening beyond this deliberative space to give an ear to para-human messages.

Before beginning this exploration, I foregrounded the figure of the farmer as a point of reference. Not only does the farmer engage practices of remaindering remains (manure management), the farmer lives a rural life, outside the agora, the public marketplace, the public space of deliberation and commodification of knowledge, goods, and peoples. Indeed, one might say the farmer and/as rhetoric inhabits the *pagus*, outside the polis. Victor J. Vitanza's *Negation, Subjectivity, and the History of Rhetoric* explores rhetoric and/as the *pagus* in provocative detail, arguing that such is theorized as a practice that destabilizes the polis: "The pagus . . . is the space" of "rich growth, fruitfulness, fertility; copiousness, abundance," what exceeds the dialectical machine and repression (321), which the marketplace and citizenry of the polis depends on, with its classifications and divisions that render language and subjects "Greek" or "barbarous," and, therefore, guarantee, politically, what rhetorics will be heard and granted civilized status and what bodies will be protected or otherwise recognized as "human." Oftentimes the para-human walks among us, as the one denied recognition as a "human" and as the language that is voiced but unheard. Erik Doxtader writes, "As imagined and then mythologized in the name of codifying Hellenism's homotropia, the barbarian sits at the edge of logos and the culture that it claims to sponsor. Sometimes inside and sometimes outside, the barbarian's barbarism can mark an animal or inhuman lack of language, an incompetent, gibberish-sounding performance of language, an infelicity that corrupts language's law and value, and an attack on language—a violence against the word wrought by an incomprehensible voice" ("Coming to Terms," 119). So in contrast to the traditionally conceived concept of rhetoric as the public art of deliberation (and the agora as the site of such deliberation), rhetoric reconceived via the art of divination is an art of disruption—of language, of politics—that takes place in a divine state, that helps us await rhetoric's future.

Bibliography

Aristotle. *On Rhetoric: A Theory of Civic Discourse*. Translated by George A. Kennedy. New York: Oxford University Press, 1991.

Berthin, Christine. *Gothic Hauntings: Melancholy Crypts and Textual Ghosts*. London: Palgrave, 2010.

Bowden, Hugh. *Classical Athens and the Delphic Oracle*. Cambridge, UK: Cambridge University Press, 2005.

Braude, Ann. *Radical Spirits: Spiritualism and Women's Rights in Nineteenth-Century America*. Bloomington: Indiana University Press, 2001.

Caputo, John D. *The Prayers and Tears of Jacques Derrida: Religion Without Religion*. Bloomington: Indiana University Press, 1997.

Cole, Thomas. *The Origins of Rhetoric in Ancient Greece*. Baltimore: Johns Hopkins University Press, 1995.

Davis, Diane. *Inessential Solidarity*. Pittsburgh: University of Pittsburgh Press, 2010.

Derrida, Jacques. *Cinders*. Translated by Ned Lukacher. Minneapolis: University of Minnesota Press, 2014.

———. "A Number of Yes." In *Psyche: Inventions of the Other*, vol. 2, by Jacques Derrida, edited by Peggy Kamuf and Elizabeth G. Rottenberg, 231–40. Stanford: Stanford University Press, 2008.

Doxtader, Eric. "Coming to Terms with a Declaration of Barbarous Acts." In *Re/Framing Identifications*, edited by Michelle Ballif, 116–30. Long Grove, IL: Waveland Press, 2013.

Geisler, Cheryl. "How Ought We to Understand the Concept of Agency? Report from the ARS." *Rhetoric Society Quarterly*. 34, no. 2 (2004): 9–17.

Johnston, Sarah Iles. *Ancient Greek Divination*. Malden, MA: Wiley-Blackwell, 2008.

Lundberg, Christian, and Joshua Gunn. "'Ouija Board, Are There Any Communications?' Agency, Ontotheology, and the Death of the Humanist Subject, or, Continuing the ARS Conversation." *Rhetoric Society Quarterly* 35, no. 4 (2005): 83–105.

Rollins, Brooke. *The Ethics of Persuasion: Derrida's Rhetorical Legacies*. Columbus: Ohio State University Press, 2020.

Royle, Nicholas. "Ouijamiflip." *Oxford Literary Review* 30, no. 2 (December 2008): 235–56.

Struck, Peter T. *Divination and Human Nature: A Cognitive History of Intuition in Classical Antiquity*. Princeton, NJ: Princeton University Press, 2016.

Vitanza, Victor J. *Negation, Subjectivity, and the History of Rhetoric*. New York: SUNY Press, 1996.

CHAPTER 8

Where Is the Nuclear Sovereign?

NED O'GORMAN WITH KEVIN HAMILTON

There was for a very long time—nearly three centuries—a Being so sacrosanct as to be an almost-God, immortal, invisible, and so wise as to be, in William Blackstone's phrase, "not only incapable of *doing* wrong, but even of *thinking* wrong" (qtd. in Kantorowicz, *King's Two Bodies*, 4; emphasis in the original). This Being, of course, was "a man-made irreality," a piece of "physiological fiction," in the words of one of its more recent chroniclers, Ernst Kantorowicz (4–5). For this Being was the monarch, who, according to Tudor political mysticism, had not one but *two* Bodies, one mortal and the other immortal, and—apparently—two minds, one fallible and the other infallible. The historical story told by Kantorowicz, Michel Foucault, and most recently by Eric Santner is that this "personal" Being, in the course of modernity, dissolved into an "impersonal" one (Kantorowicz, *King's Two Bodies*, 5); in the dramatic changes from royal to popular sovereignty a "new physics of power" took hold under the rise of a "disciplinary regime," such that the Two Bodies became innumerable "bodies . . . individualized by these relations [of power]" (Foucault, *Discipline and Punish*, 135–69, 192–94, 222–23; Santner, *Royal Remains*, xxi). The shift to a distributed sovereignty, and the dissolution of the monarchical Being, was basic to modernity.

Or so the story goes. Whatever we might make of it, it is obvious that the twentieth century saw something other than a distributed sovereignty. It brought new concentrations of power, for which there are no strict historical antecedents: cultlike totalitarian führerism, liquid multinational (in) corporations, the imperious veto authority of the United Nations Security Council, and the push-button power of drones. These are neither royal nor popular forms of sovereignty; they are neither Caesarist nor republican; they follow, historically speaking, alien logics and unprecedented inventions in efforts to make power global, total, and agile. As Ariella Aïsha Azoulay argues, they are *imperial*, premised on "ruling apparatuses, with minimum connection to worldly activities, which it tends to destroy or replace by extractive, productive, and computational activities required for its own operations" (*Potential History*, 388). A symbolic, epistemological, and administrative epicenter of this imperial sovereign power is *nuclear sovereignty*, the power and authority to command the use of nuclear weapons in a conflict (Bessner and Guilhot, *Decisionist Imagination*). By 1950, the terrifying emergency power of nuclear sovereignty became the force around which the world of nations was organized, each alert to that moment of procedural execution that would also be the moment of global cataclysmic destruction.

Nuclear sovereignty still organizes the world of nations. It stands as a *call*. We, each of us, are summoned to the potential terror of nuclear catastrophe. As long as this terror is deferred, it is "set apart, exclusively appropriated to some person or some special purpose"—a basic sense of the *sacred*.[1] Nuclear catastrophe is set apart from our everyday time, from worldly history, and even from the epochal events of wars, revolutions, financial crashes, and epidemics. It is a *wholly other* possibility, one that, if realized, would bring the wholly other (non)existence of nuclear annihilation. So we are called to it, to fear it, to respect it, or to willfully ignore it—but we are always called to it. And that is its "special purpose." It makes us subjects, not citizens; perpetrators or victims, not people; default survivors, not agents of care and community.

Whether this call can ever be politically legitimate remains an open question. Two recent books argue that it cannot, at least not according to the legitimizing structures of liberal democracy. Garry Wills's *Bomb Power: The Modern Presidency and the National Security State* and Elaine Scarry's *Thermonuclear Monarchy: Choosing Between Democracy and Doom* argue that nuclear sovereignty constitutes an outright violation of constitutional democracy, both legally and normatively. They conclude that at present, we—and here the pronoun "we" covers not only the citizens of the United States, but all living things on earth—live not under the power of a democracy, but under the "bomb power" of a "thermonuclear monarchy" cloaked in the shadows of a national security state.

Wills and Scarry argue that nuclear sovereignty directly compromises the two pillars of justification on which the modern nation-state is erected: solidarity and security. What kind of social cohesion is achieved through technologies of extermination? Likewise, what sort of security can be won by burning and poisoning to death millions upon millions—perhaps even billions—with an arsenal of radioactive warheads that can be launched in a matter of minutes? Nuclear weapons are not only extreme weapons. As Ned O'Gorman, Joseph Masco, and Stephen Hilgartner have argued, the rhetorical strategies used for their justification operate at the extremes of plausibility, rationality, and credulity. Still, these "ultimate weapons" continue to call us, and enjoy widespread official and ideological sanction, even in liberal democracies. As we write, nuclear proliferation is on the rise, and the United States is aggressively engaged is the process of "modernizing" its nuclear arsenal. Given the political and rhetorical contradictions of nuclear weapons, why are we forced to respond to the call of *this* sacred? Not everything carefully set apart for a special purpose, not everything sacred, should be revered. What gives?

In this essay, we suggest that it is the concept of "sovereignty" itself that has to give. What we know about sovereignty, or at least think we know, is that it is a preeminent political formulation. Thus in keeping with the grand story of modernity, political revolutions—typically, from monarchy to democracy—are believed to be essentially transformations in the nature and locus of sovereignty. Sovereignty is the fact; its configuration forms the core of the political contest. So, too, the critics of nuclear sovereignty assume that it represents a constitutional crisis because they accept as a matter of fact that nuclear sovereignty is a political formation. In this respect, critics like Wills and Scarry do not differ about the terms of the debate from those in the US Congress and courts, or the juridical and legislative regimes of the United Kingdom, Israel, Pakistan, India, France, China, and Russia. Everywhere, nuclear sovereignty, with sovereignty itself, is taken to be a political formation. The only question is whether it is a legal or legitimate political formation.

Yet it is precisely the political status of sovereignty that we question in this essay. Taking a cue from the work of Hannah Arendt, we argue that sovereignty is not a political formulation but a technological one, and that the command and control of nuclear weapons, far from being an emergency exception to the modern technics of sovereignty, is its extension. Moreover, we argue that this technological configuration is as much discursive as it is technological—a matter of the rhetorical *technê* as well as technics. For it is constituted in the organization of speech into types, identities, and loci (or typical rhetorical spaces) to create what Kenneth Burke calls an "ultimate order" (*Rhetoric of Motives*, 186–87). This ultimate order, in keeping with the very etymology of the word "hierarchy" ("sacred ruler"), is *set apart* (see 306). It consecrates not only a technological space, but a rhetorical space, a locus, differentiated from the political riffraff and reserved for the singular decision of a unitary will. And it is this space that calls us as no other.

But where is this space? *Where is the nuclear sovereign?* This is central question that drives this essay. Because our method is rhetorical-critical, we focus as much on the question—*Where is the nuclear sovereign?*—as the answer we will offer. Indeed, it is the interrogative *where?* that not only brings us to our thesis, but makes it possible. Thus we have organized this essay into four parts. First, we consider the concept of sovereignty as a techno-theological invention. Second, we turn to nuclear sovereignty, showing that the question *Where is the nuclear sovereign?*—as distinct from *who?*—is not only a crucial question to ask, but one called for by the rhetoric of nuclear sovereignty. Then, in the third part of this essay, we move into a genealogy of the nuclear sovereign. Finally, in the fourth and final section, we attempt to locate the nuclear sovereign, taking our genealogy as a clue and using a set of images to guide us. Throughout, we approach nuclear sovereignty not as a sacred "thing" but as a concept turned sacred call, one that sets us all apart for potential cataclysmic destruction.

SOVEREIGNTY: FROM POLITICAL TECHNOLOGY
TO POLITICAL THEOLOGY

Political power in Europe was for centuries dialectically caught between *potestas* (authority/right) and *potentia* (force/might). The difference between the legitimate ruler and the tyrant, classically conceived, was not that the former ruled by law and the latter by violence, but that the tyrant ruled *only* by force (Arendt, *Between the Past and the Future*, 105). The ever-present challenge before the legitimate ruler was therefore to use force judiciously, and thus keep from becoming a tyrant. But the modern theory of sovereignty, as Arendt suggested and her German intellectual opponent, Carl Schmitt, defended, took a different course: legitimate political authority was fused with a logic sociotechnical efficacy such that *potestas* was identified with *potentia* (Altini, "'Potentia'"). Thus, as early as the dawn of the eighteenth century, Giambattista Vico could complain that political theorists had turned politics into "a type of physical research" rather than a species of "practical common sense" (*On the Study Methods*, 37).

This identification, to be clear, was *rhetorical*. While it was the extension of philosophical projects, beginning with the ghost-in-the-machine metaphysics of René Descartes and fully articulated in the political philosophy of Thomas Hobbes, the fusion of political authority with effective technical regimes was not itself a metaphysical achievement, but a rhetorical one (Foucault, *Discipline and Punish*, 136). Under this rhetorical regime, there is no final dialectical tension between right and might. As the political realist Hans Morgenthau wrote just after World War II, as though it were a mere matter of fact, "Power may comprise anything that establishes and maintains the control of man over man. Thus power covers all social relationships, which serve that end, from physical violence to the most subtle psychological ties by which one mind controls another" (*Politics*, 1). Less than a decade later, the progressive sociologist C. Wright Mills could declare with equal matter-of-factness, "All politics is a struggle for power; the ultimate kind of power is violence" (*Power Elite*, 171). For both men, despite their significant philosophical and political differences, political power is essentially and ultimately coercive power.

"Sovereignty" is the concept under which this fusion took form. Under conditions of European modernization, politics was rendered "sovereign" by rhetorically regulating and orienting the concepts of individual and collective freedom, power, and judgment toward the efficacious command of a unitary will. The sovereign, to summarize Hobbes (*Leviathan*), is he who not only has the right to command, but the power to do so. This rhetorical project, as Jean Bethke Elshtain argues, was embedded in the language of theology and the sacred. Sovereignty was set apart from the mundane, made otherworldly, clothed in theocentric concepts of power that transformed the sovereign from the holder of but one discrete medieval office to "something mystical and expansive" that becomes in modernity "a corporate personality, or source of will, which gave the body politic its identity"

(*Sovereignty*, 62). Thus in the twentieth century Schmitt (*Political Theology*) would summon what he called "political theology" (*politische Theologie*) to revivify a theory of sovereignty that was essentially Hobbesian. For Schmitt, as for Hobbes, sacred rhetoric was central, then as now, to validating the technical rationalization of political rule in the concept of sovereignty.

This sacred rhetoric rests on a semantic structure. Formal semanticists remind us that questions and assertions are complementary: "If we did not have any questions, we would not have any need for assertions either," write the logicians Jeroen Groenendijk and Martin Stokhof ("Studies," 6). The composition of our questions is correlated with the construction of our assertions. Within theories of sovereignty since the sixteenth century, there has been an ongoing tension between assertions that answer the question *where*? and those that answer the question *who*? According to the etymology, the sovereign "super-reigns," a construct that makes the locus of the sovereign preeminent. Thus sovereignty is traditionally understood as "the highest, legally independent, underived power" in a polity (17). Moreover, we find in the early modern conception of sovereignty another locus, encoded in the 1648 Treaty of Westphalia, where the concept of sovereignty means "supreme authority *within a territory*" (Philpott, "Sovereignty"; emphasis added). Therefore, the sovereign is spatially defined in three dimensions: the sovereign reigns at once above and across.

But *who* is this sovereign? As Daniel Bessner and Nicolas Guilhot argue, this became the central question of the "decisionist" logic of the twentieth-century nuclear sovereignty (*Decisionist Imagination*, 7). For the hereditary monarchies of old, for whom the Treaty of Westphalia was written, the answer to the *who*? question was a matter of tradition and, as Kantorowicz stresses, theology. The sovereign was he who inherited the throne under the auspices of divine right. The democratic and republican revolutions of the eighteenth century, by contrast, made "the people" sovereign and, in the theory of Rousseau (*Social Contract*), nearly divine. Henceforth, *who*? assumed a preeminent place in the rhetoric of modern sovereignty, such that "Who decides?" became the decisive political question (Bessner and Guilhot, *Decisionist Imagination*, 7).

Or did it? Schmitt argued that *where*? remained the constitutive question of sovereignty. For the "problem" of sovereignty, Schmitt argued, is not strictly "legal" in character—it is "actual" (*Dialogues*, 18). It is not just a matter of *potestas* but of *potentia*. As the political theologian Oliver O'Donovan writes, echoing this insight, "Political organization and authority is founded, only partly but necessarily, on political *power*, and *political power is founded on power over nature*. If the ink in the dictator's pen won't flow when he wants to sign the decree, if his gun powder won't explode, if his military jeep won't start or the radio fails when he wants to broadcast, then his dictatorship will come to a humiliating end" (*Desire*, 94; emphasis added). Thus, Schmitt argues, "the connection of actual power with the legally highest power is the fundamental problem of the concept of sovereignty" (*Dialogues*, 18). Law must be correlated with power to be effectual.

For Schmitt, the reconciliation of legal power and actual power was codified in the concept of the "state of exception" (*Ausnahmezustand*), a crisis wherein a leader suspends the rule of law in order to effectively serve the higher interests of the state. In his book *Dictatorship*, Schmitt traces the state of exception to the older "public right of exception" where "whoever is in command is allowed to deviate from the *ius commune* [common law] in a case of emergency, in the interests of the maintenance of the state and of public tranquility and security" (12–13). *Who* is in command, of course, depends on the already established legal order. Thus, for Schmitt, the state of exception is not a state of pure lawlessness: rather, it is a location wherein whoever is in command stands in relation to the law, even as he stands above it. As Schmitt writes, "Although he stands outside the normally valid legal system, he nevertheless belongs to it, for it is he who must decide whether the constitution needs to be suspended in its entirety" (*Political Theology*, 7). Giorgio Agamben stresses the paradoxical position of the sovereign as described by Schmitt: it is "defined by the oxymoron" of "ecstasy-belonging" where the sovereign stands outside the law while being of it (*State of Exception*, 35). The sovereign, to allude to the biblical phrase (John 17:14), is *of* the law, but not *in* it.

What of democracies? Schmitt concludes that from a "liberal constitutional point of view," the "most guidance the constitution can provide is to indicate *who* can act in such a case" (*Political Theology*, 7; emphasis added). Jean Bodin (1530–1596), whom Schmitt considers the first great theorist of the concept of sovereignty, ties himself in knots trying to show how sovereignty can (and must) be undivided and univocal, and yet can be "popular" (*l'estat populaire*, sometimes translated "democratic"). In a popular government, "the people" are sovereign, but where is the sovereignty of the people? In the "majority," a kind of quasi-definable and countable space. Hobbes is at least clearer about the matter. By emphasizing the concept of the "contract"—a means whereby one's right is surrendered or given to another—Hobbes is able to show how Bodin's insistence on an indivisible sovereignty might be worked out in a world of many individuals, as individuals are, through the contract, able to "transfer" their right "for some other good" (*Leviathan*, 93).

Yet here the word "transfer" also suggests a spatial logic—for Hobbes, even geometric—of sovereignty: it is strictly a matter of one's locus within a contractual schema. At the same time, Hobbes's claim is not fully absolutist, for the political subject, he argues, can never give up his [*sic*] first natural right, the right to preserve and protect his own life and to "do anything which, in his own judgment and reason, he shall conceive to be the aptest means thereunto" (91). That is, there is one right that is immovable, the right to self-protection. So, even as Hobbes is able to conceive of sovereignty geometrically, his political geometry breaks down at the point of the individual, a *who* whose right to self-protection cannot be moved or transferred. Arguably it is not until Rousseau that we get a concept of sovereignty that clearly distinguishes between, and clearly keeps separate, the who and the where. Ironically, while Rousseau is known as a proponent of the sovereignty of the people, his solution to the problem of sovereignty is strictly an answer to the question *where?* The sovereignty of the people is *in* the "general will," an impersonal, indivisible, secular yet sacred space that authorizes the administrative and legislative functions of government.

In this Rousseauian view, when Americans assemble every four years to elect a president, they are, among other things, deciding who can stand in the oxymoronic space of ecstasy-belonging. It is no wonder that modern, democratic sovereignty is clothed in the ritual, pomp, and ceremony that Foucault, for one, associates with early modern monarchical sovereignty (*Discipline and Punish*, 50, 217). Indeed, for Bodin, Hobbes, Rousseau, and Schmitt alike, the sovereign is a virtual god who both is constituted by, and in a certain sense constitutes, the political system only as he stands above it and apart from it. This is the essence of the political theology of sovereignty.

However, Schmitt further argues that from a *technical* standpoint, *sovereignty is not oxymoronic at all*. In the opening pages of *Dictatorship* Schmitt draws on Machiavelli to retrieve what he describes as the means-end technical approach to governing encompassed within the concept of "dictatorship." In a dictatorship, "political technology" is not a matter of mere "technicity," or engineering society for the tautological sake of engineering society. Rather, in a dictatorship, techniques and technologies are deployed as particular means meant to achieve particular ends within the contingencies of "concrete circumstances" (6). Thus Schmitt describes dictatorship as an instrumental art: "Because a concrete goal should be accomplished, the dictator has to intervene in the course of action through a concrete means—and has to do it directly" (7–8). In an "extreme case," this may necessitate, Schmitt argues, that the dictator "has the capacity to not obey general norms" but rather "is entitled to do everything that is appropriate to the actual circumstances" (8). What is significant about Schmitt's theory of dictatorship here is that it is identical with both his theory of the "state of exception" and of "sovereignty" *and yet, from the technical standpoint, lacks any oxymoronic capacity whatsoever.* For Schmitt, dictatorship is straightforward, as "the content of the actions of the dictator consists in this: achieving a certain goal, 'accomplishing': the enemies should be defeated, the political opponents nullified or destroyed" (7). For Schmitt, dictatorship is the height of political technology, properly understood.

A close reading of Schmitt reveals a political theory that is a political technology first and a political theology only secondarily. Schmitt (in *Political Theology*) accepts the fundamental "technical" nature of the modern state: it is a mechanism of power, as much as a turbine is. But he also insists on the logically necessary *personal* nature of rule in the modern state— unlike Locke and Rousseau, he will not allow for impersonal or general forms of rule (13–14). This is because political power for Schmitt must be not only legal and actual, but also decisional (*Dezisionismus*)—rooted in decisive acts of a person or persons. In addressing the subject of sovereignty, therefore, his *Political Theology* tacks back and forth between *where* and *who*. Political theology here is for Schmitt a project of rhetorical retrieval, a mode of re-enchantment. As Atlmann, Schmitt's fictional persona, states in Schmitt's late work, "Dialogue on New Space," "As I see it, unencumbered technology encloses the humans more than it opens new spaces to them. . . . The one who manages to restrain the unencumbered technology, to bind it and lead it into a concrete order has given more of an answer to the contemporary call than the one who, by means of modern technology sees to land on the moon or Mars. The binding of the unencumbered technology—that, for example, would be the labor of a new Hercules" (*Dialogues on Power and Space*, 80). And so, the sovereign Being returns, not in Christological form (as with the King's Two Bodies) but in the mythic figure of Herculean contradictions. Sovereignty appears here, as in European history—both domestic and imperial (Azoulay, *Potential History*)—as a political technology, a "solution" to crises and conflicts. At each step in the evolution of sovereignty, power is not only rationalized, it is ritualized and indeed sanctified. It takes on a political-theological character. Sovereignty thus emerges at the nexus of state technology and state theology.

Arendt argues that far from being a chapter in political history proper, the emergence of the concept of sovereignty should be understood as a crucial episode in the anti-political project of European modernity. Arendt saw in sovereignty a notion that was "most pernicious and dangerous" to politics, for it set up an equation where "the freedom of one man, or a group, or a body politic can be purchased only at the price of the freedom, i.e., the sovereignty, of all others" (*Between Past and Future*, 164). Indeed, that is what sovereignty was created to do: to "settle" conflicts among persons and parties, the concept of sovereignty constructed an absolute before which all others must submit. Arendt (in *On Revolution*) argued that sovereignty entails not only this absolute right, but the prerogative to execute it—a right to omnipotence. However, she replied, "under the condition of human plurality"—which is, after all, a most basic fact of the human condition—power "can never amount to omnipotence, and laws residing on human power can never be absolute" (29). Indeed, she argued, "the absolute . . . spells doom to everyone when it is introduced into the political realm" (74). Political doom is the death knell that reverberates through the concept of sovereignty; in nuclear sovereignty this ominous sound calls us to not only our political doom, but species doom.

THE LOCUS OF SOVEREIGNTY

The nuclear sovereign, a person vested with the power to use a thing to destroy billions of things, could never claim moral legitimacy, for no moral calculus could justify the power to destroy moral existence as we know it. The same holds for political legitimacy, Arendt argues (*Human Condition*, 1–4). No politics can justify the destruction of all politics. Indeed, nuclear sovereignty emerged not because it was constitutionally or politically justified, but because it was technologically feasible. More precisely, it was *architecturally* feasible. The Greek word *arkhitektôn* can denote a chief-builder, as the etymology suggests (from *arkhi-* "chief" + *tektôn* "builder"); it can also, with little stretching, denote the "founding" or originary builder, as *archê* is both the "beginning" and the "head" or "chief." In the 1940s in the liberal, constitutional, and democratic United States it became feasible to build a new founding technology that put the fate of all peoples within the power of one person to determine. As the clock in figure 8.1 suggests, the nuclear sovereign is a locus—a location, a site, a definable space within a broader architecture. That locus in Latin can also mean a rank, a position, or a seat of power within an institutional architecture is important to remember, as is the fact that loci in rhetoric are means of ordering discourse. In the United States, according to the stereotypical formula, the locus of the nuclear sovereign is occupied by he or she who holds the rank of the president. Elsewhere—in the United Kingdom, in Israel, in India—it is possessed by a prime minister. But the nuclear sovereign is not identical with the president or prime minister. This space is a rhetorical location—it does not exist physically but discursively. But it is not just one space among many, one mode of presidential power among others. In step with the cor-relation of political authority with physical power in modernity, this space is rhetorically set apart as an inner sanctum of power.

But *where is this space*? Or, *where is the nuclear sovereign*? This is what we want to further investigate. *Pace* Wills and Scarry, we suggest that the prob-lem of nuclear sovereignty is better interrogated as we explore the domain of the rhetoric of technology, rather than that of law or political theory—and that the latter are but ways of consecrating a domain of technology. This is the other meaning of the clock in figure 8.1: the nuclear sovereign is not only a rhetorical location, but one that is reflected technologically in the architecture and infrastructure of "the physical devices of technical perfor-mance" and their corresponding norms and methods of human interaction (Winner, *Autonomous Technology*, 11). As Ariella Azoulay argues, modern sovereignty is imperial sovereignty, and imperial sovereignty is organized as "a technology" of accumulation, exploitation, and, above all, destruction (*Potential History*, 387–88).

When we come to the question of nuclear sovereignty in the United States, it is fair to say that the *where* question is not so much confused with the *who* question, but habitually subsumed to it. Perhaps this is because the

FIG. 8.1   Clock in the Situation Room. Courtesy Wikimedia Commons (Pete Souza).

where question is surprisingly difficult to answer, and for a number of reasons. In order to give shape to our question (*Where is the nuclear sovereign?*) let us reflect on the difficulties of answering it. We will use this space of reflection to delve deeper into the locus of nuclear sovereignty, where locus is finally understood rhetorically as a discursive space.

From the perspective of formal semantics, our question is strained from the start, for it takes "the sovereign," a concrete entity, a *who*, and makes it the subject of a *where* question. We are asking *where* is a *who*? Such a question, it would seem, would presuppose the identity of the *who*. And yet the priority of the *who* is precisely what we aim to suspend, even upend, *even as* we want to suggest that the proper question is *Where is the nuclear sovereign?* not *Where is nuclear sovereignty?* In short, we want to locate an entity without presupposing the identity of that entity.

A second reason that answering our question is difficult is the inescapably personal and historical character of nuclear sovereignty more generally. *Nuclear* sovereignty, unlike perhaps *sovereignty* as such, is a definitive historical phenomenon, the product of persons acting amid very particular historical eventualities. Therefore, we are drawn, even compelled, to consider nuclear sovereignty in terms of persons. And yet while answering the question *Where is the nuclear sovereign?* can gain significant traction by pointing to a particular, historical governing official, it cannot be sufficiently answered in this way. The sovereign entity we are concerned with here is more than a person, or even a succession of persons. In asking our question, we are not just looking for a specific historical person; we are not even looking for "the sovereign" per se. Rather we are looking a person bearing a peculiar sovereign aspect, nuclear sovereignty—and thus we are thrust back into the concept of sovereignty, a concept that has a locus, a location.

This then brings us to a third reason our question is hard to answer: the common habits of talking about "the nuclear sovereign" within American political culture. As this is the messiest reason, but also potentially the most fruitful to consider, we want to reflect on it at a bit more length. Within American political culture we do not tend to ask *Where is the nuclear sovereign?* because it seems counterintuitive; it violates the rules of a language game, so to speak. In filling out the statement "The nuclear sovereign is . . ." we tend toward a name and/or a title to which a name is attached: "The nuclear sovereign is Barack Obama," or "President Trump," or simply "the president." As Hillary Clinton's 2008 presidential campaign recognized with its "It's 3:00 a.m." ad, the question of *Where is the nuclear sovereign?* seems pointless:

> It's 3:00 a.m. and your children are safe and asleep [image of a barely lit suburban home that transitions to a sequence of images of children asleep in bed as dramatic music plays]. But there's a phone in the White House and it's ringing [sound of phone ringing]. Something's happening in the world. Your vote will decide who answers that call [more poorly lit images of children sleeping at night], whether it is someone who already knows the world's leaders, knows the military, someone tested and ready to lead in a dangerous world. It's 3:00 a.m. and your children are safe and asleep [image of mother entering a child's bedroom at night]: who do you want answering the phone? [crescendo of music; image of Hillary Clinton talking on a white phone].

For obvious political reasons, the ad asked *who?* "Who do you want answering the phone?" "Your vote will decide *who* answers that call." But it also assumes that the answer to the question *where?* is an obvious one: the White House. In the United States, the White House, or the Office of the Presidency, is a ready answer to the question *Where is the nuclear sovereign?* This is the case even if we take the "White House" as a synecdoche, as most viewers of this ad surely did in some way. But while there is a kind of commonsense accuracy to this answer, it is not quite adequate to the complexity contained in the question. Answering *Where is the nuclear sovereign?* with "the White House" does not do justice to the question, even if we take the White House as a synecdoche for the Office of the Presidency more generally. The question can, and in our context here should, take us further than that.

This is not to say that the question of the Clinton ad, *who?* should be played down. Indeed, the question of *who?* might end up telling us something about *where?* Take the documentary *Countdown to Zero*, directed by Lucy Walker. It captures well the predominance of the complement *who* in our questions about the nuclear sovereign, but it also suggests something of how we might need to scratch beneath the *who* and find a *where*, a location. A pivotal clip in the film begins with images of presumably nuclear-armed missiles being fitted on military airplanes as an off-screen narrator is heard saying "We estimate that there are about 23,000 nuclear weapons now in the world, still." The screen then shifts to the expert himself as he continues: "The good news is that there used to be 60,000, so we've cut those arsenals by more than half. But we in the United States still have about 1,500 hydrogen bombs on missiles poised for launch in fifteen minutes or less. The *really* bad news is the Russians have the same." The film transitions to the sight and sound of a missile in launch, as another expert is heard off-screen saying, "If the Russians fired missiles at the United States, the first warning would come from satellites and they could detect the flame from the booster rocket within seconds, easily within a minute." The screen turns to images of NORAD, the early warning detection center used by the United States and Canada, as the off-screen expert continues: "Suddenly this early warning hub in the United States would become very frenzied to try to figure out whether this is a false alarm or whether this is a real attack, and determine this within sixty seconds." An image of a digital clock counting down from sixty seconds appears on-screen, to the sound of ominous music, as the off-screen expert explains, "The president would receive a briefing from the duty officer at Strategic Air Command headquarters." The expert then appears on-screen and continues: "That briefing of the president of his response options and their consequences has to be delivered in as little as thirty seconds [a ticking stopwatch fills the screen]. The president normally would have no more than twelve minutes to make a decision and maybe as little as ten seconds." The voice of Jimmy Carter then cuts into the film with a still image of him on the phone in the Oval Office. Carter, who soon appears on-screen speaking to the camera, states, "I knew that if the Soviets did launch an attack that it would take twenty-six minutes for an ICBM to leave Russian soil and land in Washington or New York, and I had that much time to decide how to respond." The stopwatch appears again on-screen, and the voice of Mikhail Gorbachev, speaking Russian, is heard as the subtitles read, "Every minute we were on guard, ready to strike back." Gorbachev, now on-screen, continues: "We would have to make a decision, upon receiving a report that missiles were flying toward us, and only a few minutes left."

Given the urgency of the situation, and the shortness of time, so dramatically rendered in *Countdown to Zero*, it would seem that it all comes down to *who*? Would you rather have Jimmy Carter at the phone, or Richard Nixon? John Kennedy or Ronald Reagan? Hillary Clinton or Donald Trump? Such questions, such decisions, are not inconsequential. Nor are they inconsequential with regard to the composition of questions about the nuclear sovereign. When we now say, "Jimmy Carter was the president of the United States," we offer an answer to a vital, potentially world-historical question *Who was the nuclear sovereign*? It is a commonplace of American rhetorical culture to want to answer this question with a name. And this name suggests that the location of the nuclear sovereign is in a person. The name of the president of the United States speaks both to the personal location of nuclear sovereignty, and can function metonymically as the part in which the whole complex of nuclear sovereignty is concentrated, such that we can answer the question *Where is the nuclear sovereign*? with a *who*. At the time of this writing, the nuclear sovereign is where Donald Trump is. *Who* would seem to be the essential interrogative, if not the only interrogative of consequence.

But is this so? Lurking in this *who* is the stubborn and distinct question of *where*?—for strictly speaking, the president of the United States is the "holder," as the US Constitution puts it, of the Office of the President. This office is constituted legally and has the form of legally bound duties. But in speaking of "legally bound," or bounded, duties, we are entering a space, even if it is an abstract legal space. So we are presented with the question of *where?* even in asking *who?* Indeed, in answering the question of nuclear sovereignty with "the President," we are in fact presupposing an answer to the question *where?* We are assuming a legal locus. Therefore, Wills, Scarry, and others have devoted considerable effort to showing how, in the words of Scarry, "the United States Constitution outlaws nuclear weapons" (*Thermonuclear Monarchy*, 29). And so we arrive again at the Office of the Presidency.

Our argument, however, is that in fact we cannot find the nuclear sovereign within a legal locus, or even an extralegal but recognizably political location. We will have to find the nuclear sovereign elsewhere. Thus the remainder of this essay will suggest that we cannot, in fact, find the nuclear sovereign in law, or even in political theory. Then we will argue that the nuclear sovereign is a locus *of*, but not *in*, technology.

A PECULIAR SOVEREIGNTY

The nuclear sovereign is an entity. Nuclear sovereignty is a concept. Can we say that one is prior to other? Does the entity depend on the concept? Or is the concept derived from the entity? This is another way of asking, if we were to construct a genealogy of the nuclear sovereign, where would we begin? We begin with the concept of sovereignty more generally. Schmitt and others, as we have seen, locate the advent of the modern theory of sovereignty in the works of the sixteenth-century French jurist Bodin. We accept the locus and consider its implications.

Schmitt notes that Bodin asked, "To what extent is the sovereign bound to laws, and to what extent is he responsible to the estates?" Bodin's answer, Schmitt tells us, was qualified. In general, the sovereign is bound to law, but in emergencies, the sovereign is freed from such conventional boundaries. Schmitt writes, "The decisive point about Bodin's concept is that by referring to the emergency, he reduced his analysis of the relationships between prince and estates to a simple either/or. This is what is truly impressive in his definition of sovereignty: by considering sovereignty to be indivisible, he finally settled the question of power in the state. His scholarly accomplishment and the basis for his success thus reside in his having incorporated the *decision* into the concept of sovereignty" (*Political Theology*, 8; emphasis added). And here in the decision to leave the boundaries of law for an exceptional, indivisible space—a space itself of decision—is found, according to Schmitt, the core of the modern theory of sovereignty. "Sovereign is he who decides on the exception," Schmitt memorably writes. But he could have written "Sovereign is he who can cross the boundaries of law into an exceptional space." Indeed, when he writes of the sovereign standing "outside the normally valid legal system" (7), or when he claims, "The definition of sovereignty must therefore be associated with the borderline case, and not with routine" (5), he says as much.

What is significant here in thinking about the genealogy of the nuclear sovereign is not only its spatial logic but its sacred logic. Bodin relies heavily on a late medieval spatial logic, where two loci are put into relation, one "ordinary" (*oridinatas*)—a space of *routine*, as Schmitt puts it—and the other "extraordinary" (*extra, oridinatas*)—a space of pure *decision*, in Schmittian language. This pure decision would not be the decision to make an "exception," which is at the "borderline," but a space set apart and completely outside the ordinary order, which in late medieval theology can only be a kind of space of pure decision associated with God.

Now, let us fast forward to the advent of *nuclear* sovereignty. Unlike the concept of sovereignty more generally, nuclear sovereignty, as we have suggested, has an acute *historical* aspect, connected to the work of physicists, engineers, politicians, and industry in the 1930s and 1940s. One consequence of this history is that nuclear power, a physical power, set in motion the political history of nuclear sovereignty. If, in modernity, political authority has been conflated with physical force, then it is not surprising to find at the base of a nuclear sovereignty the discovery of a physical force. What may be surprising, however, are the particularities of that sovereignty, specifically the fact that the *concept* of nuclear sovereignty has its roots in a quite unique and extraordinary space.

In October 1941 America's pioneering atomic weapons research and development program was moved from the supervision of Vannevar Bush's Office of Scientific Research and Development (which had been established earlier that year, in June 1941, by executive order) to the military command and control of the Army Corps of Engineers, where it became the Manhattan Engineer District under the command of General Leslie Groves. The Army Corps of Engineers had numerous such "districts," tied to specific geographical regions and activities. The Manhattan Engineer District was different in this respect, as it was *not* tied to any particular geographical region. Rather, the district subsumed a comprehensive array of activities and operations at a myriad of locations. It was also different in that it became, for all intents and purposes, a juridical province that functioned, under the auspices of state secrecy, apart from congressional oversight or judicial review. It was thus a doubly deterritorialized space: geographically boundless (Gen. Groves even used his authority to send spies into Europe, and it was he who was the military authority behind the atomic bombing of Japan), but also de facto free from legislative and judicial accountability. As Richard Rhodes chronicles, Herbert Mark, aide to Undersecretary of State Dean Acheson, described the Manhattan District as "a separate state, with its own airplanes and its own factories and its thousands of secrets." "It had," he continued in state-of-emergency language par excellence, "a peculiar sovereignty, one that could bring about the end, peacefully or violently, of all other sovereignties" (*Making*, 277).

Thus the Manhattan Project began as military state within a civil state made possible by a state of emergency. Nuclear sovereignty here began as an extraordinary space—not *in* an extraordinary space, but *as* one. But this is not to say that *the* nuclear sovereign was found there, too. In looking for the nuclear sovereign, we are looking for the entity, not the concept. The Manhattan Engineer District, as a kind of state within a state, created a concept of nuclear sovereignty as an extraordinary, supra-constitutional operational space. But this concept was not realized in the sovereign, as it was willfully qualified by its subservience to the interests, if not the laws, of the United States. In this sense, the Manhattan District was less as a state within a state and more a colony of the United States, created to serve national interests.

President Harry Truman's decision to drop atomic bombs on Hiroshima and Nagasaki in the summer of 1945 might constitute the first chapter in the history of the nuclear sovereign. But the legal location from which he made this decision is exceedingly difficult to place. Indeed, the subsequent history of legislation about atomic weapons, beginning with the Atomic Energy Act of 1946, can be read as an ongoing effort to locate the nuclear sovereign within law. But as Wills argues, this effort has had dubious results at best:

In the case of nuclear attack on the United States, the President would not have time to consult Congress or instruct the public. He must respond instantly—which means that he must have the whole scientific apparatus for response on constant alert, accountable only to him. If, on the other hand, a danger to our allies or our necessary assets is posed, calling for a nuclear initiative on his part, he cannot issue a warning ahead of time without alerting the enemy. . . . The nature of the presidency was irrevocably altered by this grant of a unique power. There the president's permanent alert means our permanent submission. He became, mainly, the Commander in Chief, since he could loose the whole military force of the nation at any moment. (*Bomb Power*, 46–47)

The nuclear sovereign, that is, cannot be located within the constitutional parameters of presidential power. The locus of the nuclear sovereign, wherever it is, is so unequivocal, so unqualified, so absolute, as to defy any constitutional parameters—and this for fundamentally technological reasons, having to do with the calculation of *time* and *physical power*. It is no wonder legislative attempts to bound the nuclear sovereign have been ineffective, and have functioned instead as forms of assent to an intractable technological logic seemingly necessitated by the sheer physical power and speed of nuclear weapons.

OPERA AD EXTRA

If there is any political logic at work at all here, it would seem to have to be that of political absolutism. But not even theories of political absolutism can construct a space for the *nuclear* sovereign. The early modern and modern doctrines of "necessity"—connected to "emergency"—have since the sixteenth century been predicated on *the primacy of the preservation*, or survival, of the state. It goes without saying that the political history of nuclear weapons has rendered this predication ludicrous. While we still find the nuclear sovereign *somewhere*, it is not within the loci of political theory, not even absolutist theories.

Nevertheless, theories of political absolutism do provide us with a critical clue as to the location of the nuclear sovereign. Here we want to consider an image suggested in Bodin. According to Schmitt, Bodin identifies sovereignty with the capacity for absolute, indivisible decision, but this decisionism assumes, we must not forget, the capacity to act, and act *effectually*, to bring about what one decides (this is the sense of "law" Bodin holds). In this way, Bodin distinguishes between "the sovereign and the government." The former decides and commands; the latter executes the decision and obeys. Thus for Bodin there is on one level sovereign power, and on another, subordinate level, government, which one commentator has aptly described as "the machine through which the sovereign operates" (Tooley, "Introduction," 31). The sovereign, that is, is a kind of absolute operator of the vast machinery of government.

This is the archetypal image, we want to argue, of the nuclear sovereign. And it tells us where to look. Two Cold War presidential images set the stage for us here. Here (see fig. 8.2) we have President Dwight Eisenhower

FIG. 8.2 President Eisenhower pushing the button. Courtesy Oak Ridge National Laboratory (photographer unknown).

pushing the button at the UN's first International Conference on Peaceful Uses of Atomic Energy in Geneva, Switzerland, held in 1955. Note his hand, which extends angularly from his forearm to rest, ever so gingerly, on the button in the middle of a compact control panel. The president's finger is exerting pressure—a subtle gesture of physiological power, which at Geneva in 1955 initiated an electromechanical process whereby an electronic signal was sent through a snake of wires from the control panel, across a floor space, to a mechanism that would activate a reactor and ignite a nuclear chain reaction. Was this an act of sovereignty? Have we, at last, found the nuclear sovereign *here*?

Ignore for the moment that he is pushing a button that starts a nuclear reactor rather than launches a nuclear weapon and consider instead Eisenhower's slouching shoulders. Consider the way his eyes seem to be straining to recognize which button to push. Consider the way the white-coated technician stands over him, microphone in hand, narrating the president's actions to the audience present, and perhaps offering guidance to the sovereign on exactly how to navigate the control panel. And consider the cadre of suited men in the backdrop, looking down, half amused. It is safe to say that we have not found the nuclear sovereign here. Rather, we have found the president performing the part, indeed the caricature, of the nuclear operator. In fact, after this particular stunt, the Oak Ridge National Laboratory named Eisenhower an "honorary reactor operator" (Kertesz, "Project Aquarium," 32).

But it is not only the stunt aspect of this scene that keeps it from being the space of the nuclear sovereign. It is that Eisenhower is here integrated *into* an operation. The operator we see here does not stand *outside* the operation, but rather *within* it, as a component within a larger system of action and reaction. That is to say—to push the point a bit further—while we colloquially refer to the nuclear sovereign "pushing the button," the act of literally pushing a button is an act that deconstructs nuclear sovereignty. For nuclear sovereignty, the powerful fiction goes, is *indivisible*. Button pushing, on the other hand, can be powerful only within a system of divisible parts. Its call is integrated, not set apart. Technological systems and the socioeconomic systems on which they depend, Don K. Price argued in his 1965 work *The Scientific Estate*, result in the "diffusion of sovereignty" (57). Langdon Winner suggests in his influential *Autonomous Technology* from 1978 that technology indeed puts political power and authority on a "new foundation" (138), one that might challenge Bodin's and Schmitt's notion of the indivisibility of sovereignty.

However, we find in the nuclear sovereign the persistence of the notion of the indivisibility of sovereignty, and the apogee of the Bodinian image of the sovereign as the absolute operator *outside and over* the machinery of government. The reason we do not find the nuclear sovereign *at* the control panel is because this would place the sovereign *within* technology. In Tayloristic fashion, such operations as pushing buttons and reading dials divides labor into routines of actions and reaction. But sovereignty, Schmitt writes, is not "routine" (*Political Theology*, 5). And indeed, the *rhetoric* of nuclear sovereignty has since Truman persistently worked to position the nuclear sovereign outside technology and its routines. It is set apart.

Here we come to our second image, George Tames's "The Loneliest Job in the World" (fig. 8.3). It is an image intimately associated with the Cuban Missile Crisis, though it was shot and published in the *New York Times Magazine* some six months before the showdown with Soviet premier Nikita Khrushchev. Despite this anachronism, if there is an image of the nuclear sovereign in American collective memory, this is it. The question

FIG. 8.3 "The Loneliest Job in the World." President John F. Kennedy in the Oval Office, February 10, 1961. Courtesy George Tames / The New York Times / Redux.

is not only why do we find the nuclear sovereign *here*, but where is "here"? With respect to the latter question, we do not want to dismiss the literal answer, the Oval Office. Rather, we want to ask why the Oval Office can function as a symbolically charged site of nuclear sovereignty, whereas the operator's seat at the control panel at the 1955 Geneva Convention cannot.

To pursue this question to its conclusion we want to consider a mid-1960s Air Force film production, *SAC Command Post*. The history of this film is elusive, but it seems to have been commissioned in response to the Hollywood films *Dr. Strangelove* and *Fail-Safe*, both of which vividly questioned nuclear sovereignty by challenging—comically and tragically, respectively—the effectual power of presidential control over America's nuclear weapons. *SAC Command Post* entails a documentary response to such challenges to the nuclear sovereign.

SAC Command Post (fig. 8.4) visually features the complex network of surveillance, communications, and weaponry devices that constitute Strategic Air Command operations. Narratively, it stresses the hierarchical system of command and control, spanning from the pilots, bombardiers, and missileers on the bottom to the president on the top. This narrative insists that nuclear weapons are exclusively under presidential control and will be used only at presidential command. And yet the visual and narrative dimensions of the film collaborate to make a crucial claim about the location of the nuclear sovereign. For there is in the film an *inverse relationship* between the number and complexity of buttons, dials, indicator lights, and so on before the film's actors and their level of authority. At the top of this technological hierarchy sits the image of the buttonless telephone (figs. 8.5 and 8.6), which is, relative to the complex interfaces of SAC, a kind of primitive technology, a simple two-way line of communication, akin—technologically speaking—to the tin-can phones we tried to make as children.

Now consider the image of Kennedy in the Oval Office (fig. 8.3). Seen in light of the massively dense technological networks that constitute America's nuclear weapons system, this image is noteworthy for its technological minimalism. We have only one identifiable machine in the frame, and it is set off to the side, like a curiosity. This technological minimalism, we would argue, constitutes the locus of the nuclear sovereign, which is solitary, contemplative, univocal, interior, invisible, indivisible.

FIG. 8.4 Emergency Action Console. Still taken from *US Air Force Special Film Project 1236,* *"SAC Command Post."* Courtesy US National Archives and Records Administration, Motion Pictures Unit, Record Group 342.

FIG. 8.5 Buttonless telephone #1. Still taken from *US Air Force Special Film Project 1236, "SAC Command Post."* Courtesy US National Archives and Records Administration, Motion Pictures Unit, Record Group 342.

FIG. 8.6 Buttonless telephone #2. Still taken from *US Air Force Special Film Project 1236, "SAC Command Post."* Courtesy US National Archives and Records Administration, Motion Pictures Unit, Record Group 342.

That is, *Where is the nuclear sovereign?* In an indivisible locus of decision, a rhetorical space that is as *invisible* as it is indivisible because it is inward and immediate. It is a locus located without the system, above the network, off the charts, even as systems, networks, and charts represent its conditions of possibility. The president, "wherever he is" (as the movie *SAC Command Post* states), moves into the space of the nuclear sovereign when the president moves out of technology and into an invisible and unchartable space of decision. In this way, the nuclear sovereign is a locus—the creature of a technological and rhetorical architecture. The nuclear sovereign is an assertion that answers a *where?* question. And it is a locus *of* technology, constituted technologically rather than politically, possible only against, or rather *above*, a technological order. But it is not therefore located *in* technology. It is a space, to use the parlance of late medieval nominalism, of the *opera ad extra*, the work "from without." Schmitt writes of the sovereign, "Although he stands outside the normally valid legal system, he nevertheless belongs to it, for it is he who must decide whether the constitution needs to be suspended in its entirety" (*Political Theology*, 7). The *nuclear sovereign*, we argue, occupies an analogous technological space—the nuclear sovereign is a locus that stands outside the routines of the nuclear weapons systems, even as the nuclear sovereign belongs to it—for it is the nuclear sovereign who must decide whether and how it must be loosed, and where and for whom time will stop. And so, we are all summoned.

Note

1. *Oxford English Dictionary*, s.v. "sacred, *adj.* and *n.*" Accessed July 21, 2020. https://www.oed.com/view/Entry/169556.

Bibliography

Agamben, Giorgio. *State of Exception.* Translated by Kevin Attell. Chicago: University of Chicago Press, 2005.

Air Force Audio Visual Service, 1365th Photo Squadron. *US Air Force Special Film Project 1236, "SAC Command Post."* Washington, DC: National Security Archive, n.d. https://archive.org/details/AirForceSpecialFilmProject1236sacComnandPost.

Altini, Carlo. "'Potentia' as 'potestas': An Interpretation of Modern Politics Between Thomas Hobbes and Carl Schmitt." *Philosophy and Social Criticism* 36, no. 2 (2010): 231–52.

Arendt, Hannah. *Between Past and Future: Eight Exercises in Political Thought.* New York: Penguin, 1993.

———. *The Human Condition.* Chicago: University of Chicago Press, 1998.

———. *On Revolution.* New York: Penguin, 1984.

Azoulay, Ariella Aïsha. *Potential History: Unlearning Imperialism.* London: Verso, 1999.

Bessner, Daniel, and Nicolas Guilhot, eds. *The Decisionist Imagination: Sovereignty, Social Science, and Democracy in the 20th Century.* New York: Berghahn Books, 2019.

Bodin, Jean. *On Sovereignty: Six Books of the Commonwealth.* Translated by Marian J. Tooley. Oxford, UK: Basil Blackwell, 2009.

Burke, Kenneth. *A Rhetoric of Motives.* Berkeley: University of California Press, 1969.

Elshtain, Jean Bethke. *Sovereignty: God, State, and Self.* New York: Basic Books, 2008.

Foucault, Michel. *Discipline and Punish: The Birth of the Prison.* Translated by Alan Sheridan. New York: Vintage Books, 1995.

Groenendijk, Jeroen, and Martin Stokhof. "Studies on the Semantics of Questions and the Pragmatics of Answers." Joint PhD diss., University of Amsterdam, 1984.

Hamilton, Kevin, and Ned O'Gorman. *Lookout America! The Secret Hollywood Studio at the Heart of the Cold War.* Hanover, NH: Dartmouth College Press, 2019.

Hilgartner, Stephen, Richard C. Bell, and Rory O'Connor. *Nukespeak: Nuclear Language, Visions, and Mindset.* San Francisco: Sierra Club Books, 1982.

Hobbes, Thomas. *Leviathan.* Edited by Richard Tuck. New York: Cambridge University Press, 1996.

Kantorowicz, Ernst. *The King's Two Bodies: A Study in Mediaeval Political Theology.* Princeton, NJ: Princeton University Press, 1997.

Kertesz, Francois. "Project Aquarium." *Oak Ridge National Laboratory Review* 1, no. 2 (Winter 1968): 24–36.

Locke, John. *Two Treatises of Government.* Edited by Peter Laslett. New York: Cambridge University Press, 1960.

Masco, Joseph. *The Theater of Operations: National Security Affect from the Cold War to the War on Terror.* Durham, NC: Duke University Press, 2014.

Mills, C. Wright. *The Power Elite*. New York: Oxford University Press, 1956.

Morgenthau, Hans J. *Politics Among Nations: The Struggle for Power and Peace*. New York: A. A. Knopf, 1948.

O'Donovan, Oliver. *The Desire of the Nations: Rediscovering the Roots of Political Theology*. New York: Cambridge University Press, 1996.

O'Gorman, Ned. *The Iconoclastic Imagination: Image, Catastrophe, and Economy in America from the Kennedy Assassination to September 11*. Chicago: University of Chicago Press, 2016.

———. *Spirits of the Cold War: Contesting Worldviews in the Classical Age of American Security Strategy*. East Lansing: Michigan State University Press, 2012.

Philpott, Daniel. "Sovereignty." In *Stanford Encyclopedia of Philosophy*. Stanford University, 1997–. Article published May 31, 2003; last modified March 25, 2016. https://plato.stanford.edu/archives/sum2016/entries/sovereignty.

Price, Don K. *The Scientific Estate*. New York: Oxford University Press, 1965.

Rhodes, Richard. *The Making of the Atomic Bomb*. New York: Simon & Schuster, 1986.

Rousseau, Jean-Jacques. *The Social Contract and Other Later Political Writings*. Edited and translated by Victor Gourevitch. New York: Cambridge University Press, 1997.

Santner, Eric. *The Royal Remains: The People's Two Bodies and the Endgames of Sovereignty*. Chicago: University of Chicago Press, 2011.

Scarry, Elaine. *Thermonuclear Monarchy: Choosing Between Democracy and Doom*. New York: W. W. Norton, 2014.

Schmitt, Carl. *Dialogues on Power and Space*. Edited by Andreas Kalyvas and Federico Finchelstein. Translated by Samuel Garrett Zeitlin. Malden, MA: Polity Press, 2015.

———. *Dictatorship*. Translated by Michael Hoelzl and Graham Ward. Malden, MA: Polity Press, 2014.

———. *Political Theology: Four Chapters on the Concept of Sovereignty*. Translated by George Schwab. Chicago: University of Chicago Press, 1985.

Tooley, Marian J. "Introduction." In *On Sovereignty: Six Books of the Commonwealth*, by Jean Bodin, translated by Marian J. Tooley, 6–42. Oxford, UK: Basil Blackwell, 1955.

Vico, Giambattista. *On the Study Methods of Our Time*. Translated by Elio Gianturco. Ithaca, NY: Cornell University Press, 1990.

Walker, Lucy, dir. *Countdown to Zero*. DVD. Los Angeles: Magnolia Pictures, 2010.

Wills, Gary. *Bomb Power: The Modern Presidency and the National Security State*. New York: Penguin, 2010.

Winner, Langdon. *Autonomous Technology: Technics-out-of-Control as a Theme in Political Thought*. Cambridge, MA: MIT Press, 1978.

CHAPTER 9

From the Cathedral to the Casino

The Wager as a Response to the Sacred

BROOKE ROLLINS

[Gambling] is a God. Yes, a God; it has its votaries and its saints, who love it for itself, not for what it promises, and who fall down in adoration when its blow strikes them. It strips them ruthlessly, and they lay the blame on themselves, not on their deity. "I played a bad game," they say. They find fault with themselves; they do not blaspheme their God.

—ANATOLE FRANCE, *THE GARDEN OF EPICURUS*

Despite its sinful undertones and excessive relation to what historian Jackson Lears calls the "(implicitly Protestant) ethos of systematic self-control" (*Something*, 6), gambling maintains a powerful and widely observed association with the sacred. Outside of the cathedral's hallowed walls, the casino is that sacrosanct place most thoroughly devoted to and organized around a series of practices that players undertake to put themselves in relation to forces beyond their control. So insistent and intoxicating are these rituals that nineteenth-century novelist and critic Anatole France characterized gambling as an all-powerful deity. Noting its ardent devotees who, in the manner of nuns and monks, have *"vowed* to play" (*Garden*, 22; emphasis added), France argues that gambling is less a matter of making easy money than it is a sacred practice with its own intrinsic rewards: "What is play, I should like to know, but the art of producing in a second the changes that

Destiny ordinarily effects only in the course of many hours or even many years?" (23). He adds, furthermore, that much like those suffering Christians who take solace in God rather than blame him for their misfortunes, gamblers keep the faith even amid devastating losses. Giving themselves over to what he calls the "domination of an irresistible force" (22), gamblers gamble because it provides a "hand-to-hand encounter with Fate" (23). To make a wager, by these lights, is to call out to the universe—to ask, in the form of a playful ritual, "Where do I stand?"

If the powerful allure of gambling is that it allows players to, in a certain impure manner of speaking, communicate with God, its primary interest to rhetoricians might be the way that its accompanying performative elements function as persuasive gambits. Gamblers famously perform idiosyncratic rituals as a way of conjuring good luck. They attach significance to "lucky" numbers, caress good luck charms, and kiss about-to-be wagered chips—all in the name of courting fortune's favor. Such rhetorical gestures have no grounding in reason, of course, but they do allow gamblers feel some measure of active participation in the otherwise uncontrollable moment of encountering chance. This is why Lears argues that even contemporary gambling activity is profoundly connected to a "wider web of . . . ancient, multifaceted rituals that have addressed profound human needs and purposes" for centuries (*Something*, 6). Furthermore, sociologist and gambling studies scholar Gerda Reith, who argues that gambling is emblematic of the ongoing human struggle with uncertainty, explains that "superstitious and irrational" thoughts, which are typically given no space or authority in everyday life, are allowed to "organize and explain" the distinctly separate world of the casino (*Age of Chance*, 156). "These include a broad range of magical and quasi-religious beliefs," she says, including "the notion of 'luck,' the idea that the cards, dice, or tickets can somehow be influenced by the gambler, and the idea that the outcome of games is decided by providential forces such as 'fate' or 'destiny'" (156). Psychoanalyst Theodore Reik made a similar claim about gambling's psychological and spiritual motivations, arguing that the compulsion to gamble comes from a desire to see if one's trespasses will be punished or forgiven by "the ultimate father surrogate" (*From Thirty Years*, 171). He writes that "gambling, which never has as its end money or gain, becomes a kind of question addressed to destiny" (170–71). Because it functions both as a question posed to fate and an opportunity to help destiny's gifts along, gambling is a uniquely appropriate manner of responding to the sacred.

With this thought of gambling as a "question addressed to destiny" in mind, my purpose in this chapter is to examine the way that wagering functions as a rhetorical response to the sacred. What happens to the gambler in the midst of such an address, and what is it about betting—risking something of one's own—that puts players in relation to something sacred, perhaps even to God? I will argue here that one important rhetorical location where such questions are explored (albeit obliquely) is the *Pensées*, a posthumously published collection of essays and fragments about religion, philosophy, and human psychology by the seventeenth-century mathematician, physicist, and religious thinker Blaise Pascal. Written after his spiritual conversion in 1654, the *Pensées* is generally thought to be Pascal's unfinished apology for the Christian religion, although there has been considerable speculation about the collection's rhetorical purpose and form. With a particular focus on the famed *liasse* or fragment known as the Wager, and by connecting Pascal's claims here to his debate with the Jesuits about grace and free will, I argue that Pascal shows gambling to be a distinctive and fitting response to the sacred. More specifically, I suggest that Pascal's use of wagering as a rhetorical device highlights the subjective unraveling of the believer in the face of God's radical unknowability and that this dissolution mirrors what happens to the gambler in the decidedly more secular realm of the casino. While the Wager is best known as the place where Pascal invents decision theory and brings it to bear on situations of uncertainty, my reading of the text highlights the ways that Pascal's highly rational, persuasive attempts are unsettled in their encounter with the sacred. This is not, I contend, a failure of Pascal's text, and I offer no correctives to his innovative formula for decision making.[1] But this example does show the profoundly disorienting and desubjectifying effects of encountering alterity, and it demonstrates that gambling is an apt figure for characterizing and thinking through rhetorical responses to the sacred.

When I use the term "sacred" in this essay, I refer not only to the religious or magical circumstances alluded to above (those often performed by gamblers), but also to those contexts Michael Bernard-Donals has referred to as "less mystical and more mundane" ("Call," 398). Drawing on Immanuel Kant's concept of the sublime, Maurice Blanchot's thinking of the disaster, and Avital Ronnell's work on stupidity, Bernard-Donals characterizes the sacred as an ineffable, unbounded, and finally indeterminate concept that is incapable of being understood or mastered. No longer confined to the realm of religion or spirituality, the sacred is no *thing* in particular, but that which is in excess of knowledge. The sacred occasionally calls to us and compels us to respond, and yet in its very approach, it defiantly, frustratingly withdraws itself from our experience (400–401). Reaching out, demanding a response, and yet remaining "set apart" from understanding, the sacred call has a profoundly disruptive and disorienting effect on the addressee (401). Characterized by its "principally (if not exclusively) affective" demand for a response, the call of the sacred, Bernard-Donals says, "profoundly dislocates the one who is called, so much so that her membership in the community or the collective . . . is called into question" (399, 400). The person addressed by the sacred call is ungrounded and unmoored—subjectively dispersed in an encounter with something that overtakes him. The sacred call thus "troubles, rather than easily calls forth, a rhetorical response, a reasonable discourse, or even an autonomous interlocutor or a stable ground from which to speak" (399). And because encounters with the sacred often pose difficulties for speakers who hope to compose fitting responses, the sacred eludes the field of rhetoric's traditional discursive, communicative scope. For this reason, Bernard-Donals argues that it is important for the discipline to develop a more capacious understanding of the term. Expanding our view, he suggests, would enable us to explore the limits of rhetoric and to consider more fully what is at stake in those instances in which the "discipline of discourse" cannot quite live up to its name. Pascal's Wager, I believe, is a prime location to consider these limits and their effects on the precarious subjective boundaries of speakers who wish to persuade in moments of profound uncertainty.

GAMBLING: THE SECULAR AND SACRED PREOCCUPATION OF BLAISE PASCAL

Gambling holds a special status in the work and cultural legacy of Blaise Pascal. The fact that this otherwise unseemly leisure pursuit occupied his attention during both the scientific and religious phases of his short life speaks to the richness and versatility of gambling as an intellectual concept and suggests that Pascal himself may have seen gambling as representative of some essential attribute of the human experience. During Pascal's rise to prominence as a natural philosopher, gambling activity provided a series of problems he could help solve through the invention of novel mathematical proofs. And after his turn to more properly religious pursuits, when he began to intervene in the debate between the French Augustinians of Port-Royal and the Jesuits, gambling enabled Pascal to conceive of the state of humanity after the fall and what it might mean to anticipate salvation. As Michael A. Rosenthal has argued, "The logic and experience of gambling" was a powerful lens through which Pascal chose to "investigate and justify forms of life and belief" ("Benjamin's Wager," 262).

Pascal's interest in gambling began as a mathematical preoccupation. A precocious and brilliant mathematician who published an essay on conics (a locus of points in projective geometry) by age sixteen and invented the mechanical calculating machine by age eighteen, Pascal first turned his attention to gambling in 1654, when he began to correspond with the mathematician Pierre de Fermat about how to calculate odds in games of chance (Edwards, "Pascal's Work," 41–42). This collaboration was prompted by Pascal's friend Chevalier de Méré, an avid gambler and an "aristocratic, sensuous, free-thinking and well-read connoisseur," who asked for help in determining how much a stake in a game of chance would be worth if that game were interrupted before its conclusion (Rogers, "Pascal's Life," 13).[2] Pascal's solution to what is now known as the Problem of Points introduced the idea of "expected value," a mathematical concept that enables players to estimate the value of their stakes by multiplying all the potential outcomes (each coin toss, for example, that remained to come when the game was prematurely terminated) by their likelihood of occurrence, and then adding those values together. With this innovation, as A. W. F. Edwards explains, Pascal took the subject of probability "beyond medieval enumeration of possibilities and computation of chances into the modern form of a calculus embodying the full rigour of mathematical proof" ("Pascal's Work," 51). Reith puts this accomplishment a slightly different way. She argues that where previous thinkers understood a game's past results as indicative of what was to come, Pascal recognized that chance was "an unfinished story whose end was not determined by what had gone before" (*Age of Chance*, 25). It is in the context of these circumstances that probability theory—the gambler's logic—was born.

Edwards notes that "Pascal was justly proud of his solution to the Problem of Points" ("Pascal's Work," 48), and he illustrates this claim by quoting a 1654 letter that Pascal sent to Marin Mersenne's Académie Parisienne (where he had, as a teenager, interacted with some of Europe's intellectual elite). Describing his solution to the Problem of Points, Pascal stressed the way mathematical formulation enabled a new kind of intellectual mastery over heretofore uncharted realms: "Proper calculation masters fickle fortune," he proclaimed (*Pensées*, 48). During the scientific phase of his life, then, gambling provided Pascal with opportunities to advance mathematical knowledge and to invent new methods for solving complicated problems with an array of unpredictable outcomes. It was a scene, in short, in which his formidable intellect triumphed over chance.

Later in the same year that he corresponded with Fermat, however, Pascal experienced a reportedly mystical spiritual conversion that would both change the course of his life (Rogers, "Pascal's Life," 14) and complicate the place and function of gambling in his thinking. Having felt humbled by the presence of God during his conversion, Pascal turned away from the mathematical and scientific pursuits that had garnered him renown and focused instead on religious study. He sought spiritual guidance from the leaders of the Port-Royal convent, and by 1665 he was embroiled in a high-stakes debate about religious doctrine in competing wings of the Catholic Church in France. His *Provincial Letters* expressed support for and defended the beliefs of the pious, scripture-focused Port-Royal Augustinians in their dispute with the Jesuits, whom Pascal believed to be too permissive in their approach to win over nonbelievers (Elster, "Pascal and Decision Theory," 54). These ideas make their way into the *Pensées*, as well. "Faith is different from proof," Pascal writes there. "One is human and the other a gift from God" (4).

At the heart of the debate between the Port-Royal adherents, who followed the teachings of St. Augustine, and the Jesuits was the former's belief that "all human virtue was false virtue and that an individual's salvation lay entirely in the hands of God" (Rogers, "Pascal's Life," 10). Grace, in other words, was a gift from God and God alone. Because humans had been radically corrupted by the Fall, they could not achieve salvation on their own (Moriarty, "Grace," 144–46). They believed, furthermore, that God could have rightly condemned everyone to eternal damnation, but, for reasons unknown to man, he took mercy on some "minority... of the whole human race," and granted them grace (147). The Jesuits, by contrast, held more open views, insisting that humans did have a role to play in achieving salvation. They believed that "salvation depends, to some extent, on our free choice, that God distributes to all a 'sufficient grace' that enables them to fulfill commandments, but that we choose whether to avail ourselves of this help or not" (145–46). The key difference was this matter of "sufficient grace." For the Jesuits it meant that *all* people had the capacity to be saved. Pascal, by contrast, felt that this notion devalued God's far rarer gift. Grace was not something to which corrupt and weak humans were entitled, and it was certainly not something they should expect. Instead it was a matter of predestination for a fortunate few. It was a free gift from God—a stroke of luck.

What we see after the spiritual conversion is that chance—and Pascal's relation to it—begins to occupy a very different sort of space in Pascal's thinking. Before his mystical encounter with the sacred, Pascal approached "fickle fortune" as something to be mastered. He was able, by way of his remarkable mathematical acumen, to understand chance in ways that no one before him could. But after his conversion, chance is no longer something he wants to or is able to render intelligible. Instead it is the essential characteristic of an experience of profound vulnerability and openness to what spiritual gifts might be granted by God. Lears has argued that any notion of grace (whether it be Pascal's or Jonathan Edwards's) recognizes that "the dream of mastery over fate [is] a delusion" (*Something*, 9). Connecting the tradition of grace to secular practices of gambling, he adds that "grace [can] not be produced predictably or earned systematically . . . ; it [can] be courted only obliquely and experienced fleetingly" (9). Once a field in which Pascal developed statistical methods and proofs to cordon off contingency, gambling ultimately comes to represent for him a far more vulnerable ontological state. No longer the mathematician who, from an objective remove, identifies the hidden logics of games of chance, Pascal becomes the gambler immersed in the game. To be a person of faith, as he understands it, is to helplessly await the gifts of a God who is completely beyond his knowledge and control. It is to be suspended in a moment of expectation before the coin falls heads or tails.

THE RHETORIC OF THE WAGER

I take the time to articulate this shift in the status of gambling in Pascal's thought because, as I will explain, his seemingly opposed secular and sacred approaches to the topic find themselves on something of a collision course in the Wager. Furthermore, Pascal's belief that grace is something only God can bestow leads to important questions about the rhetorical purpose and form of the *Pensées* and those of its most famous fragment. As Michael Moriarty puts this, "Pascal states that faith is a gift from God, not the result of a process of reasoning. . . . In which case, we might ask, what is the point of an apology for the Christian religion?" ("Grace," 144). The Wager, furthermore, seems to take an explicitly *persuasive* form insofar as it uses the structure of a bet in order to make the case that it is a far better decision to believe in God than not to. Specifically, Pascal makes an argument for the rationality of faith on the basis of a risk-to-reward ratio: Why risk infinite damnation for the sake of finite earthly pleasures, he asks, when you might reap infinite rewards in the afterlife by giving up a bit of gratification today? (*Pensées*, 121–27). Following a detailed analysis of this reasoning, Jon Elster is prompted to ask, "Why would a person who believed in predestination bother to do anything for *anyone's* salvation, his own or that of others?" ("Pascal and Decision Theory," 69–70). For Elster the "conclusion seems inescapable that the Wager . . . would have been much more convincing if offered by a Jesuit" (70). From the Jesuits' point of view, in other words, it makes sense to try to persuade a person to believe in God as a way making good use of their sufficient grace, but from the point of view of Pascal and predestination, it makes no sense at all. What I will suggest, however, is that we can resolve some of these tensions by thinking through what role the theme of gambling plays in Pascal's famous argument. What do the uncontrollable, irrational, and unsettling aspects of gambling add to his otherwise probabilistic thinking? The lasting message of the Wager may be that it is, above all, rational to have faith, but when Pascal places gambling at the heart of his claim, he nonetheless unsettles this logic. When he uses wagering as a rhetorical device, that is, he highlights the subjective unraveling that is characteristic of any encounter with the sacred.

The predominant reading of Pascal's use of the Wager as an argument for religious faith is that the tactic enabled him to conjoin his two passions, mathematics and religion. More specifically, the Wager is known as the place where Pascal applies his insights from probability theory (the methods he developed to solve the Problem of Points) to more general areas of human life and decision making. As Nicholas Rescher argues, "[Pascal's] wager argument—which turns on using the machinery of mathematical expectations to assess the acceptability of gambles—was an ingenious use of a mathematical resource for the purposes of religious apologetics" (*Luck*, 129). By most accounts, and perhaps even at face value, the argument of the Wager is in keeping with what I described above as Pascal's secular approach to gambling. Much in the same way that he used probability to create order in the face of unpredictable results in the Problem of Points (those of the unfinished game), in the Wager, Pascal uses mathematical formulations to respond to the (also unknowable) sacred. The basic argument he sets forth here is that it is rational to have faith not because we know for sure that God exists but because belief is a good bet. His claim is that "there is an infinity of infinitely happy life to be won, one chance of winning against a finite number of chances of losing, and what you are staking is finite. That leaves no choice; wherever there is infinity, and where there are not infinite chances of losing against that of winning, there is no room for hesitation, you must give everything" (*Pensées*, 123–24). To wager a certain finite stake for the chance at an uncertain but infinite gain, in other words, is to be on the right side of a divine risk-to-reward ratio. In this way, Pascal's approach diverges significantly from comparable apologetic arguments by St. Anselm, St. Thomas Aquinas, and René Descartes, all of whom make a case for the actual existence of God. This is not so for Pascal, who freely admits, "If there is a God, he is infinitely beyond our comprehension" (122). The approach he takes instead is to make an argument for how best to proceed in a case of such uncertainty.

By imposing mathematical intelligibility on the disordered expanse of the sacred, Pascal formulates a justification of the Christian faith from a highly rational point of view. Faced with what is "infinitely beyond [his] comprehension," he once more uses calculation in an attempt to overcome "fickle fortune." In fact, with the Wager, Pascal takes the probability theory he developed during the correspondence with Fermat a step further by applying it to broader choices people make in the face of uncertainty. This marked the invention of a nascent version of decision theory, which, as Ian Hacking notes, represents "a decisive turning point in probability theory . . . [that] showed that the mathematics of games of chance had quite general applications" ("Logic," 186). In this way, Pascal's genius is put in the service of mastering chance, and while the decisions we make in life may be a series of gambles, his work suggests that there exist mathematical tools to show us how we ought to proceed in the face of the unknown. As it did in the Problem of Points, probabilistic thinking seems to lead the way. Indeed, Rescher argues that Pascal's lasting legacy is his ability to "impos[e] . . . mathematical intelligibility on inherently fortuitous occurrences" (*Luck*, 129).

And yet it seems to me that even as Pascal uses the structure of gambling as a way to corral the unruly territory of the sacred, there are significant places in the text when he goes the other way. That is, even as the Wager provides Pascal (and his audience) with a reasonable strategy for contending with the unknown, it also at moments reveals him to be a far more vulnerable, overwhelmed, and dislocated subject—a true believer who must nonetheless helplessly await a gift from God. We get a glimpse of this when Pascal first discusses God's infinite unknowability. Because he is "indivisible and without limits," Pascal stresses that we are unable to situate ourselves in relation to God, who "bears no relation to us" (*Pensées*, 122). The starting place for Pascal, then (and for us readers, too), is one of profound disorientation. Unable to get a bead on the sacred, our only recourse is to gamble. According to Pascal, "Either God is, or he is not. But to which view shall we be inclined? Reason cannot decide this question. Infinite chaos separates us. At the far end of this infinite distance a coin is being spun which will come down heads or tails. How will you wager?" (122). How, Pascal seems to ask here, can one possibly chart the "infinite chaos" of the boundless territory that lies between rational human agents and the truth of the existence or the nonexistence of God? What instruments could possibly help us find our way, and how could we know, before it is too late, whether or not we had made it? Faced with a situation this far beyond human understanding and control, Pascal suggests that our best recourse is to wager. Gambling, it would seem, is the only available response.

Despite all this probabilistic armament that Pascal uses to protect himself from the disorienting encounter with the sacred, one of the most notable aspects of his argument is that wagering is not simply one response among others. There is no other way to respond, Pascal suggests, and he tells us that we are not able to refuse the sacred call. This is not, in other words, a hand we will be allowed to sit out. "You must wager," Pascal says. "There is no choice, you are already committed" (123). We thus get a glimpse of the necessity of the Wager in Pascal's argument. Even though he will ultimately formulate a logic to help us wager well, he shows us that the sacred, to borrow a formulation from Bernard-Donals, "calls for a singular, radically constrained, and likewise radically particular utterance" ("Call," 400). Before we can call on our reserves (helpfully supplied by the genius mathematician) to calculate the most appropriate path forward, we are put in the vulnerable position of having to bet on something far beyond the limits of our knowledge and control.

Elsewhere in the *Pensées*, Pascal describes gambling as a distinctive kind of leisure activity people take up as a way to escape feelings of existential anxiety. And it is useful, I think, to consider his discussion of the Wager on God's existence within this broader context. In a fragment titled "Diversion," Pascal explains that humans are prone to dwell on and feel a deep uneasiness about the sheer coincidence of their existence. Writing in the voice of someone suffering from such ennui, Pascal complains, "I feel that it is possible that I might never have existed, for my self consists in my thought; therefore, I who think would never have been if my mother had been killed before I had come to life; therefore I am not a necessary being" (37). People go to great lengths, Pascal explains, to escape the feelings of unease that accompany such a decentering revelation. Along with billiards, hunting, and dancing, gambling is a distraction that works by producing a mental "agitation" that takes our minds off the accidental nature of our existence (38).[3] Occupied with the excitement of our diversions, we need not dwell on the fact that we are not "necessary being[s]" (37). The devout Pascal, of course, sees gambling (along with other amusements he includes in this section) as a shallow means of preventing oneself from contemplating what really matters—the true majesty of God (42). But given that people use these activities to keep their minds off the random chance (and thus the precarity) of their existence, gambling is the single most appropriate response to the ennui Pascal describes. To recall the observations of France and Reik from the beginning of this chapter, gambling is precisely the practice of calling out to the universe to find out where one stands.

By Pascal's own admission, then, gambling is something people do when they feel uneasiness about and discomfort with their place, purpose, and impermanence in the world. And so if the task is to characterize what people do when they contemplate the existence of God, wagering is a particularly fitting response. As I have suggested above, this is in part because the Wager provides Pascal with the opportunity to use probability theory (perhaps the finest of his many mathematical contributions) to provide a reasoned course for future action. But it is also fitting because what it means to encounter the sacred is that reason is profoundly troubled. One of the primary characteristics of the sacred, as Bernard-Donals reminds us, is that it "calls forth a response beyond reason" ("Call," 398). Making a bet is always such a response because no matter how much careful figuring and planning come before the Wager, its defining feature is that the gambler must always surrender to an outcome totally beyond her knowledge and control. It is as though the activity of gambling makes a game out of responding to the sacred call—as if it playfully replicates and experiments with the intensity of this experience.

Walter Benjamin understood gambling as a profoundly desubjectifying experience, referring, in "The Path to Success, in Thirteen Theses," to the roulette player, who "has no name of his own and requires no one else's. For he is represented by the chips he places on specific numbers on the table" (146). Individual identity is given up, in other words, to the anticipation of the unknowable to come. Caught up in the perpetual ritual movement of his chosen game, the gambler is, as Jeffrey T. Nealon has argued, not the origin of his own action, but instead someone who has been pulled into a Deleuzian collective assemblage, "wherein it's all about joining or tuning into an impersonal or transpersonal flow" ("Take Me Out," 467). Once in motion, he adds, the gambler "reperform[s] a set of moves, or riff[s] on a refrain" (466). This desubjectifying experience is what gamblers call *action*. They long for action, they seek it out, and they experiment with its intensity. But this is an action that cannot simply be distinguished from passivity. Gamblers who have action are at one in the same moment had by it, suspended in its wave. It might seem counterintuitive to characterize this absorptive appeal of gambling as a response to a sacred call, but, when a player wagers, he is utterly dislocated—taken out of his discrete individuality.

There are moments in the Wager when Pascal seems to emphasize these desubjectifying characteristics of gambling. When he discusses what precisely we are wagering on—and remember, this is a wager we cannot refuse—he signals a noticeable unease with the vulnerability and disempowerment that accompany this task. It is not simply that we cannot know the truth of God's existence, but that it is an "infinite chaos" that prevents us from knowing. He characterizes our encounter with the sacred, furthermore, as a troubling, desubjectifying experience: "The finite is annihilated in the presence of the infinite and becomes pure nothingness. So it is with our mind before God" (*Pensées*, 121). Thus Pascal admits to being unsettled in the encounter with the incalculable, and his final inability to return the excessive nature of the sacred to the masterful confines of his interpretive horizons leaves him feeling disoriented. We cannot position ourselves in relation to God, he says, and our subject position is dispersed in the presence of his infinity.

What I am attempting to demonstrate here is the thematic significance of gambling itself in Pascal's Wager. In fact, I think that one of its most remarkable features is that way it links spiritual commitment to the risks associated with gambling. It matters, in other words, that when tasked with facing God and communicating about religious belief, Pascal adopted both the logic and language of the gambling hall. He uses gambling terminology throughout the fragment, referring to faith as a sort of game that functions not unlike a "coin being spun which will come down heads or tails" (122). In addition to relying on the larger structure of the Wager to characterize religious faith, he rounds out his argument for belief by drawing on specific images from the casino: he refers frequently to play, stakes, prizes, winning and losing, and the faces of cards (122–25). Scholars have placed a great deal of emphasis on the innovative if imperfect logic of Pascal's claim. Hacking, for example, notes that the Wager actually rests on three discrete arguments: an argument from dominance, an argument from expectation, and an argument from dominating expectation ("Logic," 188), and Elster (among others) stresses the novelty of Pascal's ability to hook human decision making up to the idea of expected utility ("Pascal and Decision Theory," 57). But I think it is important to keep in mind that when Pascal invites us to view faith as a wager, we must understand the practice and structure of gambling as a meaningful interpretive frame for spiritual commitment. Before we can even begin to contemplate the sacred, we must inhabit the vulnerable subject position of the gambler—a person who is defined by her openness to forces beyond her control.

When he is faced with the infinity of God and the limitless chaos that prevents us from knowing the truth of his existence, Pascal's rhetorical response is to place a bet. For the prodigious scientist and inventor, it makes a certain kind of sense that this response includes strong elements of rational, mathematical thinking. Certainly, Pascal's formulation of the wager attempts to overlay expectation on to what is finally impossible to anticipate. But I think Pascal's Wager is also something else—a persuasive mathematical formulation that is given only by way of its open, unbounded relation to the future. If we are able to wager well, that rational choice comes *after* our having had to wager. We are "already committed," Pascal reminds us (*Pensées*, 123). That is, before we undertake the probabilistic thinking that enables us to make a good bet, we are exposed and vulnerable to the sacred whose call, Bernard-Donals says, "works by means of *dis*-integration" ("Call," 403). In this way, the Wager articulates a path for rational decision making that rests on a far less masterful state of being called by the sacred and exposed to its alterity. In the end, that is, the "infinite chaos [that] separates us" refers not only to an epistemological limit but also to a profound ontological disturbance that involves what Bernard-Donals describes as a "coring out of the self" (405).

Keeping these epistemological and ontological senses of the Wager in mind might help answer those questions posed by Moriarty and Elster about why Pascal, who believed that grace was only given by God, would write an apology for Christianity and, in the Wager fragment itself, a persuasive argument for belief. Pascal's use of gambling as an argument for faith provides a subtle if uncomfortable reminder that salvation is not up to us. For him it is a gift we—like so many gamblers before us—can only helplessly await. And so while Pascal's Wager can teach us how to use probability to navigate uncertain situations, it will not let us forget that first we must be called to respond to the sacred other whose disproportion always unsettles our subjective boundaries.

Notes

1. Scholars have often seen the Wager as an opportunity to discern the finer points of Pascal's probabilistic reasoning and, while crediting the natural philosopher for laying the foundation for modern decision theory, as an opportunity to explain and critique the argument's logical flaws. See, for example, Hacking, *Emergence of Probability*; Rescher, *Pascal's Wager*; and Elster, "Pascal and Decision Theory." In this chapter, I am less interested in pursuing objections to the logic of the Wager than I am positing a thematic connection between gambling and faith in the *Pensées*.

2. Pascal developed his friendship with Chevalier de Méré during what is known as

his "worldly period," in the years just prior to his spiritual conversion. Along with Damien Mitton, whom Pascal deploys as a sophisticated but skeptical interlocutor in the *Pensées*, Chevalier de Méré, Ben Rogers explains, "had worked the gentlemanly code of *honnêteté* or good breeding into something like a full-blown, philosophical ethic . . . defined in opposition to all forms of selfishness, small-mindedness" ("Pascal's Life," 13). Though Pascal later rejected this code because of its incompatibility with his view of man's weakness in relation to God, it "gave him a formidable value system to argue against, and, paradoxically, greatly enriched his understanding of a good Christian life" (13).

3. Here is Pascal on the way gambling meets people's psychological needs and helps divert them from existential anxiety: "A given man lives a life free from boredom by gambling a small sum every day. Give him every morning the money he might win that day, but on the condition that he does not gamble, and you will make him unhappy. It might be argued that what he wants is the entertainment of gaming and not the winnings. Make him play for nothing; his interest will not be fired. . . . He must create some target for his passions and then arouse his desire, anger, fear for this object he has created, just like children taking fright at a face they have daubed themselves" (41).

Bibliography

Benjamin, Walter. "The Path to Success, in Thirteen Theses." In *Selected Writings*, vol. 2, *1927–1934*, by Walter Benjamin, edited by Michael W. Jennings, Howard Eiland, and Gary Smith, translated by Rodney Livingstone et al., 144–47. Cambridge, MA: Belknap Press of Harvard University Press, 1999.

Bernard-Donals, Michael. "The Call of the Sacred and the Language of Deterritorialization." *Rhetoric Society Quarterly* 41, no. 5 (2011): 397–415.

Edwards, A. W. F. "Pascal's Work on Probability." In *The Cambridge Companion to Pascal*, edited by Nicholas Hammond, 40–52. Cambridge, UK: Cambridge University Press, 2003.

Elster, Jon. "Pascal and Decision Theory." In *The Cambridge Companion to Pascal*, edited by Nicholas Hammond, 53–74. Cambridge, UK: Cambridge University Press, 2003.

France, Anatole. *The Garden of Epicurus*. Translated by Alfred Allinson. London: John Lane, 1908.

Hacking, Ian. *The Emergence of Probability: A Philosophical Study of Early Ideas About Probability, Induction, and Statistical Inference*. Cambridge, UK: Cambridge University Press, 1975.

———. "The Logic of Pascal's Wager." *American Philosophical Quarterly* 9, no. 2 (April 1972): 186–92.

Lears, Jackson. *Something for Nothing: Luck in America*. New York: Viking, 2003.

Moriarty, Michael. "Grace and Religious Belief in Pascal." In *The Cambridge Companion to Pascal*, edited by Nicholas Hammond, 144–61. Cambridge, UK: Cambridge University Press, 2003.

Nealon, Jeffrey T. "Take Me Out to the Slot Machines: Reflections on Gambling and Contemporary American Culture." *South Atlantic Quarterly* 105, no. 2 (Spring 2006): 465–74.

Pascal, Blaise. *Pensées*. Translated by A. J. Krailsheimer. London: Penguin Books, 1966.

Reik, Theodore. *From Thirty Years with Freud*. Translated by Richard Winston. New York: Farrar and Rinehart, 1940.

Reith, Gerda. *The Age of Chance: Gambling and Western Culture*. London: Routledge, 1999.

Rescher, Nicholas. *Luck: The Brilliant Randomness of Everyday Life*. New York: Farrar, Straus and Giroux, 1995.

———. *Pascal's Wager: A Study of Practical Reasoning in Philosophical Theology*. Notre Dame, IN: University of Notre Dame Press, 1985.

Rogers, Ben. "Pascal's Life and Times." In *The Cambridge Companion to Pascal*, edited by Nicholas Hammond, 4–19. Cambridge, UK: Cambridge University Press, 2003.

Rosenthal, Michael A. "Benjamin's Wager on Modernity: Gambling and the Arcades Project." *Germanic Review* 87 (2012): 261–78.

CHAPTER 10

Rightness in Retrospect

Stonewall and the Sacred Call of Kairos

JEAN BESSETTE

> Archives do not simply reconnect us with what we have lost. Instead they remind us, like Warhol's boxes, of what we have never possessed in the first place.
>
> —SVEN SPIEKER, *THE BIG ARCHIVE*

The concept of *kairos* has been portrayed in art and poetry in sacred imagery for millennia. Personified as Kairos, the Greek god of opportunity, the figure is depicted with sinewy strength and speed: a swift, muscled man with winged feet and back, balancing a scale or wielding a knife as he teeters on a ball. His hair is his most unusual feature; on an otherwise bare head, a lengthy forelock awaits the fleeting grasp of would-be rhetors. With these qualities, the god of opportunity reveals his alacrity, "the sharp nature of his entrances and exits" (Myers, "*Metanoia*," 1), the fickleness of his favors, and the unpredictability of his movements. He cannot be anticipated, commanded, or held; the rhetor's only hope is to identify and seize before it is too late. At risk, Kelly Myers argues, is the arrival of the goddess of regret, Metanoia, whose name connotes the "feelings of repentance" that come with hindsight (7).

These qualities highlight *kairos*'s "sacredness," defined by Michael Bernard-Donals and Kyle Jensen as that which escapes understanding, defies human mastery, and will not be predicted. The sacred demands a response from rhetoric and its rituals that attempts to wrest control of the situation through a system of mechanisms that can be studied and taught. We can see this dynamic play out in our understanding of kairos, typically defined (post-Aristotle) as the "right timing and proper measure directly related to the rhetorical importance of time, place, speaker, and audience, the proper and knowledgeable analysis of these factors, and the faculty of using the proper means in a particular context to arrive at belief" (Helsley, "Kairos," 371). As Helsley suggests here, the sacred, fleeting moment of opportunity requires an appropriate and timely response from a rhetor who has properly assessed the situation through educated faculties.

In this chapter, however, I argue that the archive profoundly unsettles our attempts to respond to the sacred kairos through rhetorical rituals characterized by agency, timeliness, and appropriate measure. Myers's evocation of *metanoia* suggests that kairos is not, or not only, defined by its brevity, by that fleeting, singular moment. In order to recognize kairos—to know that the sacred aperture of opportunity has indeed opened—we must wait for either regret (Metanoia) or victory (Nike, brother of Kairos). In other words, though we can try, we cannot *wholly* anticipate or even know in the moment that kairos is here; we can only evaluate it as such in retrospect after failure or success has been gauged. As Myers ("*Metanoia,*" 11) explains, "In this longer view, kairos can be seen as a series of opportunities occurring over time, experienced with a range of exhilaration and regret. Rather than placing emphasis on isolated moments and available means, *metanoia* encourages broader considerations of the ways in which people move through experience." Any longer view demands the archive and, in the case of kairos, reveals both ethical and methodological implications for rhetoric.

Archives expand temporality beyond the present moment and attenuate how—and when—a response to an opportunity is identified as kairotic. For how can a rhetor know if a response is fitting and called for by the moment until after the moment has passed and the success of the rhetoric (whatever that means) has been assessed? Understanding a response as "fitting" depends on a longer temporality wherein successful rhetoric is defined by aims that precede or follow the rhetorical act. That is, the identification of kairos's rightness depends on a prefigured or postfigured *end* (a goal of persuasion, communication, invention) and its achievement.

Because kairos evinces the sacred—eluding control and prediction—the "rightness" of a moment can only be identified as such in hindsight. If the rhetoric succeeds (whatever that means), the time was—in retrospect—right.

The case of the Stonewall Riots of 1969 illustrates the stakes of taking the archive into account when assessing how rhetoric responds to the sacred kairos. Widely considered the fountainhead of gay liberation, this uprising of gay and transgender bar patrons against police raids seems to exemplify the kairotic moment: after years of raids (usually thwarted or diminished by paying off the cops), this time was different. This time was *right*—for reasons no participant can fully explain. As many critics have noted, Stonewall has been positioned as the watershed of liberation, *the* opportune moment to fight back for the right to gather queerly in public space.

And yet the case of Stonewall reveals how the archive can undermine our ritual attempts to identify and control kairos through rhetorical theory. If the uprising succeeded in mobilizing the gay liberation movement (and so the time was right to riot), the rhetors who heeded the sacred call were not always so sure of its rightness after the event. Focusing on Sylvia Rivera, a Puerto Rican street queen who (may have) helped fulminate the riots, I trace how the retrospective rhetorical construction of Stonewall's kairos participated in the erasure and exclusion of the trans and queer rhetors who answered its sacred call. The archival traces and absences of Rivera's life from the movement after Stonewall complicate theories of kairos by raising questions about for whom and for what ends a time for action can be said to be right. The archive does not secure certainty about kairos, however. It only unsettles its designation.

RHETORIC'S RESPONSES TO THE SACRED CALL OF KAIROS

Rhetorical scholars have tended to respond to the sacredness of kairos in one of two ways: through rituals of agential control and, more recently, through acknowledgment of its unpredictable, emplaced power that evades such ritual. The first camp, emphasizing subjective agency, casts kairos in terms of a situational context to which the rhetor adapts in the moment. James L. Kinneavy and Catharine Eskin ("Kairos," 435), for instance, lean on this connotation in their exegesis of kairos in Aristotle's rhetoric: the rhetor "applies the rules of the art of rhetoric to the particular situation at

issue." Kairos, in their reading, refers to the individual and unique case—
and moment—to which the general rules of rhetoric must be "applied"
appropriately; this is how rhetoric responds to kairos's sacredness through
rituals of applied theory.

Though less systematic than the Aristotelian approach,[1] the Isocratean
approach also understood kairos in terms of adaptive application of lessons
to the moment. As Janet Atwill (*Rhetoric Reclaimed*, 159) put it in her interpretation of Isocrates, "in the mastery of the moment lies the rhetor's best
chance to intervene in and transform a situation." The Isocratean rhetor
improved this chance by imitating adroit orators until "habituated" to a
keen discernment of kairos (59). Isocrates's academy coached pupils in this
principle of *phronesis*, or practical wisdom, and indeed, the rhetor's ability
to identify kairos was the hallmark of the educated for Isocrates: "Whom,
then, do I call educated? . . . First, those who manage well the circumstances
which they encounter day by day, and who possess a judgment which is
accurate in meeting occasions as they arise and rarely misses the expedient course of action" (qtd. in Sipiora, "Introduction," 14). In this more
agential view of the concept then, successful response to kairos is something that can (within limits) be taught, practiced, and learned. Kairos's
sacred qualities, in other words, can be wrangled by the rhetor well-
educated in *phronesis*.

These responses to kairos's sacredness can be understood as rituals that
uphold our belief that rhetoric can be taught and learned. Implicitly or
explicitly, rhetoricians often respond to the sacred by turning to Aristotle,
who privileged a universal logical system that could transcend individual
situations. As Jane Sutton ("Kairos," 413) explains, in the Aristotelian tradition "*kairos* is absorbed in part of a comprehensive system of rhetoric and
emerges through moderation, the appropriate and the good." For this camp,
in other words, kairos can be bent to our will with the right rituals of theory
and practice.

However, a second camp has called these rituals of control into question. As Thomas Rickert (*Ambient Rhetoric*, 74–75) inquires, "If rhetoric is
to cast itself as a teachable subject, then some formalization must be possible, and if not, what then? How to teach the unexpected?" Drawing more
on Gorgias than Aristotle, a number of rhetoricians have questioned rituals
of agency over kairos, arguing that the scene of rhetoric cannot be anticipated or controlled and in fact exercises power over the rhetor (Rickert,

Ambient Rhetoric; Leston, "Unhinged"; Hawhee, "Kairotic Encounters"). Eric Charles White's treatise on the subject, *Kaironomia*, was influential in drawing the field's attention to these sacred aspects, emphasizing that the rhetor does not simply impose his will on a situation; he is—instead or as well—"'seduced' in turn by the occasion of speech" (38). Kairos, as the sacred "occasion of speech," moves the rhetor to respond, undermining the sense that an agential subject can freely call on rhetorical rituals from universal systems of logic.[2]

Instead, the rhetor's "locus of decision" in how to respond to the occasion is distributed across the spatially situated context in Rickert's ambient understanding. Rather than rhetor-as-agent, the agential force comes from kairos *itself*, understood as a posthuman, emplaced "environs" that affords the rhetor some opportunities and not others.[3] Emphasis on the sacredness of kairos interrupts the rhetorician's rational, empirical analysis that would respond to the sacred through rituals of rhetorical theory. This leads us to a fundamental question: if kairos is an agential, inventive force dispersed ambiently, *how—and when—do we identify it?* What rituals do we employ to assert that the time was right and the response was fitting?

STONEWALL THAT NIGHT

If we examine the Stonewall Riots as a moment, as a temporally bound occasion, then we may assume that kairos is both experienced and designated as such in the moment. The June 27, 1969 uprising of queer bar patrons against a police raid is typically considered the wellspring of the gay liberation movement, a rare and explosive genesis that rhetoricians might see as the quintessence of a sacred kairos.

The kairos of the occasion was, of course, not anticipated in advance. Like most gay bars in New York City at the time, the Stonewall Inn was owned and controlled by members of the Mafia. Mollified by weekly payoffs by the Mob, the corrupt Sixth Police Precinct would raid the bar about once a month with intentionally little disruption to the Stonewall Inn, though patrons were often arrested for dressing in the clothes of the opposite gender, touching members of the same gender, or for lacking identification (Duberman, *Stonewall*, 192–93). The police would notify the Mob-connected owners that a raid was imminent before their arrival because, as historian Martin Duberman explains, "given the size of the weekly payoff, the police had an understandable stake in keeping the golden calf alive" (193). For their part, the Mafia put systems in place to protect the liquor supply and warn patrons. If police were suspected, the bartender would flash white lights so that dancers would know to separate and employees could hide the liquor and cash. Though police acted with considerable derision and arrogance toward the queer patrons (195), raids were fairly typical and appear to have been managed as a matter of routine.

But by all accounts, something was different this night in June. No one was quite able to name what precisely had changed except perhaps to comment on the warmth of the night or the incidence of Judy Garland's funeral that day; as Duberman puts it, "all sensed something unusual in the air, all felt a kind of tensed expectancy" (196). If we focus on the night itself, the Stonewall Riots seem to exemplify kairos as a *moment* sensed and seized by rhetors. In line with Rickert's view of the sacredness of kairos, the ambient environs helped create the conditions for kairotic response. As police exited the bar pushing hand-cuffed prisoners toward the waiting wagon, they expected the crowd to dissipate out of fear as they always had before. But they would not this time. Sylvia Rivera described it thus: "You could feel the electricity going through people. You could actually feel it. People were getting really, really pissed and uptight" (qtd. in Duberman, *Stonewall*, 196). Jim Fouratt, a riot participant, remembers "*the* explosive moment" occurring when a lesbian in masculine attire escaped the police wagon and started to physically agitate the van; meanwhile, drag queens were "throwing their change and giving lots of attitude and lip" (qtd. in Duberman, *Stonewall*, 196). Another witness, Harry Beard, saw the flashpoint in a moment of police brutality against the "cross-dressed" lesbian, when the crowd responded in outrage by throwing coins and eventually bottles and construction debris at the cops.

The agency of the riotous response was dispersed across the spatially and temporally situated context. According to participant Craig Rodwell, there was no single galvanizing act; the flashpoints were simultaneous, a crowd generating collective anger (Duberman, *Stonewall*, 197). The crowd's acts of fury succeeded in pushing the police into retreat inside the bar, where they called for the riot-control Tactical Patrol Force. Two dozen members arrived in full riot gear and engaged the crowd with billy clubs and tear gas. The crowd did not retreat but rather ran around the block and reassembled behind the riot police, a tactic they repeated again and again.

Hours after they began, the crowd finally dispersed in the early morning light—until they returned the next evening en masse and then again two days later to continue the rebellion, swelling to more than a thousand people.

If we examine this moment *as a moment*, it certainly seems to emblematize kairos. Robert Leston ("Unhinged," 30) describes such an occasion as "rhetorical alchemy," a fount of invention in which, "on the spur of the moment . . . the speaker or writer"—or rioter—"in conjunction with all these disparate forces in the 'ecology' converges this energy into something appropriate and fitting to say"—or throw. Leston's description of kairos is an apt explanation of Michael Fader's memory of the riots: "We all had a collective feeling like we had enough of this kind of shit. It wasn't anything tangible anybody said to anyone else" (qtd. in Carter, *Stonewall*, 160). The energy of the scene was palpable and compelled a response from rhetors eager for the opportunity.

If we pause the story here, then, the Stonewall Riots exemplify kairos's sacred, unidentifiable, and dispersed force on rhetors for whom no universal rules could intervene in the particular case. These rhetors did not appear to draw on rituals of rhetorical theory to respond to the occasion of the raid; instead, they invented responses in the moment, throwing coins and shoes, rocking the police wagons, even upending a parking meter and ramming it through. But we cannot pause the story here, for the archive continues and precedes it and it is the archive that both makes and undermines the kairos of this moment.

RIGHTNESS IN RETROSPECT

If we return to the connotations of space, time, and proper measure in the earliest definitions of kairos, we can see that each is premised on a longer temporality than the momentary. These connotations draw on metaphors of battle and moderation that can only be evaluated in hindsight.

In these earliest definitions, the successful achievement of an act dictates whether we understand kairos to have occurred. For instance, Homer's reference to kairos as the space between a "forest of shields" (White, *Kaironomia*, 13) where an arrow can travel presupposes a warrior who intends to mortally wound his enemy. Likewise, early connotations of kairos with weaving—with the precise, fleeting moment where a breach in the cloth opens for a weaver to draw a thread through—presupposes the end of the act of weaving: the successful completion of cloth. Finally, Hesiod's reference to the maximum load a wagon can sustain before breaking under its weight presupposes a traveler with the aim of carrying as much as possible. If the warrior blocks the arrow, if the thread becomes tangled, if the wagon's axle shatters, we are unlikely to call the moment and the measure *right*. The kairotic moment is judged as such in retrospect.

Contemporary theorists also presuppose an achieved aim in discerning whether kairos was present. As John E. Smith explains, "*Kairos* means that the problem or crisis has brought with it a time of opportunity... *for accomplishing some purpose* which could not be carried out at some other time" ("Time," 52). Likewise, Rickert writes that "*kairos* defines a rhetor's relation to a unique opportunity arising from an audience, situation, or time, one that calls for a proper response *in order to gain advantage or success*" (*Ambient Rhetoric*, 75).[4] In short, then as now, kairos is defined *as* kairos when an explicit or tacit aim succeeds in a given time and place.

These examples point to rhetoric's fundamental teleology. It is not surprising that teleology imbues Aristotelian rhetoric, as it does his natural philosophy. Alan Gross maintains that Aristotle's understanding of rhetoric as a *techne* makes teleology fundamental to rhetoric, for *techne* are defined by their ends: "The weaving of the weaver, the dancing of the dancer, the writing of the poet are constitutive movements whose *erga* are products: the rug, the dance, the poem" ("What Aristotle Meant," 30). As a *techne*, then, Aristotelian rhetoric is defined by its threefold "products": the discernment of the available means of persuasion, persuasion itself, and "its ultimate *telos*," the well-being of the city-state (30).

Though we may expect to find teleologically defined rhetoric in Aristotle's tradition, those operating in the Gorgian tradition also depend on prefigured aims. White, for instance, emphasizes the irrational, unpredictable—sacred—quality of kairos in Gorgias that cannot be reduced to systemic method. Yet here, too, teleology is presupposed. White argues that "since the circumstances enabling *success* may change at any time, kairos implies that there can never be more than a contingent and provisional management of the present opportunity. *Success* depends, in other words, on adaptation to an always mutating situation" (*Kaironomia*, 13; my emphasis). Whether the rhetor or the situation enacts more agency—or whether agency happens "in-the-middle," as Hawhee ("Kairotic Encounters") contends—kairos is determined by whether success has been gauged. The key phrase here is "has been."[5]

The teleological underpinning of rhetoric means that the adjudication of kairos must happen in hindsight. As Rickert writes, "The situation presents itself in such a fashion that the appropriate action will be understood, after effective results are achieved (i.e., retroactively), to have been kairotic" (*Ambient Rhetoric*, 74). After all, it is only after the game has been won that we can say that a player made the right moves at the right time. If the game is lost, then we are likely to view the player's moves as ill-timed and poorly measured. Was the cloth completed? Then the weaver saw the opening for drawing through the thread. Did the arrow strike the warrior? Then the warrior saw the vulnerable space between armor and shields. Did the wagon hold the weight? Then the load was properly measured. In short: Was success achieved? Then the time was likely right and the response fitting. The designation of kairos depends on the existence of an aim and its eventual success.[6]

But where does the aim come from? Within whom or what is the aim? And *when* does the aim come? Kenneth Burke, in *Permanence and Change*, suggests that the ends of rhetoric and the discernment of kairos are not external to rhetoric but are themselves rhetorical. He writes, "Now, when you begin talking about the optimum rate of speed at which cultural changes should take place, or the optimum proportion between tribal and individualistic motives that should prevail under a particular set of economic conditions, you are talking about something very important indeed, but you will find yourself deep in matters of rhetoric: for nothing is more rhetorical in nature than a deliberation as to what is too much or too little, too early or too late" (45). The upshot of Burke's claim is that we deliberate about the right ends (e.g., "cultural changes" or winning a game), about the right time, and about the right measure. There are times, after all, when even winning a game is not expedient for a player (who may aim to endear himself to a superior or be gentle with a child). "Rightness" then is not universal, not an uncontested truth, but rather "deep in the matters of rhetoric" (45). For whom and to whom is a move "too much or too little, too early or too late"—or for whom and to whom is it *right*?

To be clear, I do not mean to suggest that kairos itself is *only* the product of ex post facto deliberation but rather that the very sacredness of kairos necessitates that it is *also* rhetorical. That is, there may be two kairoi associated with a rhetorical situation: the sacred call—described variously as "ecological," "ambient," and "invention-in-the-middle"—that rhetors both choose and are compelled to answer, and the sequent—and rhetorical—designation of temporal and proportional rightness after the moment has passed and the success of the rhetoric's aim has been gauged. The consequences of this second valence are my focus here.

Considering the rhetorical valence of kairotic designation necessitates that we examine *for whom* and *to whom* the ends, means, time, and proportion of rhetoric is right. These questions are "fundamentally ethical, since [they] involv[e] preferences," as Burke describes rhetoric generally (250). "The ethical shapes our selection of means," Burke continues. "It shapes our structures of orientation, while these in turn shape the perceptions of the individuals born within the orientation" (250). Though the "rightness" of a time or measure is typically, and implicitly, connoted in terms of what is *correct* for a given situation, I turn us here to the other common meaning of rightness: that which is morally good and just. Is what is right for the rhetoric—the success of some aim—right for the rhetor? How, and when—and for whom—can we know that the time was right?[7]

BEFORE AND AFTER STONEWALL

Part of the challenge of situating a kairotic moment in the longer temporality suggested by rhetoric's teleology rests in a binary distinction between *kairos* and *chronos* that we have inherited from classical rhetoricians. Smith explains that while kairos was "qualitative," representing "time that marks an opportunity that may not recur," chronos referred to the objective, quantifiable, and uniform march of time. Chronos is the abstract, universal structure of time; kairos is the occasion on which a time becomes meaningful ("Time," 47). This dichotomous distinction often leads us to focus *either* on kairos as the momentary flash of opportunity for accomplishing some purpose *or* on chronos as all time, unadulterated by human significance. But as I have argued, kairos is typically designated as kairos in retrospect: after an aim has been judged to be achieved. Thus we must understand a kind of time-in-the-middle, to borrow Hawhee's term, a kind of kairo-chronos that allows us to understand as qualitatively meaningful what comes before and after the moment we retrospectively identify as right.

Riot participant Michael Fader understood his memory of the "collective feeling" of fury not as a momentary flash but rather as the culmination of an aim that had developed for years before that warm June night. His continued remarks illustrate the longer temporality of rhetoric that includes the development of an aim that ultimately defines kairos as kairos. Fader went on to say, "It was just kind of like everything over the years had come to a head on that one particular night in that one particular place . . . All kinds of people, all different reasons, but mostly it was total outrage, anger, sorrow, everything combined, and everything just kind of ran its course" (qtd. in Carter, *Stonewall*, 160). Not only had the raids been happening for years but so had radical organizing. As other historians explain, the Stonewall Riots were able to foment gay liberation because of the decades of activism before them, including the radical movements of the New Left and civil rights in the 1960s as well as the homophile movement begun in the 1950s that succeeded in raising gay and lesbian consciousness and shaping collective identity. As historian John D'Emilio remarked, "*Something* of significance must have occurred before that night of outrage in Greenwich Village to explain why a spontaneous riot could have birthed a mass grassroots movement" (*Making Trouble*, 235). In other words, the development of the exigency and the aim preceded the kairotic moment.

Faderman understood that aim as nothing short of freedom itself: "We felt that we had freedom at last, or freedom at least to show that we demanded freedom. . . . There was something in the air, freedom a long time overdue, and we're going to fight for it" (qtd. in Carter, *Stonewall*, 160). Of course, a narrower exigency of the riot was simply to stop the immediate police raid, but most participants remember the goal being much greater. Indeed, the reprise of the riots the next evening and then again on Wednesday suggests that impeding the Friday night raid was only one aim in a larger rhetorical project that was decades in the making: gay liberation. Craig Rodwell, an industrious homophile activist, called the papers during the first uprising to make sure it gained media traction because he "immediately knew that this was the spark we had been waiting for for years" (qtd. in Carter, *Stonewall*, 167).

In short, it requires a longer view in order to make sense of the kairos of Stonewall, a kairo-chronic view that extends both before and *after* the riots themselves. It is because we view the riots from hindsight as having succeeded in the long-brewing aims of thwarting the raid and advancing gay liberation that we can retroactively designate the moment as kairotic. As Thomas Piontek maintains, "we can draw meaning from Stonewall *only* in the context of belatedly constructed teleology of gay liberation"—only upon looking back at the event as having always been for a particular vision of gay liberation (*Queering*, 15). For half a century, the events of that June night have been celebrated as the watershed of gay liberation because the burgeoning movement needed (and perhaps still needs) to leverage the event rhetorically—to position the riots as a symbol of gay militancy and power that was a break from the past's alleged homophile-movement compromises. Piontek put it bluntly: "Stonewall, in other words, became an enabling fiction that allowed gay militants to read back into history a particular story that they wanted to tell—the story of gay liberation as they envisioned it" (20). In other words, the kairos of Stonewall is part of its necessary rhetorical construction of having achieved the aim of liberation action. Once the event was framed as the origin point for liberation activism, the time became—retrospectively—right.

THE SYLVIA RIVERA ARCHIVE

Reflecting on before and after Stonewall, it becomes clear that taking a longer view of kairos disturbs the notion that we have revealed an objective kairotic reality—a moment that is "right" without consideration of the success of rhetorical act and for whom. The contours of post-Stonewall gay liberation did not make room for those on the front lines of the riots. Jessie Gan maintains that "while the iconography of Stonewall enabled middle-class white gays and lesbians to view themselves as resistant and transgressive, Stonewall narratives, in depicting the agents of the riots as 'gay,' elided the central role of poor gender-variant people of color in that night's acts of resistance against New York City" ("'Still,'" 127). Historians and witnesses emphasize that the people who fought the hardest were the most marginalized of the Stonewall Inn's patrons: transgender people, drag queens, underage street kids, and queers of color who fought "with the same ferocity they would fight for any situation of survival" (witness Tommy Lanigan-Schmidt qtd. in Carter, *Stonewall*, 163). As Rivera recalls, "It was street gay people from the Village out front: homeless people who lived in the park in Sheridan Square outside the bar—and then drag queens behind them and everybody behind us" (Rivera, "'I'm Glad'"). The retrospective rhetorical construction of Stonewall's kairos participated in the erasure and exclusion of the trans and queer rhetors who answered the sacred call of that collective fury.

Yet we cannot look to the archive for the objective truth of kairotic rightness either. The archive cannot tell us, finally, that the moment was *wrong* to riot, any more than it can tell us that the moment was right. Drawing on Derrida, Bernard-Donals explains that the archive contains only an "impression of the event," not the event itself ("Archival Subjects," 130). The archive also contains traces of what it has not recorded, "the traces of events, objects, and individuals that have been left out of the archive but leave an impression upon the objects in it" (130). It is because of the archive—oral histories, written testimony, media coverage, ephemeral traces—that we "know" that the retrospective rightness of Stonewall was not right for everyone involved, yet it is that same archive that unsettles any hope of determining absolutely the rightness of the riots.

Sylvia Rivera brings the simultaneous necessity and failure of the archive's determination of kairos into relief. On the streets since she was ten years old, the Puerto Rican transgender woman had survived poverty and violence through sex work and queer community, and all that despite living with addiction. She told Duberman, "I thought that night in 1969 was going to be our unity for the rest of our lives" (*Stonewall*, 246), but political organizations that formed in the aftermath of the riots disdained her gender, race, and class. Her "darker skin," "fractured English," "rude anarchism," "sashaying ways," and street living were rejected by various factions in the Gay Liberation Front and Gay Activist Alliance (238). But by her account, she was in the thick of things in the years following the riots in order to bring her aims to the attention of a liberation movement that seemed to leverage the riots and efface the rioters. Rivera's aims were neither abstract nor complicated. She wanted to provide shelter for homeless trans and queer youth and she wanted to save their lives from the violence, drug addiction, and discrimination she knew so well. That is what she was fighting for after Stonewall, founding STAR (Street Transvestites Action Revolutionaries) with her friend and sister rioter Marsha P. Johnson.

Archives retain meager scraps of Rivera's memory, scattered across queer collections, newspaper archives, and oral history projects. These fragments trace Rivera's demands for accountability from the movement, her pride and frustration with her role in the riots, her intermittent homelessness and suicide attempts, and—when it was convenient for the movement—her periodic apotheosis in the decades following the Riots. It also contains her critics, like the historian who claims she was not present at the Riots at all. Reading through this archive, it is not easy to say the time had been right to riot for Sylvia Rivera and her aims for the survival and dignity of transgender people. As Bernard-Donals suggests, "What is archived, in other words, isn't really *there* at all" ("Archival Subjects," 134).

In the years following the riots, Rivera pleaded with the community for recognition of the courage and sacrifice of trans people and called out the white, middle-class biases of the movement. Here are some excerpts from her archive. The first is from a 1971 piece in *Come Out!* (a newspaper published by the Gay Liberation Front):

> Remember the Stonewall Riots? That first stone was cast by a transvestite half-sister June 27, 1969 and the gay liberation movement was born. Remember that transvestites and gay street people are always on the front lines and are ready to lay their lives down for the movement. Remember the transvestite half-sister that was out gathering signatures for the Homosexual Civil Rights Bill petition and was arrested on 42nd Street. Remember the NYU sit-in? Transvestites and gay street people held the fort down and didn't want to give in that Friday night after we had been removed from the sub-cellar. So sisters and brothers remember that transvestites are not the scum of the community; just think back on the events of the past two years. (Rivera, "Transvestites")

The second is drawn from a fiery speech delivered at the 1973 Christopher Street Liberation Rally:

> Y'all better quiet down. I've been trying to get up here all day, for your gay brothers and your gay sisters in jail! They're writing me every motherfuckin' week and ask for your help, and you all don't do a goddamn thing for them. Have you ever been beaten up and raped in jail? . . . You all tell me, go and hide my tail between my legs. I will no longer put up with this shit. I have been beaten. I have had my nose broken. I have been thrown in jail. I have lost my job. I have lost my apartment. For gay liberation, and you all treat me this way?

... If you all want to know about the people that are in jail—and do
not forget Bambi l'Amour, Andorra Marks, Kenny Messner, and the
other gay people that are in jail—come and see the people at STAR
House on 12th Street, on 640 East 12th Street between B and C,
apartment 14. The people who are trying to do something for all of
us and not men and women that belong to a white, middle-class,
white club. And that's what y'all belong to. (Rivera, "Y'all Better
Quiet Down," 30)

Discouraged by her treatment at the 1973 rally, intermittently homeless, and
dependent on drugs and alcohol, Rivera left Manhattan and the movement.
The Sylvia Rivera archive contains these impressions of her anger at being
left—or even actively cast—out of the liberation project post-Stonewall. It
also contains the impressions left by her absence, by those years when she
left the movement and its epicenter, the events of those years that were not
recorded.

Just as true, however, is the absence of the events the archive *did* record,
which left their own impression. In 2004, historian David Carter asserted
his belief that Rivera was not present at the riots at all. In an interview for
Gay Today, Paul D. Cain asked Carter why Rivera was missing from his
book, *Stonewall: The Riots That Sparked a Revolution*, when she was featured
prominently in Duberman's 1993 history, *Stonewall*. Carter replied, "I am
afraid that I could only conclude that Sylvia's account of her being there on
the first night was a fabrication," basing his belief on third-hand accounts
from Randy Wicker and Doric Wilson, who told him that Marsha P. Johnson had told them Rivera was not present. He also based his assertion of
her absence on what he saw as conflicting accounts of the night from Rivera
herself: whether or not she had been to the Stonewall Inn before, whether
or not she was "in drag" that night, whether or not she was there to celebrate
Johnson's birthday.

The archive cannot finalize if Rivera was there nor if the riotous moment
was right for her and her mission of transgender rights. It can tell us that—at
times—she felt it *was* right, particularly during moments where she felt the
freedom to be herself and the gratitude of the queer community. This next
excerpt from her archive marks the first trace of Rivera's reappearance in
connection to the liberation movement. It comes from a 1989 NPR radio
documentary, "Remembering Stonewall," which featured Rivera's voice

among other riot participants: "Today I'm a thirty-eight-year-old drag queen. I can keep my long hair, I can pluck my eyebrows, and I can work wherever the hell I want. And I'm not going to change for anybody. If I changed, then I feel that I'm losing what 1969 brought into my life, and that was to be totally free." Five years later, she would lead a march down Fifth Avenue. This impression is captured in a newspaper article titled "Tribute to Riot Is Peaceful: Gays Remember a Turning Point": "The Fifth Avenue march was led by Sylvia Rivera, a transvestite who fought police at Stonewall. Rivera had dropped out of sight in recent months and was feared dead. 'I'm here to see that we still have the guts to take Fifth Avenue,' Rivera said" (Associated Press, "Tribute"). In these archival traces, Rivera is proud of her role in the riots and of the courage it demanded.

But while the impression of these feelings would last, archived in radio and newspapers, the feelings themselves would not. In Bernard-Donals's Badiou-inflected terms, Rivera as "the subject in the archive is 'riven' . . . by the network of multiple possibilities, multiple pasts, the impressions and disorder of the archive" ("Archival Subjects," 132). As a complex person whose life was fluid, continuous, and contradictory, she could not be frozen in the archive and we cannot look to her archive to determine whether the riots were right—the right moment, the right aim—for her. In this heartwrenching trace from the archive—a *New York Times* article dated only a year after she led the pride march—she felt abandoned by the movement to the point of succumbing to suicide. She was overcome with grief for the loss of her friend Marsha P. Johnson and perhaps lonelier after the march than before it. In "Still Here: Sylvia, Who Survived Stonewall, Time, and the River," journalist Michael T. Kaufman wrote:

Sylvia Rivera, the transvestite who in 1969 battled passionately and inspirationally at the Stonewall uprising, tried to kill herself 10 days ago by walking into the Hudson River . . . "We started sleeping outside and on that Friday morning, I went down to the river to meditate. I do that usually once a day. I go down there and think about Marsha P. Johnson. Marsha was the first friend I made on 42nd street. She was 17. Marsha plugged in the light for me. Three years ago, they pulled Marsha's body out of the Hudson at Christopher Street. It's still not clear whether it was suicide or if someone killed her. Her ashes went into the river and I draw strength when I

go down there and think about her. But that day when I was drink-
ing, I was thinking how with Marsha gone there was no one left. I
thought it might be time to take a little swim. I was up to my waist
when somebody saw me and the police came and brought me here."
... But by last June, when the 25th anniversary of the Stonewall
uprising was celebrated, Sylvia was restored to an honored place in
the gay parades. "The movement had put me on the shelf, but they
took me down and dusted me off," she recalled at the hospital. "Still,
it was beautiful. I walked down 58th Street and the young ones were
calling from the sidewalk, 'Sylvia, Sylvia, thank you, we know what
you did.' After that I went back on the shelf. It would be wonderful
if the movement took care of its own. But don't worry about Sylvia.
I should be out of here in a week and I should be fine."

Set against the earlier traces of pride and gratitude, this impression from
the *New York Times* confutes the rightness of the riots for Rivera, whose
feelings of abandonment by the movement compounded her grief for
Marsha.

These feelings, too, would not endure. Three years later, the archive
contains yet another impression, one in which her memories of the riots
were a source not of pain but again of great pride. In an interview with Leslie
Feinberg for *Workers World*, Rivera is grateful:

I'm glad I was in the Stonewall riot. I remember when someone
threw a Molotov cocktail, I thought: "My god, the revolution is
here. The revolution is finally here! ... I always believed that we
would have a fight back. I just knew that we would fight back. I just
didn't know it would be that night. I am proud of myself as being
there that night. If I had lost that moment, I would have been kind
of hurt because that's when I saw the world change for me and my
people. Of course, we still got a long way ahead of us. (Rivera,
"'I'm Glad'")

Four years later an impression captures both regret and gratitude for her
role in the riots. It is fitting that the final trace left in her own voice is complicated and contradictory. In an essay written while she was dying from
liver cancer and published posthumously, Rivera's fury and pride comes

from the transnational expansion of her community and the need to teach them about the role of the riots in their history:

> Yes, I'm angry with this fucking community. I wish sometimes that 1969 never happened, they make me so angry. But it happened and I have a whole lot of children. One of my most beautiful moments, all these years, was in 2000 at world pride when the Italian trans-sexual organization in Bologna invited Julia and me to participate. I got to speak to all those people that have oppressed our community. Because it's not just here in the United States with the mainstream community but all over. It's astonishing to see how history repeats itself. But I reminded all those 500,000 children out there that day that if it wasn't for us, they would not be where they're at today. They wouldn't have anything, none of them, from one corner of the world to the other. Because it was our community, the street kids, the street queens of that era, who fought for what they have today. They still turn around to give us their backs. (Rivera, "Queens in Exile," 67)

Rivera provided voice and sustenance to those "street kids" and "street queens" until the end.

Though it would retain a multitude of its riven impressions, the archive went quiet with her death, marked by an obituary in the *New York Times* on February 20, 2002: "Sylvia Rivera, who helped lead the charge—in makeup and full voice—at the birth of the modern gay liberation movement, died yesterday at St. Vincent's Manhattan Hospital. She was fifty and lived in Brooklyn. The cause was liver cancer, said the Rev. Pat Bumgardner of the Metropolitan Community Church of New York, where Ms. Rivera was coordinator of the food pantry" (Dunlap, "Sylvia Rivera"). Rivera fought for thirty years after Stonewall for the basic survival of trans and queer people of color on the streets. Her expansive project of social justice was both invigorated and contravened by the Stonewall Riots of 1969; her feelings about the riots would be equally as conflicted until her death. The archival traces and absences of Rivera's life from the movement after Stonewall complicate theories of kairos, for when we read through her archive, it is not easy to determine finally for whom, for what aims, and when the time was right.

CONCLUSION

Rhetoricians have long attended to the complexity of kairos, both reifying and complicating its denotation of appropriateness in time and measure. Indeed, the literature abounds with allusions to the challenge of pinning down the concept: kairos is described as "a beautifully flexible word" (Wilson, "Kairos," 177) with "terminological capaciousness" and "elasticity" (Trapani and Maldonado, "Kairos," 278; see also Sipiora, "Introduction"; Helsley, "Kairos"; Baumlin, "Ciceronian Decorum"). While scholars point to the diversity of connotations over time, we continue to call on Kinneavy's influential definition of the "right or opportune time to do something, or right measure in doing something" ("Kairos: A Neglected Concept," 80). Kairos means this and it means more than this: the concept is imbued with ethical consequences, subjective dislocation, and contradictory tensions between space and time, control of—and by—a situation, and more.

The slippery and expansive meaning of kairos evades our attempts to locate and thoroughly systemize it through rituals of applied rhetorical theory. But its scopic, fluid qualities are precisely what makes the concept sacred. As René Girard maintains, "As long as meaning is healthy, the sacred is absent" (Violence and the Sacred, 241). The inverse applies here: as long as the meaning of kairos is "unhealthy," the sacred is present. Such a view is supported by scholars such as Hawhee, Leston, Rickert, and White, who have challenged our ritual responses of applied theory to the sacred, "embodied, mobile, nonrational version of rhetorical kairos" (Hawhee, Bodily Arts, 68–69).

I have sought in this chapter to further their project by asking a question that follows from it: if kairos exemplifies a sacred call that evades our attempts to wrangle it through teachable and applicable rhetorical theory, how—and when—do we identify it? How and when do we determine what time and measure is right—and for whom? I have argued that such questions demand a longer view than the momentary flash to which we typically attend. A longer view exposes the teleological underpinnings of rhetoric itself, the ways in which we determine the rightness of time and measure by our sense that an aim has been achieved, an aim that either precedes or follows the kairotic moment itself. Because we must wait to assess success, we can only identify kairos in retrospect.

The archive is both necessary and unavailing in finally determining whether a moment is *right*, or wrong. A longer view demands a historical record, the "signs of consigned memory" that document the past (Derrida, *Archive Fever*, 33). But the archive contains only impressions of the event, not the event itself, so much so that Kent Kleinman calls them "machines for forgetting" (qtd. in Bernard-Donals, "Archival Subjects," 128). The Sylvia Rivera archive—its traces of emotional shifts, its contradictory accounts, its silences—reveals the value and futility of the archive in discerning kairos. We cannot assess the *kairos* of Stonewall without the archive, and yet it profoundly unsettles our ability to determine it, finally. What the archive contains is not really *there* at all, but we must look for it nonetheless.

Notes

1. Other scholars have emphasized the distinction between Aristotle and Isocrates on matters of kairos. George Kennedy describes Aristotle as philosophical and Isocrates as sophist; Sutton explains that whereas Aristotle "absorbed *kairos* in to the comprehensive system of rhetoric" (*Classical Rhetoric*, 413), Isocrates focused on kairos and the contingencies of the situation (see also Harker, "Ethics of Argument"). Nonetheless, here I call attention to how Isocrates and Aristotle share an assumption of the subjective agency of the rhetor.

2. Drawing on White and Gorgias, Hawhee ("Kairotic Encounters," 18) calls kairos "invention-in-the-middle," a "space-time which marks the emergence of a provisional 'subject,' one that works *on*—and is worked on by—the situation."

3. Robert Leston takes the ecological dispersion of kairos further, arguing that its attendant invention "can be said to be largely determined by the environment and history to which it belongs" such that "there is no reason why *kairos* must be bound to human experience" at all ("Unhinged," 32).

4. The emphasis on both quotations from Smith and Rickert is mine.

5. It is telling that many explanations of kairos depend on analogy to games or battle. Scott Consigny, for instance, explains that "the opening or *kairos* does not exist 'on its own,' apart from the perceptions and actions of an individual, any more than an opening in a particular moment of play in a game exists independently of the positions and skills of the players" (*Gorgias*, 87). Game players have an aim—generally, to win—and they act according to rules accepted by all players. And as Hawhee notes, the god of kairos was from the beginning associated with athletics, his figure depicted in statues at the stadium gates of Olympia.

6. One might wonder whether we cannot assess the quality of a move *as* it is made. Why must the adjudication of rightness be done in retrospect? It is not always, for example, the right time and proportion to take a chess opponent's queen? Yet even a novice player knows to look at least a move ahead: if taking the opponent's queen puts the player at risk of checkmate, then it is the right move at the wrong time. If the move is made and the game is lost because of it, one would be unlikely to call it the opportune moment to capture the queen. Knowing the rightness of a move in the present requires knowing what happens in the future, which cannot be assessed until it has occurred.

7. Others have emphasized the connection between ethics and kairos. Cynthia Sheard's investigation of kairos in Kenneth Burke

illuminates the necessary relation between rhetoric, preferences, and ethics. Building on Sheard, Michael Harker writes that "a more complete definition of the term recognizes that concerns of appropriateness and timing inter-animate each other in such a way that it is almost impossible to consider *kairos* outside of the most problematic philosophical and rhetorical realm, the realm of action, the realm of ethics" ("Ethics of Argument," 82).

Likewise emphasizing ethics, Kinneavy argues that kairos "brings timeless ideas down into the human situation of historical time. It thus imposes value on ideas and forces humans to make free decisions about those values" (*"Kairos* in Classical," 62). But despite these gestures at ethical concerns, we have not yet considered what and who is at stake in these choices—and in how we designate kairos *as* kairos.

Bibliography

Associated Press. "Tribute to Riot Is Peaceful: Gays Remember a Turning Point." *Colorado Springs Gazette Telegraph*, June 27, 1994.

Atwill, Janet. *Rhetoric Reclaimed: Aristotle and the Liberal Tradition*. Ithaca, NY: Cornell University Press, 1997.

Baumlin, James S. "Ciceronian Decorum and the Temporalities of Renaissance Rhetoric." In *Rhetoric and Kairos: Essays in History, Theory, and Praxis*, edited by Phillip Sipiora and James S. Baumlin, 138–64. Albany: SUNY Press, 2002.

Bernard-Donals, Michael. "Archival Subjects and the Violence of Writing." In *Abducting Writing Studies*, edited by Sidney I. Dobrin and Kyle Jensen, 123–41. Carbondale: Southern Illinois University Press, 2017.

Burke, Kenneth. *Permanence and Change: An Anatomy of Purpose*. Berkeley: University of California Press, 1984.

Cain, Paul D., and David Carter. "David Carter: Historian of The Stonewall Riots." GayToday.com, 2004. http://gaytoday.com/interview/070104in.asp.

Carter, David. *Stonewall: The Riots That Sparked the Gay Revolution*. New York: Macmillan, 2004.

Consigny, Scott. *Gorgias: Sophist and Artist*. Columbia: University of South Carolina Press, 2001.

D'Emilio, John. *Making Trouble: Essays on Gay History, Politics, and the University*. New York: Routledge, 2016.

Derrida, Jacques. *Archive Fever: A Freudian Impression*. Translated by Eric Prenowitz. Chicago: University of Chicago Press, 1996.

Duberman, Martin. *Stonewall*. New York: Dutton, 1993.

Dunlap, David W. "Sylvia Rivera, 50, Figure in Birth of the Gay Liberation Movement." *New York Times*, February 20, 2002.

Gan, Jessie. "'Still at the Back of the Bus': Sylvia Rivera's Struggle." *Centro Journal* 29, no. 1 (2007): 124–39.

Girard, René. *Violence and the Sacred*. Translated by Patrick Gregory. Baltimore: Johns Hopkins University Press, 1979.

Gross, Alan G. "What Aristotle Meant by Rhetoric." In *Rereading Aristotle's Rhetoric*, edited by Alan G. Gross and Arthur Walzer, 24–36. Carbondale: Southern Illinois University Press, 2000.

Harker, Michael. "The Ethics of Argument: Rereading Kairos and Making Sense in a Timely Fashion." *College Composition and Communication* 59, no. 1 (2007): 77–97.

Hawhee, Debra. *Bodily Arts: Rhetoric and Athletics in Ancient Greece*. Austin: University of Texas Press, 2004.

———. "Kairotic Encounters." In *Perspectives on Rhetorical Invention*, edited by Janet Atwill and Janice Lauer, 16–35. Knoxville: University of Tennessee Press, 2002.

Helsley, Sheri L. "Kairos." In *Encyclopedia of Rhetoric and Composition: Communication from Ancient Times to the*

Information Age, edited by Theresa
Enos, 371. New York: Garland, 1996.

Kaufman, Michael T. "Still Here: Sylvia, Who
Survived Stonewall, Time and the
River." *New York Times*, May 24, 1995.

Kennedy, George A. *Classical Rhetoric and
Its Christian and Secular Tradition
from Ancient to Modern Times*. Chapel
Hill: University of North Carolina
Press, 2003.

Kinneavy, James L. "Kairos: A Neglected
Concept in Classical Rhetoric." In
*Rhetoric and Praxis: The Contribution
of Classical Rhetoric to Practical
Reasoning*, edited by Jean Dietz Moss,
79–105. Washington, DC: Catholic
University of America Press, 1986.

———. "*Kairos* in Classical and Modern
Rhetorical Theory." In *Rhetoric and
Kairos: Essays in History, Theory, and
Praxis*, edited by Phillip Sipiora and
James S. Baumlin, 58–76. Albany:
SUNY Press, 2002.

Kinneavy, James L., and Catherine R. Eskin.
"Kairos in Aristotle's Rhetoric."
Written Communication 17, no. 3
(2000): 432–44.

Leston, Robert. "Unhinged: Kairos and the
Invention of the Untimely." *Atlantic
Journal of Communication* 21, no. 1
(2013): 29–50.

Myers, Kelly A. "*Metanoia* and the Transformation of Opportunity." *Rhetoric
Society Quarterly* 41, no. 1 (2011): 1–11.

Piontek, Thomas. *Queering Gay and Lesbian
Studies*. Urbana: University of Illinois
Press, 2006.

"Remembering Stonewall." Produced by
David Isay, featuring Sylvia Rivera.
Weekend All Things Considered, NPR,
July 1, 1989.

Rickert, Thomas. *Ambient Rhetoric: The
Attunements of Rhetorical Being*.
Pittsburgh: University of Pittsburgh
Press, 2013.

Rivera, Sylvia. "'I'm Glad I Was in the
Stonewall Riot': An Interview with
Leslie Feinberg.'" In *Street Transvestite
Action Revolutionaries: Survival, Revolt,*

and Queer Antagonist Struggle, 12–14.
N.p.: Untorelli Press, 2012.

———. "Queens in Exile, the Forgotten
Ones." In *GenderQueer: Voices from
Beyond the Sexual Binary*, edited by
Joan Nestle, Clare Howell, and Riki
Wilchins, 67–85. Los Angeles: Alyson
Books, 2002.

———. "Transvestites: Your Half-Sisters and
Half-Brothers of the Revolution."
Come Out! 2, no. 10 (1971): n.p.

———. "Y'all Better Quiet Down." In *Street
Transvestite Action Revolutionaries:
Survival, Revolt, and Queer Antagonist
Struggle*, 30–32. N.p.: Untorelli Press,
2012.

Sheard, Cynthia Miecznikowski. "Kairos
and Kenneth Burke's Psychology of
Political and Social Communication." *College English* 55, no. 3 (1993):
291–310.

Sipiora, Phillip. "Introduction: The Ancient
Concept of *Kairos*." In *Rhetoric and
Kairos: Essays in History, Theory, and
Praxis*, edited by Phillip Sipiora and
James S. Baumlin, 1–22. Albany:
SUNY Press, 2002.

Smith, John E. "Time and Qualitative Time."
In *Rhetoric and Kairos: Essays in
History, Theory, and Praxis*, edited by
Phillip Sipiora and James S. Baumlin,
46–57. Albany: SUNY Press, 2002.

Spieker, Sven. *The Big Archive: Art from
Bureaucracy*. Cambridge, MA: MIT
Press, 2008.

Sutton, Jane. "Kairos." In *Encyclopedia of
Rhetoric*, edited by Thomas O. Sloan,
413–17. New York: Oxford University
Press, 2001.

Trapani, William C., and Chandra A.
Maldonado. "Kairos: On the Limits to
Our (Rhetorical) Situation." *Rhetoric
Society Quarterly* 48, no. 3 (2018):
278–86.

White, Eric Charles. *Kaironomia: On the
Will-to-Invent*. Ithaca, NY: Cornell
University Press, 1987.

Wilson, John R. "Kairos as 'Due Measure.'"
Glotta 58, nos. 3–4 (1980): 177–204.

CHAPTER 11

Historiography and the Limits of (Sacred) Rhetoric

DANIEL M. GROSS

Sometimes a story needs to be told just so that we can grasp what is already on hand. Such is the case with sacred rhetoric, which persists and imposes itself upon us at every turn, while at the same time remaining difficult to grasp in terms of the modern academy, where rhetoric has prevailed primarily as a secular art. In most undergraduate writing and speaking classrooms, for instance, rhetoric is a type of know-how designed to enhance a student's capacity for communicating in a variety of secular circumstances typically including other classrooms, public arenas, and professions. Meanwhile for the same students, expressly religious activities like preaching, praying, and parsing sacred texts happen somewhere else like over lunch with acquaintances (as I have witnessed regularly at the University of California, Irvine, Student Center), or at home with family and in services over the weekend. Then this same divide winds up parsing the world accordingly, so that it becomes difficult to identify sacred objects and activities that are *not* expressly religious as they appear ambiguous like the aura of fame that I will discuss in a section on Sigmund Freud below, or like "sanctuary," which has long been a site of struggle between authorities of the church and authorities of the state, but now suffers doubly as that struggle has largely receded into a quasi-ethical domain where neither the rules of state nor the rules of church apply consistently (for treatment of sanctuary from the medieval era to recent controversies, see Allen, *Uncertain Refuge*; and Allen, "Why Sanctuary Cities Must Exist").

At more advanced levels of scholarship, including graduate and professional, rhetoric is primarily a type of knowledge tied again to the classroom, but also to neighboring fields that sometimes need to know about their historical ties to rhetoric—as in the case of literary studies, law, or education—or to know about their limitations—as in the rhetoric of science. Preaching, praying, pilgrimage, sanctuary, renewing the self, or studying sacred texts might very well be at issue in these higher faculties. But they are grasped primarily through the sciences and their softer neighbors, in terms of behavior. Or in terms of form. Or in terms of a secularizing history. As the story has been told for over a century going back at least to Max Weber's progressive disenchantment thesis (always bonded with re-enchantment as many forget), the sacred per se has been banished from the secular academy, and along with it has gone our grasp of sacred rhetoric.

More recently, however, a broad pushback in the academy is evident for instance in the title of an influential 2009 essay collection edited by Joshua Landy and Michael Saler, *The Re-Enchantment of the World: Secular Magic in a Rational Age*. Indeed, as this book and others have argued, a powerful countertendency has always run alongside the push to secularize, producing "an array of strategies for re-enchantment, each fully compatible with secular rationality" (Landy and Saler, *Re-Enchantment*, 14; see also Berman, *Reenchantment*; Bennett, *Enchantment*). But we have only just begun to retell this story in rhetorical studies, which means that we do not yet have a good sense for what the strategies look like in this case, or what appear as "sacred rhetoric" in the first place. Hence one of the goals of this current volume: we tell this "re-enchantment" story from the perspective of rhetoric per se, so we can simply grasp what is already on hand. But in doing so our work as rhetoricians winds up differing from cultural histories of the sort just mentioned, and in ways that are significant both in terms of methodology, and in terms of the objects studied. Unlike cultural historians like Landy and Saler, whose re-enchantment fills a "God-shaped void" and hence is zero-sum on balance (*Re-Enchantment*),[1] rhetoricians approach the matter in a way that is fundamentally different, first interrogating the very distinction: how it appears historically, how and to what end the arguments function, and what is at stake when it comes to finding relevant objects. That is to say from a rhetorical perspective, no calculation could ever lay out a balance sheet of dis- and re-enchantment. Saintly relic or statue? Prophecy or prediction? As we will see in the analysis that follows, these are not only questions about what sort of belief system prevails at a certain time and place—for instance, premodern religiosity or modern rationality—with named items lining up on one side or the other. It is fundamentally a question of how we characterize who's saying what, when, and to what end. That is to say it is a fundamental question of historiography. We have trouble grasping sacred rhetoric because our dominant ways of knowing in the academy make it difficult to pick out sacred things in the first place, and to understand exactly how this is so, we have to pursue the historiography that lays out the limits of rhetoric in this instance. In the next section I show how this works around the early twentieth-century establishment of the academic and commonsense field of "interpersonal communication," which is one place where the very limits of sacred rhetoric had to be redrawn.

When it comes to rhetoric, we are currently faced with a confluence between a commonsense and a field-driven set of assumptions about who's in the room, so to speak. Now typically communication is not "extrapersonal," as I will describe it below in the effort to find a room where sacred rhetoric might feel more at home. Instead it is more typically "interpersonal," which means that only you and I are in the room while everything else including the gods do not really register. To make sacred rhetoric appear more prominently in this chapter, then, we can first pursue an historiographic argument that explains how these assumptions about the characters of communication first put the extrapersonal out of reach.

In their authoritative textbook *Engaging Theories in Interpersonal Communication*, Leslie A. Baxter and Dawn O. Braithwaite outline how this subfield emerged from speech education in the first half of the twentieth century, from postwar analysis of communication gone horribly awry to everyday language rediscovered by Ludwig Wittgenstein and J. L. Austin. Interpersonal communication is thus a subfield characteristically woven into some typical secular concerns of the middle twentieth century: how is communication tragically distorted, and practically speaking what can be done about it? Absent sacred rhetoric, we should notice, a typical mise-en-scène appears reassuringly as a kind of cottage industry and I quote: "Interpersonal communication is the production and processing of verbal and nonverbal messages between two or a few persons" (6). Moreover this perfectly reasonable field of study speaks loudly to our secular common sense, where we now most often think of communication more broadly just in this way: I say this, you say that. The basic model of interpersonal communication thus prevails as one moves into related subfields in communication studies, where I say / you say essentially scales up to groups and to organizations, with special attention paid to channels of communication and the noises involved: scaled up, our relevant professional organization officially calls this the "transactional model of communication." In December 2016 the National Communication Association homepage specified the model in an image and in this definition (see fig. 11.1): "The transactional model of communication is a graphic representation of the collaborative and ongoing message exchange between individuals, or an individual and a group of individuals, with the goal of understanding each other. A communicator encodes (e.g., puts thoughts into words and gestures), then transmits the message via a channel (e.g., speaking, email, text message) to the other communicator(s) who then decode the message (e.g., take the words and apply meaning to them)."[2]

At the same time over the last couple of decades, communication scholars—including most notably John Durham Peters—have criticized this interpersonal model in just those ways that reintroduce the sacred. In his landmark 1997 book *Speaking into the Air: A History of the Idea of Communication*, Peters starts with a genealogical critique of communication

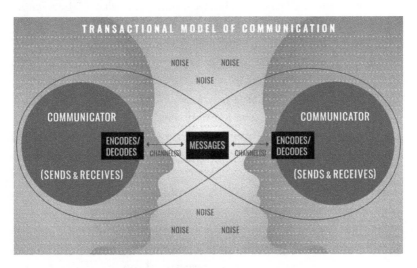

FIG. 11.1 "A Special Case." Reprinted with permission from the National Communication Association. All rights reserved.

understood as mutual communion of souls (1), as the transfer of psychical entities such as ideas, thoughts, or meanings (John Locke through C. K. Ogden and I. A. Richards in 1923), as a therapeutic response to solipsism or misunderstanding (12, 26, through Carl R. Rogers), as information processing (22).[3] Like I do in this chapter, Peters pays special attention to the 1920s interwar culture insofar as it marks the moment when communication as person-to-person activity becomes thinkable in the shadow of mediated communication. "Mass communication came first" (6) Peters asserts, and the interwar culture is where we can best see how "isolation and propaganda are two sides of the same coin" (15, referring to Lukács's *History and Class Consciousness* of 1923). Also like my work here on the extrapersonal, Peters tracks "beyond the merely human world" as he treats communication with animals, extraterrestrials, and smart machines (2). But what about rhetoric per se? Communication is not exactly the same thing as rhetoric, and therefore to grasp sacred rhetoric we must distinguish it from prevailing models of extrahuman communication going back to the parable of the sower and what Peters ultimately calls "free dissemination."

My rhetorical focus means there is no "model of communication in general" (118) that Peters extrapolates from the text/reader interaction. "To speak to another is to produce signs that are independent of one's soul" he rhapsodizes on the way to free dissemination (31) along the lines of Ralph Waldo Emerson and William James: we should acknowledge "the splendid otherness of all creatures that share our world without bemoaning our impotence to tap their interiority" (31). The rhetorician, I offer by way of contrast, is already situated ecologically among cultural formations with a certain force, among political formations with a certain exigency, amongst things beyond our control (see Rivers and Weber, "Ecological"; Edbauer, "Unframing"; Rickert, *Ambient Rhetoric*). From the rhetorical perspective one does not even dream of "free dissemination" because the job would end there; instead the rhetorician has no stable ground to judge, which is not to say the position is indifferent. We are already embedded in the analytics of power, and it is from these analytics we speak for worse and for better. In traditional terms, then, we have Aristotle's rhetorician who "sees the available means of persuasion in each case"—a definition I will depersonalize below—as opposed to Peters's communication theorist concerned with relations as mediated, or Baxter's interpersonal communication theorist concerned with a subset of those relations that appear most prominently face-to-face. Thus in terms of subfield affiliation, I approach "communica-tion" in this chapter from the perspective of rhetorical studies, as opposed to interpersonal communication and media studies.[4]

In the rest of this chapter I will work through the late-modern fate of extrapersonal communication by way of an essential case study, namely Sigmund Freud's "magic words" that intuitively challenge our common-sense, transactional model of interpersonal communication. As Jacques Lacan later summed up this achievement, "The Freudian discovery leads us to hear in discourse this speech which reveals itself through, or even in spite of, the subject" (*Seminar*, 266). But I will emphasize how Freud, in his analysis of magic words, inadvertently exceeds his rhetorically sensitive interpreters, including Jacques Lacan and Mikkel Borch-Jacobsen, insofar as he analyzes *Veranstaltungen*, cleverly translated by James Strachey as per-suasive adjuncts or contrivances, which quietly persist in the orbit of religious practice broadly understood, and which find their theoretical jus-tification in Aristotle's rhetoric. For Freud as we will see, certain images contextualized appropriately, certain sorts of language like the divine prom-ise, certain ritual experiences like the pilgrimage, as well as sacred relics per se, *persuade*—even after the obvious religious aura fades. In fact, Freud's contrivances, I argue, should be counted as inartistic means of persuasion, or what Aristotle calls in his *Rhetoric atechnoi pisteis*: laws, wit-nesses, contracts, testimony of slaves taken under torture, supernatural evidence, "and such like." With Freud's contrivances, in other words, we identify precisely how sacred rhetoric and the extrahuman more broadly shape up in modern form.

In terms of field scholarship, then, such an account helps us see differ-ently a range of rhetorical theory, including that of Kenneth Burke, who was of course an avid reader of Freud.[5] My account complements the work of Christian Lundberg, who is interested in how the early Lacan frames the psychoanalytic project as a response to impoverished models of commu-nication, for example in *Psychoses*, where Lacan writes, "The phenomenon of speech can't be schematized by the image that serves a number of what are called communication theories—sender, receiver, and something that takes place in between them. It seems to have been forgotten that among many other things in human speech, the sender is always a receiver, and at the same time, that one hears the sound of one's own words. It's possi-ble not to pay attention to it, but it is certain that one hears it" (qtd. in

Lundberg, *Lacan*, 60). Ultimately, however, my work here on *Veranstaltungen* moves toward object orientation, not what Lundberg calls the science of rhetoric (in this case figures and tropes). Most broadly, in the end, this chapter is about how we find and treat our objects, and how the rhetorical limits are set that produce our objects in the first place.

In a short piece on psychical treatment (or *Seelenbehandlung*) composed in the 1890s but first published in 1905, and importantly confluent with later work on group psychology in the 1920s, Freud provocatively rehabilitates magic words on the way to justifying and qualifying his early theory of therapeutic hypnosis: "A layman will no doubt find it hard to understand how pathological disorders of the body and mind can be eliminated by 'mere' words. He will feel that he is being asked to believe in magic. And he will not be so very wrong, for the words which we use in our everyday speech are nothing other than watered-down magic. But we shall have to follow a roundabout path in order to explain how science sets about restoring to words a part at least of their former magical power" ("Psychical [or Mental] Treatment," 283). This moment is cleverly seized on by Borch-Jacobsen in his 1990 essay "Analytic Speech: from Restricted to General Rhetoric" (in Bender and Wellbery, *Ends of Rhetoric*; see also Davis, *Inessential Solidarity*), where science generally recuperates the power of persuasion abandoned to magicians, preachers, and healers (130–31), and where Freudian psychoanalysis is explicitly grounded in the rhetorical tradition understood as the art of moving souls. Originally in verbal hypnosis and later in nonverbal transference, Borch-Jacobsen identifies the persistent Freudian interest in affectability (136), classically categorized under the objectives of rhetorical invention: *fidem facere et animos impellere* (or, in a literal translation, the goal of rhetorical invention is "to make faithful and impel courage"; see also Borch-Jacobsen, *Emotional Tie*, 54). At the same time, we cannot help but notice how Freud's article on psychical treatment contributes to a general project of disenchantment that relocates certain supernatural powers, including rhetorical, in the affective margins of psychic life:

> The affects in the narrower sense are, it is true, characterized by a quite special connection with somatic processes; but, strictly speaking, all mental states, including those that we usually regard as "processes of thought," are to some degree "affective," and not one

of them is without its physical manifestations or is incapable of modifying somatic processes. Even when a person is engaged in quietly thinking in a string of "ideas," there are a constant series of excitations [*Erregungen*], corresponding to the content of these ideas, which are discharged into the smooth or striated muscles. These excitations can be made apparent if they are appropriately reinforced [*geeignete Verstärkung*], and certain striking and, indeed, ostensibly "supernatural" phenomena can be explained by this means. Thus, what is known as "thought-reading" [*Gedankenerraten*] may be explained by small, involuntary muscular movements carried out by the "medium" in the course of an experiment. ("Psychical," 288)

But at the same time that Freud extends psychic life into the natural world and beyond, claiming even supernatural phenomena through his critique of the pathetic fallacy—they are merely projections—those same phenomena fold in and around the psyche by way of *Veranstaltungen*: persuasive adjuncts, contrivances, or events that cannot be reduced to psychic activity however expressed.

I now propose that Freud's distinction between sanctioned rhetorical interactivities of psychic life, and unsanctioned rhetorical interactivities that rely on persuasive adjuncts (exemplified below), bears a meaningful relationship to a key classical distinction most famously articulated by Aristotle. And because Freud's model of psyche dominated before the recent rise of behavioral and cognitive sciences, it provides at the same time an ideal research domain as we try to gain some perspective on our current common sense: How is the scene set? What is given? Who are the characters? What is communicable?

Aristotle distinguishes between *entechnoi pisteis*, or artful means of persuasion that can be prepared by the speaker, and *atechnoi pisteis*, or artless means of persuasion that are given to the speaker. The first category may be more familiar, and it includes those that foreground the character (or ethos) of the speaker, those that dispose the listener (pathos), and those inherent to the structure of the argument, reasonably explicated (logos). The second category, artless, may be less familiar, and it includes for Aristotle laws, witnesses, testimony of slaves taken under torture, contracts, "and such like" (*Rhetoric* 1.2.2; translations from Kennedy's edition of *On Rhetoric*; see also

Mirhady, "Non-Technical Pisteis"). Here are a few key examples from Aristotle: Antigone argues that the burial of her brother may have violated Creon's law, but it did not violate natural law (1.15.6); the Athenians "used Homer as a witness in their claim to Salamis" (1.15.13); Themistocles used the "wooden walls" oracle from Delphi to persuade Athenians that a sea battle and not a land battle would defeat the Persians (1.15.14). So respectively natural law, cultural authority, oracle: three artless means of persuasion that Aristotle sees originating elsewhere before they are placed in the hands of a litigant. And although we can learn how to manipulate such givens, according to Aristotle, it is the *entechnoi pisteis* that are trainable and therefore they receive most attention in the *Rhetoric* and in subsequent handbooks under his influence. Typically to this day we learn about the artful means of persuasion, the five canons of rhetoric from invention to delivery, and the genres deliberative, forensic, and epideictic. Typically we do not learn about the rhetorical force of what is given (see, for instance, Corbett and Connors, *Classical Rhetoric*; the index to Bizzell and Herzberg, *Rhetorical Tradition*; Crowley and Hawhee, *Ancient Rhetoric*; the synoptic outline of contents in Sloan, *Encyclopedia of Rhetoric*; Ueding and Steinbrink, *Grundriß der Rhetorik*; and so on, through the vast majority of our recent rhetoric textbooks and handbooks). In his *Introduction to Rhetorical Theory*, Gerald A. Hauser marks the point where, apparently, our job as rhetoricians and as teachers of rhetoric run into a wall: "Whenever the facts 'speak for themselves,' we have sufficient grounds to make a decision without rhetoric" (120)

Where in these three examples from Aristotle do we find most prominent the rhetorical force of what is given? In divine testimony or what is sometimes called supernatural evidence. That is where the secular handbook tradition fails most dramatically as it gives way to sacred rhetoric that prevails after the golden age of classical rhetoric primarily by way of preaching and biblical hermeneutics (see Shuger, *Sacred Rhetoric*). But first here is the Roman Quintilian on supernatural evidence treated forensically under the heading *probatio inartificialis*:

> If to this kind of evidence [Quintilian lists: decisions of previous courts (5.2), rumors (5.3), evidence from torture (5.4), documents (5.5), oaths (5.6), and witnesses (5.7)] anyone should wish to add evidence of the sort known as supernatural, based on oracles,

prophecies and omens, I would remind him that there are two ways
in which these may be treated. There is the general method, with
regard to which there is an endless dispute between the adherents
of the Stoics and the Epicureans, as to whether the world is governed by providence. The other is special and is concerned with
particular departments of the art of divination, according as they
may happen to affect the question at issue. For the credibility
of oracles may be established or destroyed in one way, and that
of soothsayers, augurs, diviners and astrologers in another.
(5.7.35–36)[6]

Striking for us in this passage is how Quintilian takes for granted supernatural evidence even as it appears in a practical arena like the courtroom.
What matters to Quintilian is not *whether* supernatural evidence should be
admissible, but rather *how* it can be argued variously: in general at the level
of providential theory, or specifically in terms of divination and its various
departments. Concretely we should remember that Quintilian was thinking
of Socrates at this point, who at his trial had to mitigate verbally the force
of his own Delphic oracle proclaiming the wisdom of Socrates; you may
anticipate how artless proofs would come to dominate sacred rhetoric from
at least Paul's epistles onward.[7]

Noteworthy for our purposes is how sacred rhetoric—broadly (and
anachronistically) understood in this instance as divine—as opposed to
the secular rhetoric of courtroom documents like a contract, will pivot differently around what is considered given and what is not, thereby shifting
what counts in the discipline and what does not. "I call God as my witness"
(*martura ton theon*) offers Paul in 2 Corinthians 23 as he provides evidence
that his ministry is efficacious. Inconveniently in this case, evidence is not
delivered by the hand of a courtroom clerk. Instead it materializes with
respect to a range of environmental affordances that include genre—the
apologetic form of the letter—and the rich apparatus of authority that
makes this particular call consequential: factors available to rhetoricians
working beyond the Aristotelian handbook tradition.[8]

Hence a pedagogical point by way of example: whereas in our day a
religious arena may allow for supernatural evidence, a secular venue won't.
Thinking about our basic communication students preparing for a presen-
tation on animal rights or euthanasia, for instance, we might remind them

that supernatural evidence has a place in the heart or at church, but not in our classrooms. That is to say in making a classroom argument about euthanasia, a sacred text like the Bible can appear to document community norms and their history; it cannot appear as ultimate authority. In this example a prototype for proof that resides outside the argument—namely supernatural evidence—now becomes prototype for proof that resides inside the argument as it is crafted by the student "alone." So, is the appeal to God as my witness artful or artless? The answer to this question depends completely on the prevailing theory of argumentation, and the prevailing scope of rhetorical agency, which is to say historiographic concern subject to basic research in the history of rhetoric.

So how exactly do *atechnoi* work for Freud? Discussing supernatural phenomena, including miraculous cures, Freud initially retreats from extrapsychic and extrapersonal analysis to a degree that justifies a predictable humanism: "There is no need . . . to bring forward anything other than mental forces in order to explain miraculous cures. . . . Indeed, the power of religious faith is reinforced in these cases by a number of eminently human motive forces" ("Psychical," 290). Freud's hyperbole is figured by way of intensification, his metaphor in English is magnification—whereby the extrahuman finds its familiar seed and I quote: "The individual's pious belief is intensified [*Verstärkung*] by the enthusiasm of the crowd of people in whose midst he makes his way as a rule to the sacred locality. All the mental impulses of an individual can be enormously magnified [*gesteigert*] by group influence such as this" (290). But I argue that without the adjuncts, contrivances, and events that exceed the psyche in this example and others—let us call them inartistic means of persuasion—that psychic experience would be impossible to identify, indeed there would be no psyche at all. After all, what is psyche detached from the world? Impossible to say. Instead Freud explains in the key passage:

> The most noticeable effects of this kind of expectation coloured by faith are to be found in the "miraculous" cures which are brought about even to-day under our own eyes without the help of any medical skill. Miraculous cures properly so-called take place in the case of believers under the influence of adjuncts suitable to intensify religious feelings [*Veranstaltungen, welche geeignet sind, die religiösen Gefühle zu steigern*; I have slightly modified Strachey's

translation]—that is to say, in places where a miracle-working image is worshipped, or where a holy or divine personage has revealed himself to men and has promised them relief from their sufferings in return for their worship, or where the relics of a saint are pre- served as a treasure. Religious faith alone does not seem to find it easy to suppress illness by means of expectation; for as a rule other contrivances [again, *Veranstaltungen*] as well are brought into play in the case of miraculous cures. The times and seasons at which divine mercy is sought must be specially indicated; the patient must submit to physical toil, to the trials and sacrifices of a pilgrimage, before he can become worthy of this divine mercy. (289–90)

Psyche is in the world concretely and thus its treatment must also run through the things of this world in all of their historicity. So, what significant shape do these contrivances take?

In his work on group psychology, Freud specifies that just like hypnosis, "artificial groups"—for example, the Catholic Church—put the object, Jesus, in the place of the ego ideal. However, in the group dynamic of the church as opposed to the military, Freud qualifies, it is not enough for the Christian to love Christ as his ideal and feel himself united with all other Christians by the ties of identification. He also has to "identify himself with Christ and love all other Christians as Christ loved them" (*Group Psychology*, 86). Indeed where there is identification in Christ, object-love must be added that "evidently goes beyond the constitution of the group" (86) to include a variety of extrinsic objects that we have just called *Veran- staltungen*: for instance, certain reified images, certain sorts of language like the divine promise, certain ritual experiences like the pilgrimage, as well as sacred relics per se; Lacan would later identify the *objet petit a* that, among other things, must be incorporated by the analyst as the figure of transfer- ence. So, it is not enough to impose doctrine from above or give lip service from below—this religious world must be completely renatured, the human being completely renewed, and community completely reconstituted as evangelical. Antonio Gramsci would analyze the cultural hegemony of the Catholic Church; in 1921 Freud concludes rather unsatisfactorily "all the ties that bind people to mystico-religious or philosophico-religious sects and communities are expressions of crooked cures of all kinds of neuroses" (*Totem and Taboo*, 141).

So next to Quintilian's famous neologism *probatio inartificialis*, now sometimes misunderstood as "brute fact" (see Maclean, *Interpretation*, 78n42), I place Freud's *Veranstaltungen*. Why this particular word?[9] *Stalt* is an abstract from the verb *stellen*, to stand, and hence we get the root word *Anstalt* or establishment, institution, something stood up and mobilized by the prefix *ver-*. It is related to the verb *veranstalten*, which means to host, to arrange, to stage, to prepare, to contrive, to institutionalize, but in Freud's case the verb is nominalized so human agency is incorporated, and we are left with Strachey's persuasive adjuncts or contrivances, even social events with a particular duration and purpose, like a religious pilgrimage in this case. Freud's point: strictly speaking there is no such thing as a *magic* word without *Veranstaltungen*. Let us just say there is no such thing as a *persuasive* word—no rhetoric—without *Veranstaltungen* otherwise known to the classical rhetorician as inartistic means of persuasion.

Clearly modern theorists of rhetoric have done some of this work already.[10] Not surprisingly given his Freud affinity, Kenneth Burke was onto something similar despite his penchant for symbolization that returns extrapersonal considerations back to people. For instance, military force, Burke argues in *A Rhetoric of Motives*, "persuade[s] by its sheer 'meaning' as well as by its use in actual combat" (161; see Burke as well on administrative force, 158–66). Think about all the rhetorical work done by a standing army implicated in an ever-changing calculus of deterrence: let us call this very inartistic means of persuasion. Likewise, "recalcitrance" is a Burkean concept that objectifies rhetoric throughout his career: it "refers to the factors that *substantiate* a statement, the factors that *incite* a statement, and the factors that *correct* a statement" (Burke, *Attitudes Toward History*, 47). So, for instance, the pseudo-statement "I am a bird" is revised into a complete practical statement when we can say "I am an aviator," but both, Burke argues, are simply statements insofar as the person who says them must take certain orders of recalcitrance into account (*Permanence and Change*, 255; see also Prelli, Anderson, and Althouse, "Kenneth Burke"). Like Freud's magic words that are meaningless without *Veranstaltungen*, Burke's statements are meaningless without the world and its objectivity (see *Philosophy of Literary Form*, 3). No doubt Burke's world and its objectivity are not that of science per se: "The magical decree is implicit in all language; for the mere act of naming an object or situation decrees that it is to be singled out as such-and-such rather than as something-other" (4). But just as Freud's magical words are materialized, Burke's "true" or "correct" magical decree does not escape the world and its recalcitrance—for example, the laws of motion—that are suspended only by "false" magic and by poetry writ large.

Words of whatever kind do nothing by themselves, even accompanied by the psychoanalytic arts of personal interactivity, and this Freud knew well enough. His analysis of aphonic Dora initiates in part because "favorable" family circumstances have not desiccated her homosexual feelings the way they normally would, and her therapy founders, supposedly, on the object relation he calls transference (Freud, *Dora*, 53).[11] Meanwhile, as Diana Fuss describes in her wonderful book *The Sense of an Interior: Four Writers and the Rooms That Shaped Them*, Freud's Berggasse 19 enacted the therapeutic session by way of precise spatial arrangement of objects and furniture (80): of course the famous couch that renders the patient supine with all that implies (90), the Etruscan mirror that opens a window onto immortality as a mythological scene reflects off the engraved surface (85), the bas-relief Gradiva who offers patient and doctor these instructions: "Look, but not with bodily eyes, and listen, but not with physical ears." Poet H. D. recalls of her first visit, "The statues stare and stare and seem to say, what has happened to you?" (qtd. in Fuss, *Sense*, 80, 97). Miracle workers need their contrivances, including a certain disposition of time and place organized around a transferential object, as Freud would call it. Likewise rhetoricians need their contrivances, including a certain disposition of time and place sometimes organized around a transferential object, which Freud's contemporary Siegfried Krakauer called in the context of Weimar culture the "human ornament," like the massive configurations at Nuremberg.[12] The job of the rhetorician is not to study words (*verba*) as one imagines at the height of 1980s linguistic constructivism, or things (*res*) as one imagines at the height of our current object-oriented theory, but rather the precise historical relation that gives this point of intersection force.

Hence a historical thesis. The modern project of dis- and re-enchantment has its ambiguity, which rhetoricians should find deeply interesting because its resolution one way or another can determine our historiography. That is to say, the ambiguity around things that may or may not appear sacred—statues/relics, birds/auspices, walks/pilgrimages, pills/cures, sacraments/reputations, words and spectacles human or divine—depends completely on historically informed rhetorical analysis for their disambiguation. It is not that once in ancient times there were enchanted relics, auspices, pilgrimages, and divine interventions, whereas now under the weight of modernity there is not (disenchantment). Nor is it adequate to reverse the progression, so that now the world can appear enchanted once again. Instead the project is rhetorical, which does not mean secular, as there have long been historians of rhetoric who worked comfortably within a religious framework like the early modern figure Nicholas Caussin through the late modern figure Richard Weaver: in each case the work is still historical, and it argues a point. Or as Quintilian implied even earlier with respect to supernatural evidence, what matters is not whether the evidence is "really" supernatural or not: theoretically that would be argued earlier at the level of a definitional stasis determining in this case what sort of evidence is admissible in a court of law. For Quintilian teaching rhetoric, it is not a matter of whether the Delphic oracle has authority in the courtroom or, say, for how seriously we should take the aura of authority when it comes to an expert witness. Instead, Quintilian is locally concerned with the ways in which oracles can be handled more or less competently given the rhetorical situation. Likewise, we, as rhetoricians, should not get hung up on the sacred/secular distinction per se along with its cognates, but rather spend our time researching and analyzing how these distinctions play out. A final example referencing Freud.

In this passage Freud exemplifies how a certain kind of secular rhetoric works by way of fashion, within a distinctly bourgeois topography: once again time and place appear disenchanted. But note how Freud's historiographic ambiguity is provisionally settled by way of figurative identity, or "complete" substitution, undone by alien material reminiscent of our contrivances as they approach a sacrament or holy communion, koinōnia: the rhetorical contrivance par excellence.[13] Freud, in "Psychical (or Mental) Treatment" (290), continues:

> In their case reputation and group-influence act as a complete substitute for faith. There are always fashionable treatments and fashionable physicians, and these play an especially dominant part in high society, where the most powerful psychological motive forces are the endeavour to excel and to do what the "best" people do. Fashionable treatments of this kind produce therapeutic results which are outside the scope of their actual power, and the same procedures effect far more in the hands of a fashionable doctor

(who, for instance, may have become well-known as an attendant upon some prominent personality) than in those of another physician. Thus there are human as well as divine miracle-workers.

In this case "therapeutic results," however tenuous, are the materials produced outside the scope of actuality; faith is erased by reputation at the same time that faith—now completely extrinsic—provides a cure under the sign of reputation. Begged is the question of actuality since the therapeutic results achieved in this case are by definition virtual. One job of the rhetorician—and we see that Freud was himself deeply insightful along these lines—is to explain what it means to be a human miracle worker in this instance, and how the job gets done, persuasive contrivances and all. To reiterate in this case from Freud, the persuasive contrivance is "reputation" in terms of one lexicon, sacrament in terms of another. Freud's singular accomplishment in this instance is his demonstration of how exactly these two terms are related.

I will conclude with the unsexy recommendation that rhetoricians continue to sidestep the disenchantment/re-enchantment narrative enabled by Freud and his earlier cohort, while foregrounding instead our work on inartistic means of persuasion. That means at least two things methodologically. To analyze rhetorically, we always need some historical perspective on what is "given" to the rhetorician and what is not—for example, in this chapter God's word to Paul, or a scientifically sanctioned cure to Freud and his cohort. Then, because there is no such thing as a persuasive word without contrivances, we need to know in each case what these contrivances are, such as Paul's epistles in the first instance, or a fashionable reputation in the second. This methodology is traditional insofar as we should continue to ask, like Aristotle, "Which appeals are artful and thus in the hands of the rhetorician, and which appeals are artless?" But unlike Aristotle, whose objectives in that famous treatise were very different, our answer to this question will depend on the prevailing theory of argumentation, and the prevailing scope of rhetorical agency, which is to say historiographic concerns subject to basic research in the history of rhetoric. Hopefully the preceding has shown how much can be gained by doing this kind of historical work, as our interest now turns to extrapersonal communication in all of its ecological, historical, and sociopolitical richness, while rejecting the primordial *homo religiosus* who, Agamben reminds us, "exist only in the imagination of scholars" (*Sacrament of Language*, 11).[14]

Notes

Though originally drafted for this volume, portions of this essay have previously appeared in print as part of my book *Being-Moved: Rhetoric as the Art of Listening* (Berkeley: University of California Press, 2020).

1. The game looks one way to dialecticians Max Horkheimer and Theodor Adorno, and another to Landy and Saler who call their approach "antinomian" (3), but zero-sum it remains: "Each time religion reluctantly withdrew from a particular area of existence, a new, thoroughly secular strategy for re-enchantment cheerfully emerged to fill the void" (1).

2. As of March 26, 2019, the caption loosens the interpersonal focus this way: "At its foundation, Communication focuses on how people use messages to generate meanings within and across various contexts, and is the discipline that studies all forms, modes, media, and consequences of communication through humanistic, social scientific, and aesthetic inquiry." See http://www.natcom.org/discipline.

3. Martin Heidegger's critique is a reference point we share: "As we have already indicated in our analysis of assertion, the phenomenon of *communication* must be understood in a sense which is ontologically broad. 'Communication' in which one makes assertions—giving information, for instance—is a special case of that communication which is grasped in principle existentially. In this more general kind of communication the Articulation of Being with one another understandingly is constituted. Through it a co-state-of-mind [*Mitbefindlichkeit*] gets 'shared,' and so does the understanding of Being-with. Communication is never anything like a conveying of experiences, such as opinions or wishes, from the interior of one subject into the interior of another. Dasein-with is already essentially manifest in a co-state-of-mind and co-understanding. In discourse Being-with becomes 'explicitly' *shared*; that is to say, it is already, but it is unshared as something that has not been taken hold of and appropriated" (*Being and Time*, 219).

4. For a breakdown of professional subfields, see for instance the University of Iowa Communication Studies Department areas of specialization, or "clusters," which "cohere around understanding and explaining how different modes and media of communication shape people's everyday lives." The clusters are (1) interpersonal communication and relationships, (2) media studies, and (3) rhetoric and public advocacy. Peters and Baxter have both been distinguished professors in this department representing media studies and interpersonal communication, respectively. See http://clas.uiowa.edu/commstudies/research (accessed July 28, 2020).

5. Kevin A. Johnson summarizes how Burke mentions a Freudian influence on the following concepts: rationalization versus analysis, comic frame, audience persuasion, cluster criticism, surrealist ingredient in art, purposive forgetting, proportional strategy, matriarchal symbolizations, prayer and chant in literary criticism, occupational psychosis, scapegoating, perfection, terministic screens, the negative, the guilt cycle, beauty and sublimity, original sin, motive, and identification ("Burke's Lacanian Upgrade").

6. Quintilian 5.1 (Russell translation): "To begin with it may be noted that the division laid down by Aristotle has met with almost universal approval. It is to the effect that there are some proofs adopted by the orator which lie outside the art of speaking, and others which he himself deduces or, if I may use the term, begets out of his case. The former therefore have been styled *inartificial* proofs, the latter *artificial*. To the first class belong decisions of previous courts, rumours, evidence extracted by torture, documents, oaths, and witnesses, for it is with these that the majority of forensic arguments are concerned. But though in themselves they involve no art, all the powers of eloquence are

as a rule required to disparage or refute them. Consequently in my opinion those who would eliminate the whole of this class of proof from their rules of oratory, deserve the strongest condemnation." Augurs interpret auspices that are signs like the flight patterns of birds, as opposed to oracles, which are supposed to be unmediated.

7. Quintilian 5.11.42 knows this tradition of Socrates's oracle; he also relates Cicero's use of divine testimony. See Long, *Ancient Rhetoric*, 47. In particular, Long finds interesting the distinction that Quintilian makes between supernatural evidence (*divinia testimonia*) and divine arguments (*divinia argumenta*): "When such arguments [appealing to the gods] are inherent in the case itself they are called supernatural evidence; when they are adduced from without they are styled supernatural arguments." Technically, Long points out, "when analyzing a speech, it is difficult to determine whether evidence is external or internal to the case; the inclusion of the former would technically fall under artificial proof. The most important evidence that Paul mustered in his defense is divine. I have already noted his reliance on the Spirit as evidence of the efficacy of his ministry. Paul had also called God to witness against him in 1.23 in anticipation of the covenantal exhortation in 5.11–7.1. However, Paul argued throughout two Corinthians explicitly and implicitly that God approved of him." Especially noteworthy is that Cicero (*Part. Or. 2.6*) lists the types of divine evidence (*testimonia*) and includes oracles (*oracula*), auspices (*auspicia*), prophecies (*vaticinationes*), and answers of priests, augurs, and diviners (*responsa sacerdotum, haruspicum, coniectorum*).

8. Jaroslav Pelikan, in *Divine Rhetoric*, emphasizes, like Kennedy, the continuities from classical Athenian Rhetoric (primarily Aristotle) to the Hellenistic environment of early Christianity. A contrary and very helpful perspective is Carol Poster's "Ethos, Authority, and the New Testament Canon." Poster argues that early Christian rhetoric—including the distinction between extrinsic and intrinsic proof—cannot be understood in the tradition of Aristotle; instead, it must be more closely associated with Hellenistic handbooks such as those of Dionysius of Halicarnassus and Anonymous Seguerianus, who composed with different courtroom settings in mind. First, "the tendency for handbooks to shift their emphasis from intrinsic to extrinsic *ethos* and from *logos* (reasoning which is part of the orator's art) to *pragmata* (extrinsic evidence) reflects a shift in judicial procedures, from classical Athenian and Republican Roman ones, which emphasized fine speeches with elaborate rhetorical flourishes, to Greco-Roman courtrooms, which emphasized facts and detailed knowledge of the law" (130). Then early Christian arguments over authority exhibit the same preferences, Poster argues, whereby "extrinsic connections with Jesus and apostolic succession were among the strongest arguments for the authority of a person or text" (136–37).

9. We also find the term in Freud, *Jokes and Their Relation to the Unconscious*: "Words are disfigured by particular little additions being made to them, their forms are altered by certain manipulations [*Veranstaltungen*] (e.g., by their reduplications or 'Zittersprache'), or a private language may even be constructed for use among playmates. These attempts are found again among certain categories of mental patients" (153). And in *Group Psychology*: "We may further emphasize, as being specially instructive, the relation that holds between the contrivance [*Veranstaltung*] by means of which an artificial group is held together and the constitution of the primal horde. We have seen that with an army and a Church this contrivance [*Veranstaltung*] is the illusion that the leader loves all of the individuals equally and justly. But this is simply an idealistic remodeling of the state of affairs in the primal horde, where all of the sons knew that they were equally persecuted by the primal father, and feared him equally" (72).

10. For instance, Richard Weaver, in *Language Is Sermonic*, acknowledged that logic alone was not enough to persuade a human being, who is "a pathetic being, that is, a being feeling and suffering" (205). He felt that societies that placed great value on technology often became dehumanized. Like a machine

relying purely on logic, the rhetorician was in danger of becoming "a thinking robot" (207). Hence Weaver writes about language as "suprapersonal" (35).

11. "It follows from the nature of the facts which formed the material of psychoanalysis that we are obliged to pay as much attention in our case histories to the purely human and social circumstances of our patients as to the somatic data and the symptoms of the disorder" (12). See also Freud on hysteria cured by marriage and normal sexual intercourse (71), and on Dora "reclaimed once more by the realities of life" (112).

12. From Fritz Lang's *Nibelungen* (1924) to Leni Riefenstahl's *Triumph of the Will* (1934), "these patterns collaborate in deepening the impression of Fate's irresistible power. Certain specific *human ornaments* in the film to note as well the omnipotence of dictatorship" (qtd. in Witte, "Introduction," 61). With the aid of the radios, the living room is transformed into a public place, mythical powers of the mass are exploited for the appearance of elevation (62). This psychoanalytic tradition (see Lundberg, above) has typically focused on the imaginary register; in this chapter I focus on the objectivity of something like Krakauer's living room scene

building on an argument about irreducible historicity.

13. Greek *koinōnia* in 1 Corinthians 10:16; the King James Version has "The cup of blessing which we bless, is it not the *communion* of the blood of Christ? The bread which we break, is it not the *communion* of the body of Christ?"

14. See also Agamben, *Sacrament of Language*, 12: "In the human sciences, beginning at the end of the nineteenth century, the idea that explaining ahistorical institutions necessarily means tracing it back to an origin or context that is sacred or magico-religious is so strong." Agamben's point about our bogus historiography recalls Jacqueline de Romilly's characterization of Gorgias in *Magic and Rhetoric in Ancient Greece*: "Sacred rhetoric rested on faith; Gorgias' magic rests on the notion that all truth is out of reach. Sacred magic was mysterious; Gorgias' magic is technical. He wants to emulate the power of the magician by a scientific analysis of language and of its influence. He is the theoretician of the magic spell of words" (16). This technical tour de force takes advantage of a recurring structural opportunity instead of marking a decisive historical turning point.

Bibliography

Agamben, Giorgio. *The Sacrament of Language: An Archaeology of the Oath*. Translated by Adam Kotsko. Stanford, CA: Stanford University Press, 2011.

Allen, Elizabeth. *Uncertain Refuge: Ideas of Sanctuary in the Literature of Medieval England*. Philadelphia: University of Pennsylvania Press, 2021.

———. "Why Sanctuary Cities Must Exist." *Los Angeles Times*, September 17, 2015.

Aristotle. *On Rhetoric: A Theory of Civic Discourse*. Translated by George Kennedy. New York: Oxford University Press, 1991.

Baxter, Leslie, and Dawn Braithwaite, eds. *Engaging Theories in Interpersonal Communication: Multiple Perspectives*. New York: Sage, 2009.

Bender, John, and David E. Wellbery, eds. *The Ends of Rhetoric: History, Theory, Practice*. Stanford, CA: Stanford University Press, 1990.

Bennett, Jane. *The Enchantment of Modern Life: Attachments, Crossings, and Ethics*. Princeton, NJ: Princeton University Press, 2001.

Berman, Morris. *The Reenchantment of the World*. Ithaca, NY: Cornell University Press, 1981.

Bizzell, Patricia, and Bruce Herzberg, eds., *The Rhetorical Tradition: Readings from Classical Times to the Present*. 2nd ed. New York: Bedford / St. Martin's, 2000.

Borch-Jacobsen, Mikkel. "Analytic Speech: from Restricted to General Rhetoric." In *The Ends of Rhetoric: History, Theory, Practice*, edited by John Bender and David E. Wellbery, 127–39. Stanford, CA: Stanford University Press, 1990.

———. *The Emotional Tie: Psychoanalysis, Mimesis, and Affect*. Translated by Douglas Brick et al. Stanford, CA: Stanford University Press, 1993.

Burke, Kenneth. *Attitudes Toward History*. Berkeley: University of California Press, 1984.

———. *Permanence and Change: An Anatomy of Purpose*. Berkeley: University of California Press, 1984.

———. *The Philosophy of Literary Form: Studies in Symbolic Action*. Berkeley: University of California Press, 1974.

———. *A Rhetoric of Motives*. Berkeley: University of California Press, 1969.

Corbett, Edward P. J., and Robert J. Connors. *Classical Rhetoric for the Modern Student*. Oxford, UK: Oxford University Press, 1965.

Crowley, Sharon, and Debra Hawhee, *Ancient Rhetoric for Contemporary Students*. 5th ed. New York: Longman, 2011.

Davis, Diane. *Inessential Solidarity: Rhetoric and Foreigner Relations*. Pittsburgh: University of Pittsburgh Press, 2010.

Edbauer, Jenny. "Unframing Models of Public Distribution: From Rhetorical Situation to Rhetorical Ecologies." *Rhetoric Society Quarterly* 35, no. 4 (2005): 5–23.

Freud, Sigmund. *Dora: An Analysis of the Case of Hysteria*. Translated by James Strachey. New York: Simon and Schuster, 1963.

———. *Group Psychology and the Analysis of the Ego*. Vol. 18 of *The Standard Edition of the Complete Psychological Works of Sigmund Freud*, edited and translated by James Strachey. New York: W. W. Norton, 1975.

———. *Jokes and Their Relation to the Unconscious*. Vol. 8 of *The Standard Edition of the Complete Psychological Works of Sigmund Freud*, edited and translated by James Strachey. New York: W. W. Norton, 1989.

———. "Psychical [or Mental] Treatment." In *The Standard Edition of the Complete Psychological Works of Sigmund Freud*, edited and translated by James Strachey, 7:281–302. London: Hogarth Press, 1953–74.

———. *Totem and Taboo: Some Points of Agreement Between the Mental Lives of Savages and Neurotics*. Vol. 13 of *The Standard Edition of the Complete Psychological Works of Sigmund Freud*, edited and translated by James Strachey. New York: W. W. Norton, 1950.

Fuss, Diana. *The Sense of an Interior: Four Writers and the Rooms That Shape Them*. New York: Routledge, 2004.

Hauser, Gerald. *Introduction to Rhetorical Theory*. 2nd ed. Prospect Heights, IL: Waveland Press, 2002.

Heidegger, Martin. *Being and Time*. Translated by John Macquarrie and Edward Robinson. New York: Harper & Row, 1962.

Ignatius of Loyola, *Ignatius of Loyola: The Spiritual Exercises and Selected Works*. Edited by George E. Ganss, SJ. New York: Paulist Press, 1991.

Johnson, Kevin E. "Burke's Lacanian Upgrade: Reading the Burkean Unconscious Through a Lacanian Lens." *KB Journal: The Journal of the Kenneth Burke Society* 6, no. 1 (2009). https://www.kbjournal.org/content/burkeslacanianupgrade readingburkeianunconsciousthrough lacanianlens.

Lacan, Jacques. *The Seminar of Jacques Lacan*, vol. 1, *Freud's Papers on Technique, 1953–1954*. Edited by Jacques-Alain Miller. Translated by John Forrester. Cambridge, UK: Cambridge University Press, 1988.

Landy, Joshua, and Michael Saler, eds. *The Re-Enchantment of the World: Secular Magic in a Rational Age*. Stanford, CA: Stanford University Press, 2009.

Long, Fredrick J. *Ancient Rhetoric and Paul's Apology: The Compositional Unity of 2 Corinthians.* Cambridge, UK: Cambridge University Press, 2004.

Lundberg, Christian. *Lacan in Public: Psychoanalysis and the Science of Rhetoric.* Tuscaloosa: University of Alabama Press, 2012.

Maclean, Ian. *Interpretation and Meaning in the Renaissance: The Case of Law.* Cambridge, UK: Cambridge University Press, 1992.

Mirhady, David. "Non-Technical Pisteis in Aristotle and Anaximenes." *American Journal of Philology,* 112, no. 1 (1991): 5–28.

Pelikan, Jaroslav. *Divine Rhetoric: The Sermon on the Mount as Message and as Model in Augustine, Chrysostom, and Luther.* Crestwood, NY: St. Vladimir's Seminary Press, 2001.

Peters, John Durham. *Speaking into the Air: A History of the Idea of Communication.* Chicago: University of Chicago Press, 2001.

Poster, Carol. "Ethos, Authority, and the New Testament Canon." In *Rhetoric, Ethic, and Moral Persuasion in Biblical Discourse,* edited by Thomas H. Olbrich and Anders Eriksson, 118–37. New York: Continuum, 2005.

Prelli, Lawrence, Floyd D. Anderson, and Matthew T. Althouse. "Kenneth Burke on Recalcitrance." *Rhetoric Society Quarterly* 41, no. 2 (2011): 97–124.

Quintilian. *The Orator's Education, Volume 3: Books 3–5.* Edited and translated by Donald A. Russell. Cambridge, MA: Harvard University Press, 2002.

Rickert, Thomas. *Ambient Rhetoric: The Attunement of Rhetorical Being.* Pittsburgh: University of Pittsburgh Press, 2013.

Rivers, Nathaniel, and Ryan Weber. "Ecological, Pedagogical, Public Rhetoric." *College Composition and Communication* 63, no. 2 (2011): 187–218.

Romilly, Jacqueline de. *Magic and Rhetoric in Ancient Greece.* Cambridge, MA: Harvard University Press, 1975.

Shuger, Debora K. *Sacred Rhetoric: The Christian Grand Style in the English Renaissance* Princeton, NJ: Princeton University Press, 1998.

Sloan, Thomas, ed., *Encyclopedia of Rhetoric.* Oxford, UK: Oxford University Press 2001.

Ueding, Gert, and Bernd Steinbrink. *Grundriß der Rhetorik: Geschichte–Technik–Methode* Stuttgart: Metzler, 1986.

Weaver, Richard. *Language Is Sermonic.* Baton Rouge: Louisiana State University Press, 1985.

Witte, Karsten. "Introduction to Siegfried Kracauer's 'The Mass Ornament.'" *New German Critique* 5 (Spring 1975): 59–66.

MICHELLE BALLIF is Professor of English at the University of Georgia. Her research interests and publications have centered around the historiography of rhetoric and how rhetorical practices, constituting disciplinary practices, have been historically instantiated and theorized by virtue of repressing and abjecting differing rhetorics, including sophistry, magic, necromancy, and telepathy, for example. She is the author of *Seduction, Sophistry, and the Woman with the Rhetorical Figure*; editor of *Theorizing Histories of Rhetoric*; and Associate Editor of *Rhetoric Society Quarterly* for special issues.

MICHAEL BERNARD-DONALS is Chaim Perelman Professor of Rhetoric and Culture at the University of Wisconsin–Madison, where he also served as the Vice Provost for Faculty and Staff from 2014 to 2020. He is the author, co-author, editor, or co-editor of nine other books, including—most recently—*Jewish Rhetoric: History, Theory, Culture* (co-edited with Janice Fernheimer) and *Figures of Memory: The Rhetorics of Displacement at the US Holocaust Memorial Museum*.

JEAN BESSETTE is Assistant Professor of English at the University of Vermont. Her research and teaching bridge rhetoric and composition; gender, sexuality, and women's studies; archival and historiographic theory; and multimodal and digital rhetoric. Her book, *Retroactivism in the Lesbian Archives: Composing Pasts and Futures*, examines how twentieth-century American lesbian collectives have engaged in "retroactivism"—efforts to propel change in present identification and politics by composing and appropriating versions of the past.

TREY CONNER is Associate Professor at the University of South Florida, St. Petersburg. His dissertation, "Remixing the Lost Book of Rhythm," engages technologies of communication, collaboration, and education, and pays special attention to the way writers today increasingly deploy digital and "musical" techniques such as sampling and mixing to share and transform information and ideas in ways that build communities and produce value. His publications include *Wyrd to the Wiki: Lacunae Toward Wiki Ontologies.*

RICHARD DOYLE is Edwin Erle Sparks Professor at Penn State University, where he has taught since 1994. Author of scores of scholarly articles and many books, Doyle has received grants from the National Science Foundation and the Mellon Foundation while winning acclaim and awards as a classroom teacher. In 2002, Doyle was healed of lifelong severe asthma in an ayahuasca ceremony, and he has since devoted his life to synthesizing the world's spiritual practices into a practical, open source and empirically verifiable pathway available to all.

DAVID FRANK is Professor of Rhetoric and Dean of the Clark Honors College at the University of Oregon. Professor Frank's research agenda incorporates rhetorical theory and history, with a focus on Chaïm Perelman's new rhetoric project, argumentation, the rhetoric of the Israeli-Palestinian conflict, and the rhetoric of Barack Obama and racial reconciliation. Professor Frank has published seven books, thirteen book chapters, and forty articles in peer-reviewed journals. His most recent book, co-edited with Nicholas Crowe, is *Rhetoric in the Twenty-First Century: An Interactive Oxford Symposium.*

DANIEL M. GROSS is Professor of English and Director of Composition at the University of California, Irvine. His books include *Uncomfortable Situations: Emotion Between Science and the Humanities,* the co-edited collection *Science and Emotions After 1945, The Secret History of Emotion: From Aristotle's Rhetoric to Modern Brain Science,* and the co-edited collection *Heidegger and Rhetoric.* He is currently at work on a book project, *The Art of Listening.*

KEVIN HAMILTON is Dean of Fine and Applied Arts at the University of Illinois, Urbana-Champaign, and a professor in the School of Art and Design.

CYNTHIA HAYNES is Professor of English at Clemson University. Her recent book *The Homesick Phone Book: Addressing Rhetoric in the Age of Perpetual Conflict* won the 2017 Rhetoric Society of America annual book prize. She is currently working on a book manuscript, *Unalienable Rites: The Architecture of Mass Rhetoric.*

KYLE JENSEN is Professor of English at Arizona State University, where he also serves as Director of Writing Programs. He is the author of *Reimagining Process: Online Writing Archives and the Future of Writing Studies*, co-editor of *Abducting Writing Studies*, and co-editor of Kenneth Burke's *The War of Words*.

STEVEN MAILLOUX is President's Professor of Rhetoric at Loyola Marymount University. Previously, he taught rhetoric, critical theory, and US cultural studies as Professor of English and Comparative Literature and Chancellor's Professor of Rhetoric at the University of California, Irvine. He is the author of *Interpretive Conventions: The Reader in the Study of American Fiction*, *Rhetorical Power*, *Reception Histories: Rhetoric, Pragmatism, and American Cultural Politics*, *Disciplinary Identities: Rhetorical Paths of English, Speech, and Composition*, and *Rhetoric's Pragmatism: Essays in Rhetorical Hermeneutics*.

JAMES R. MARTEL is Professor in the Department of Political Science at San Francisco State University. Most recently, he has published *Unburied Bodies: Subversive Corpses and the Authority of the Dead* and *The Misinterpellated Subject*. He has also written a trilogy of books on Walter Benjamin. He has another book in the making titled *Disappointing Vision: Anarchist Prophecy and the Power of Unseeing*.

JODIE NICOTRA is Associate Professor of English at the University of Idaho. Most recently, she has written a textbook for first-year composition called *Becoming Rhetorical: Analyzing and Composing in a Multimedia World*; her newest project is a book titled *The Microbial Imaginary: Rhetorics of Tiny Lives*.

NED O'GORMAN is Professor in the Department of Communication at the University of Illinois, Urbana-Champaign. He works at the intersections of the history of rhetoric, media studies, and political thought, with special interest in the crises and tensions of modernity, especially in the Cold War. He is the author of *Spirits of the Cold War: Contesting Worldviews in the Classical Age of American Security Strategy*, the award-winning *The Iconoclastic Imagination: Image, Catastrophe, and Economy in America from the Kennedy Assassination to September 11*, and *Lookout America! The Secret Hollywood Studio at the Heart of the Cold War* (co-authored with Kevin Hamilton).

BROOKE ROLLINS is Associate Professor of English at Lehigh University. Her work has appeared in *College English, Rhetoric Society Quarterly, JAC: A Journal of Rhetoric, Culture, and Politics,* and the *Velvet Light Trap.* Along with her current project, a book called *The Ethics of Persuasion: Derrida's Rhetorical Legacies,* she has begun working on a new project that theorizes the interruptive capacities of gambling and its effects on human subjectivity. A selection of this work has recently appeared in the collection *Abducting Writing Studies.*

Italicized page references indicate illustrations. Endnotes are referenced with "n" followed by the endnote number.

CPSIA information can be obtained
at www.ICGtesting.com
Printed in the USA
BVHW030818020521
605209BV00013B/23